# Capital, Coercion, and Crime

## BOSSISM IN THE PHILIPPINES

John T. Sidel

STANFORD UNIVERSITY PRESS
STANFORD, CALIFORNIA
1999

Stanford University Press
Stanford, California
© 1999 by the Board of Trustees
of the Leland Stanford Junior University
Printed in the United States of America
CIP data appear at the end of the book

# Capital, Coercion, and Crime

EAST-WEST CENTER
SERIES ON

# CONTEMPORARY ISSUES IN ASIA AND THE PACIFIC

Series Editor, Bruce M. Koppel

*A Series from*
*Stanford University Press and the East-West Center*

## CONTEMPORARY ISSUES IN ASIA AND THE PACIFIC

Bruce M. Koppel, Editor

A collaborative effort by Stanford University Press and the East-West Center, this series addresses contemporary issues of policy and scholarly concerns in Asia and the Pacific. The series focuses on political, social, economic, cultural, demographic, environmental, and technological change and the problems related to such change. A select group of East-West Center senior fellows—representing the fields of political science, economic development, population, and environmental studies—serves as the advisory board for the series. The decision to publish is made by Stanford.

Preference is given to comparative or regional studies that are conceptual in orientation and emphasize underlying processes and to works on a single country that address issues in a comparative or regional context. Although concerned with policy-relevant issues and written to be accessible to a relatively broad audience, books in the series are scholarly in character. We are pleased to offer here the fourth book in the series, *Capital, Coercion, and Crime: Bossism in the Philippines*, by John T. Sidel.

The East-West Center, located in Honolulu, Hawaii, is a public, non-profit educational and research institution established by the U.S. Congress in 1960 to foster understanding and cooperation among the governments and peoples of the Asia-Pacific region, including the United States.

*To my father, who couldn't be there,*
*and*
*To Lotta, who always was, and,*
*I trust, always will be.*

# Acknowledgments

The origins of this book date back to my first visit to the Philippines in the summer of 1985, when I worked for three months as a summer intern in the Political Section of the U.S. Embassy in Manila. Since that time, the company, friendship, assistance, and support of friends and colleagues from the Philippines, the United States, Australia, and various countries of Southeast Asia and Europe have sustained me in my endeavors. Without their efforts, I might have disappeared into the bowels of Foggy Bottom or Langley, and I certainly would never have written this book. For saving me from my checkered past and pushing me to a better future, I am eternally grateful to all concerned. The long list of acknowledgments below offers only a small token of my appreciation.

First, Stacey Rutledge deserves my thanks for inviting me to join her and her family in Manila in 1985, as do Steve and Cris Bosworth for their hospitality. Jim Nach shared his extensive knowledge, finely honed investigative skills, and dry wit and awakened my curiosity about local politics in the Philippines, as did John Sequeira in subsequent years.

During my four years at Yale University, a number of friends and mentors helped me to gain a measure of distance on my adolescent adventures in the Philippines. Hal Conklin shared his awe-inspiring knowledge and love of Philippine society and culture. The Yale Council on Southeast Asia introduced me to friends like the late David Ablin, Jeff Hadler, Boyet Miranda, Jeff Winters, and two close and longtime "Philippinist" cronies, Paul Hutchcroft and Mark Thompson. The formidable Kay

Mansfield, with her legendary warmth and wisdom, graced me with the benefits of matron-client relations; to this day, I remain proud to be one of her "boys." Finally, Jim Scott, through his work, encouragement, friendship, and, above all, his example, singularly inspired me to continue with my academic studies.

During my years at Cornell University, where I wrote the Ph.D. thesis upon which this book is based, I benefited greatly from the support of the Government Department and the Southeast Asia Program. The friendship and hospitality of the Kahins, the Pontussons, the Shiraishis, and the Tarrows stand out in my memory, as does the encouragement of John and Ida Wolff over the years. During my pre-fieldwork years in Ithaca and my stint in the luxurious Kahin Center, many students, staff, and faculty in the Southeast Asia Program offered encouragement and friendship. In particular, Peter Zinoman proved a very tolerant office-mate and enduring friend, while my favorite classmate, Lotta Hedman, pored over the entire dissertation, providing comprehensive criticisms and suggestions for revision.

Thanks go to the National Science Foundation and the Olin Foundation, which generously funded five of my six years of graduate school, and to several Cornell faculty members who offered abundant support. Martin Shefter helped to reawaken my interest in American politics, and Jonas Pontusson, recruited to serve as an outside reader, responded with the incisive analytical mind and the good-humored enthusiasm that I had learned to admire in him as my teacher and friend. Takashi Shiraishi, from my first year at Cornell, prodded me along with thoughtful questions and friendly advice, and Ben Anderson earned my admiration, affection, and gratitude over the many years I spent under his tutelage. My immense debt to him is apparent on every page of this book.

Research in the Philippines from 1990 through 1992 would not have been possible without the generosity of numerous friends in Manila, Cavite, and Cebu, to whom I still feel tremendously grateful. In Manila, the University of the Philippines Third World Studies Center kindly offered a visiting fellowship and provided a refuge from the demands of research in the metropolis, as did late nights at PCED and Trellis. Sunny Benitez and Jim Rush generously lent Lotta and me their home and admitted us to the ranks of the extensive Benitez clan. Jet Benitez selflessly took time off from work to help me with research in Cavite, providing insights and contacts otherwise beyond my grasp. Rosary Benitez took me and Lotta into her home and blessed us with her company and her friendship. Ben Anderson, Coeli Barry, Terry George, John Humphreys, Helen Mendoza, Apa Ongpin, Mark Thompson, Paul Hutchcroft and Edna Labra, Steve Groff and Maritess Regalado, Jaime and Therese Faustino, and many other friends were also a great source of companionship and support.

In Cebu, thanks to the intervention of a certain "Cherry Tanaka," Lotta and I spent many enjoyable months in the Guadalupe compound of Trining and Zosing Labra, who welcomed us into their extensive clan. Spoiling us with feasts and outings, teaching us local history and *laglum nga Binisaya*, and letting us loose among their children and grandchildren, they offered us a home away from home. The months we spent as part of their family will always remain the most cherished memories of my years in the Philippines.

In Manila, Cebu, and Cavite, a number of local experts were of great assistance in my research. In Cebu City, Resil Mojares allowed me to use the resources of the Cebuano Studies Center and treated me to fascinating discussions of Cebu history over coffee and *merienda*. Bernie Cañizares, Farah de José, Harold Olofson, and Emerito Calderon helped me with research on the Abines clan, and Lino Ybañez was a gracious host to me in Bantayan. In Cavite, Ferdinand Campos offered his assistance and his friendship. In Carmona, the courageous and eloquent Felix Purificacion accepted me into his *tropa* and earned my admiration and affection. At the Lopez Museum and the National Library, several members of the staff offered considerable assistance and support.

After completing the dissertation on which this book is based, I received tremendous encouragement from many different quarters. At the School of Oriental and African Studies (SOAS), colleagues Ian Brown and Steve Hopgood provided their unflagging support and, more important, their friendship. Beyond SOAS, travels, visits, conferences, and correspondence allowed me to enjoy the wisdom and occasional companionship of a wide variety of Philippine and Southeast Asia specialists such as Fenella Cannell, Mike Cullinane, Paul Hutchcroft, Sidney Jones, Ben and Melinda Kerkvliet, Bruce Koppel, Al McCoy, Ambeth Ocampo, Vince Rafael, Geoff Robinson, Jim Rush, Danilyn Rutherford, Jomo K. S., Jim Scott, Mark Thompson, and Carl Trocki. The Philippine Center for Investigative Journalism and the Institute for Popular Democracy, through their support and their outstanding work, encouraged me to persevere with the writing of this book.

Its publication would not have been possible without the unflagging enthusiasm, efforts, and encouragement of Bruce Koppel of the East-West Center. Muthiah Alagappa and Elisa Johnston of the East-West Center and Muriel Bell, Cindy Gammer, Kate Washington, and Stacey Lynn of Stanford University Press held my hand patiently but firmly throughout the process. Janet Mowery, copy editor, and Ty Koontz, indexer, were thoughtful and thorough. Two (not so anonymous) reviewers, Al McCoy and Jeffrey Riedinger, provided comments and criticisms that I hope I have at least partially addressed (or deflected) in my revisions, and that saved me from myself in a variety of ways. I am also grateful for Al McCoy's many efforts beyond the call of duty over the years.

Nick Benson, Paul Kihn, and John Stamm saw me through some rough patches and encouraged me with their unflagging support. From near and afar, my brother, Henry, has been a constant source of encouragement and entertainment, embracing me, warts and all, in the most generous, brotherly way. I hope that, in my own clumsy way, I have done the same for him over the years. My mother, whose early insistence on highbrow education and world travel yielded perhaps unintended consequences, suffered through my long absences, graced me with a gutsy visit to the Philippines, and cheered me on from the distant sidelines.

Finally, thanks go to the two people mentioned in the dedication of this book. My father, whose illness and death coincided with the onset of my interest and involvement in the Philippines, always inspired me through his capacity for warmth and friendship, his rigorous analytical mind, and his abundant humor and zest for life. I hope that some small traces of his influence remain, not only on these pages but in the ebb and flow of my everyday life. Lotta Hedman, my most treasured colleague and companion, has been by my side for nearly ten years now, imparting her wisdom and her affection with singular grace and generosity. More than anyone else mentioned in the preceding pages, her presence and her influence shaped this book and the years spent on its preparation and completion. To and for her I shall always be grateful.

J.T.S.

# Contents

1. Bossism and State Formation
   in the Philippines    1

2. Small-Town Bosses:
   The Mafia-Style Mayors of Cavite    23

3. The Provincial Warlords
   of Cavite, 1896–1995    51

4. The Small-Town Dynasties of Cebu    81

5. The District-Level Dynasties of Cebu    101

6. A Provincial Dynasty:
   The Osmeñas of Cebu City    124

7. Bossism in Comparative Perspective    140

   Notes    155

   Bibliography    195

   Index    215

   Series List    227

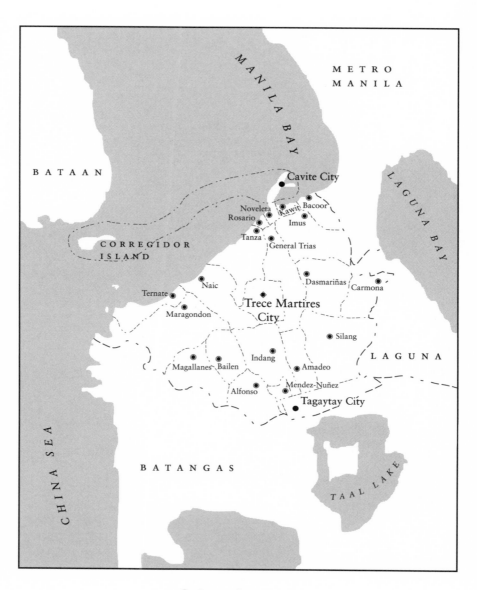

Cavite province ca. 1980

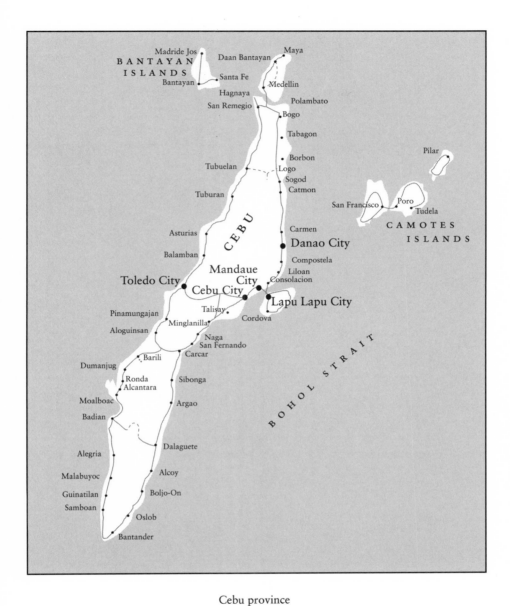

Cebu province

# Capital, Coercion, and Crime

BOSSISM IN THE PHILIPPINES

# Bossism and State Formation
# in the Philippines

In the 1990s, journalistic and scholarly scrutiny occasionally focused upon some of the more intransigent and invidious forms of local despotism to be found in various parts of the world. Urban machine bosses in the Indian city of Bombay, ranch and hacienda owners in the Mexican state of Chiapas, cocaine barons in Colombia, gangster-politicians in Thailand, mafiosi on the wane in Italy but on the rise in Russia all have featured in media accounts that highlight the plenitude and persistent influence of localized monopolies on coercive resources and economic activities. Typically lurid in their fixation on violence and condescending in their portrayal of popular acquiescence in these local tyrannies, such accounts reaffirm a smug sense of the superiority of the "civic cultures" in the industrial democracies of Western Europe and North America. In this regard, the Philippines since 1986 has offered something of a textbook example, as can be seen in the growth of local and foreign interest in so-called provincial warlords and political dynasties and the international notoriety of elections in the Asian archipelago for the use of "guns, goons, and gold."

Academic interest in these myriad manifestations of localized despotism has also enjoyed a modest resurgence, as scholars have revived some of the insights and debates raised in the political science literature of the 1960s and early 1970s on patron-client relations, political machines, "brokers," caciques, mafia, and rural banditry. Joel Migdal, for example, in his widely read and frequently cited volume *Strong Societies and Weak States* (1988), has argued that the ineffectiveness of many Third World states stems from the resilience and resistance of "chiefs, landlords, bosses, rich peasants, clan leaders, za'im, effendis, aghas, caciques, kulaks (for convenience, 'strongmen') through their various social organizations."[1] These local strongmen, Migdal claims, have, through their success at "social control," often effectively "captured" parts of Third World states.

They have succeeded in having themselves or their family members placed in critical state posts to ensure allocation of resources according to their own rules, rather than the rules propounded in the official rhetoric, policy statements, and legislation generated in the capital city or those put forth by a strong implementor.[2]

In a similar vein, Frances Hagopian, in her study of Brazil since the 1964 military coup, stressed that the "residual power" of an oligarchy or "traditional élite" in states like Minas Gerais effectively constrains the possibilities for (re)democratization in terms of "political parties, local governments, the executive-legislative relationship, electoral codes, and modes of interest association and representation."[3] Jonathan Fox, in his writings on local politics in Latin America, has likewise highlighted the persistence of "authoritarian enclaves" under formally democratic auspices and has promoted an analysis of "rural democratisation" contextualized against the backdrop of "subnational regimes."[4]

While the arguments of such authors are complex and multistranded, their essential underlying assumptions and assertions, as exemplified by Migdal's influential volume, are twofold. First, Migdal argues, local strongmen have flourished in "weblike" societies, which "host a mélange of fairly autonomous social organizations" in which "social control" is effectively "fragmented" and by which states are kept weak and ineffective. This pattern of fragmented social control, it is claimed, often crystallized in the course of colonial rule and integration into the world capitalist economy, most notably in the emergence of large landowning classes, who also occupy center stage in the accounts of authors like Hagopian and Fox:

Social control changed irrevocably as big landowners consolidated holdings and integrated themselves (and, along with them, their workers and tenants) much more fully into the world market economy. Landowners in region after region increased the resources at their disposal, which could be used to build new strategies of survival through their direct ties to the world market. Additionally, these ties often made them somewhat impervious to any attempts by ambitious political authorities to bring them under control. The stage was set for the recreation of weblike societies that would characterize so much of the Third World in the late twentieth century.[5]

In short, owing to the weblike structure of society, the capacity of state leaders to implement policies is frequently impeded or compromised, and state agencies and resources are easily captured by local strongmen.

Second, local strongmen come to exercise social control by delivering key components for the "strategies of survival" of the local population.

All people combine available symbols with opportunities to solve mundane needs for food, housing, and the like to create their strategies of survival—blueprints for action and belief in a world that hovers on the brink of a Hobbesian state of nature. Such strategies provide not only a basis for personal survival but also a link for the individual from the realm of personal identity and self-serving action (a political economy) to the sphere of group identity and collective action (a communal moral economy).

In stitching together strategies of survival, people use myths or symbols to help explain their place and prospects in an otherwise bewildering world. Their strategies rest upon concrete foundations; they provide material needs and aspirations, such as jobs, housing, and protection. These strategies of survival, sewn from the symbols, rewards and sanctions, are the roadmaps used to guide one through the maze of daily life, ensuring one's existence and, in rare instances, pointing the way toward upward mobility.[6]

In short, by this account the strongmen not only enjoy legitimacy and support among the local population but also exist to satisfy the population's needs and demands for their services. Thus authors like Hagopian and Fox frame their discussions in terms of "personalism," "clientelism," and "patron-client relations" and portray local strongmen as brokers and patrons. Hagopian, in her summary description of *coronelismo* in northeastern Brazil, offers a fine example of these two complementary arguments:

*Coronelismo* flourished under the same local economic conditions of a traditional agrarian society that generally sustain traditional political clientelism—the grossly unequal distribution of land and other material resources. Direct economic dependence and status differentials allowed local, private elites to establish political clienteles. The coroneis were usually the largest landowners in the area under their "jurisdiction."[7]

Following on the heels of such studies, this book offers a critical counterpoint to arguments that portray local despotism as reflecting the strength of society and the resilience of traditional élites and regional oligarchies. As the following chapters demonstrate, the contexts in which local strongmen thrive are shaped at least as much by the nature of the state as by that of society; élites may be less "traditional"—and oligarchies less enduring—than is often assumed. Equally, this volume takes issue with those accounts that speak in terms of "clientelism" and "personalism" and paint the political culture, predispositions, and particularistic demands of local populations as essentially causing, legitimating, and bearing responsibility for the failings of democracy on the local level. As the case studies herein suggest, the supply of local strongmen does not necessarily reflect popular demand; people do not, in other words, simply "get the government they deserve." In short, the following pages articulate arguments that highlight the decisive role of state structures on the one hand, and coercive forms of control over local populations on the other, for facilitating the emergence and entrenchment of local strongmen.

In this regard, the Philippines provides a perfect test case. Scholarly and journalistic accounts have long emphasized both the persistence of a landowning élite and the predominance of patron-client relations as features of local politics far more pronounced in the archipelago than elsewhere in Southeast Asia. Moreover, as the use of the term "bossism" suggests, this book stresses not only the often underestimated legacies of the American colonial era in the Philippines but also the curiously underrated role of violence and coercion in local strongman rule more generally.[8] Finally, in both its underlying methodology and its overarching conclusions, this book reveals the utility of the empirically rich and theoretically sophisticated scholarly work on political machines and county courthouse cliques in the United States for understanding local politics in the Philippines and elsewhere in the world.

In particular, revisionist scholars have offered a useful corrective to the conventional wisdom regarding political machines in the United States. Discrediting earlier studies that stressed the "political ethos" and interests of societal groups that supposedly benefit from machine politics, Martin Shefter instead provides an explanation for the emergence of urban political machines that focused upon "the interests of *the élites* that manage to seize the leadership of the group[s] in question."[9] Viewing urban political machines as primarily élite- rather than mass-created, he shows how the formation and entrenchment of centralized machines required *institutional structures* capable of mobilizing voters, maintaining internal discipline, and generating financial resources. Similarly, Steven Erie has elaborated an "intergovernmental theory" that explains the variation in the endurance of political machines in different American cities in terms of the *state resources* obtained through "local alliances with party leaders at the state and federal levels."[10] Offering, like Shefter, a "supply-side" view of machines, he has shown how local bosses rely on "intergovernmental alliances" with patrons at county, state, and national levels "to monopolize all public sector resources in the metropolis to strengthen their organizations and starve their opponents."[11]

Moreover, scholarship on urban machine politics in other Western industrial democracies has echoed the revisionist conclusions of Shefter and Erie. These authors find supporting evidence in Judith Chubb's work on local Christian Democrat (*Democrazia Cristiana* or DC) Party organizations in southern Italy. Explaining variation in the endurance of DC machines in Palermo and Naples, she stresses that local strongman rule may in fact reflect the weakness of society rather than its strength, and the strength of the state rather than its weakness, to use the terms favored by Migdal.

A key variable underlying DC power in Palermo is the economic structure of the city and the social fragmentation associated with it, which impede the aggregation of political demand and the organization of collective interests necessary for the emergence of an alternative model of political behavior. The monopolization of economic resources in the hands of the DC is possible because of the absence of an autonomous resource base at the local level and the consequent dependence of the local economy on the resources of the state.[12]

Moreover, against the "mass" or "exchange" theories that portray machines as working to satisfy popular demands for particularistic goods, Chubb highlights the role of machines in creating, reproducing, and manipulating scarcity for the local population at large.

Once all centers of both local and extralocal power are centralized in the hands of one party, an expanding stock of resources is no longer necessary; indeed, the power of the party rests rather on the manipulation of scarcity, on maintaining large numbers of people in competition for scarce resources, all of which are channeled through the party.[13]

Given the predominance of "strong society/weak state" and "patron-client" arguments in the literature on local strongmen in the Third World, the contrarian conclusions of scholars like Shefter, Erie, and Chubb may serve as the basis for a constructive critique. In the study of Philippine politics in particular, where oligarchical rule and political clientelism constitute the pillars of received opinion and conventional wisdom, such a critique is long overdue, as will be shown in the pages below.

## Clientelism, Oligarchy, and a "Weak" State?

As highlighted by the process and outcome of elections since the late 1980s in this Southeast Asian archipelago, the Philippines presents an important case study of local strongmen against which to reexamine the scholarly literature sketched above. In local, congressional, and national elections after the downfall of longtime president Ferdinand Marcos's authoritarian regime in 1986, three enduring aspects of Philippine democracy became apparent. First, a large number of politicians who had held office for many years in the Marcos and pre-Marcos periods won reelection, as did numerous other members of long-entrenched political families. Second, most of these politicians and "political clans" were known to enjoy not only political longevity but also economic preeminence—if not a monopolistic position—within their respective municipal, congressional, or provincial bailiwicks, through landownership, commercial networks, logging or mining concessions, transportation companies, and/or control over illegal economic activities.[14] Finally, ample evidence that fraud, vote-buying, and violence had decisively shaped the conduct and outcome of these elections led commentators to conclude that the celebrated transition from authoritarianism to democracy in Manila was less than complete in its local manifestations.[15] With the revival of electoral politics, analysts thus began to offer evocative descriptions of—and a variety of explanations for—the nature of Philippine democracy; references to political clans, dynasties, traditional politicians, caciques, warlords, and bosses appeared with great frequency in journalistic and scholarly accounts, and terms like "cacique democracy," "mafia democracy," "feudalism," "warlordism," and "bossism" gained considerable currency.

As its title suggests, this book treats these features of the social formation found in the postwar Philippines as manifestations of bossism and examines the ways in which various bosses—small-town bosses, district and provincial bosses, and even national bosses—endeavored to secure political domination and capital accumulation in their respective bailiwicks. The use of the term "boss" reflects both a rejection of accounts stressing the putative sociocultural legacies of Spanish colonial rule (caciquism) and the supposed salience of patron-client relations (clientelism) in the Philippines.[16] Use of the terms "bossism" and "bosses," moreover, emphasizes the distinctly American colonial-era institutional structures inherited by the postwar Philippine state and stresses the often underestimated and poorly understood role of violence and coercive pressures in shaping economic accumulation, political competition, and social relations in the archipelago.

This book examines first small-town and then district and provincial bosses in two provinces noteworthy for particularly dramatic socioeconomic change over the course of the twentieth century. Tracing the manifestations of bossism in a series of case studies and comparing boss rule in the two provinces and across levels of state power, the book concludes with both a reappraisal of Ferdinand Marcos's authoritarian regime and a reexamination of Philippine democracy in broader comparative historical perspective. First, however, the pages that follow discuss the two dominant contending paradigms in the scholarship on Philippine politics, attempt to formulate a counterargument stressing state formation in the archipelago, and provide a brief introductory sketch of the two provinces discussed in subsequent chapters.

Many descriptions of elected local and congressional officials in the post-Marcos era highlight their putative roles as "patrons" and "benefactors," noting that "transactions between the representative and the represented involve mostly particularistic demands ranging from jobs, medical help, and intervention in disputes, to business favors and solicitations," which elected officials attend to "because they translate into votes and political support."[17] These depictions hark back to the extensive scholarly literature on patron-client relations that dominated Philippine studies in the 1960s and that today remains largely unchallenged as a framework for understanding the dynamics of local politics in the archipelago.[18]

In the 1960s, American and American-trained Filipino scholars portrayed Philippine society and politics as structured by webs of patron-client relations. Highly personalized, multifunctional, and affect-laden in nature, patron-client ties were described as binding together individuals of unequal wealth, status, and power. Such a dyadic face-to-face relationship, perhaps exemplified by that between landlord and tenant, was defined as

an exchange relationship or instrumental friendship between two individuals of different status in which the patron uses his own influence and resources to provide for the protection and material welfare of his lower status client and his family, who, for his part, reciprocates by offering general support and assistance, including personal services, to the patron.[19]

While modernization theorists viewed patron-client ties as drawing strength from a traditional Filipino "political culture" that valorized reciprocity, smooth interpersonal relations, and kinship and fictive kinship (*compadrazgo*) bonds,[20] scholars influenced by historical materialism argued that clientelist relationships were contingent upon concrete socioeconomic circumstances: marked social inequalities, material scarcity, and the failure of kinship, village units, and state institutions to guarantee personal subsistence and security to the bulk of the population.[21] Yet all concurred in portraying patron-client relations as an essential social adhesive in Philippine society that crosscut and undermined potential cleavages based on class, corporate, or ethnic solidarities through webs of particularistic alliances based on bonds of personal reciprocity.[22]

In the eyes of these scholars, electoral politics in the Philippines thus appeared to rest on a "pyramid" or "vast network" of patron-client relationships, stretching from tenants to landlords and barrio-level ward *líders* (leaders) to mayors, congressmen, provincial governors, senators, and presidents.[23] The successful local politician skillfully used the discretionary powers at his disposal to dispense patronage to a dispersed clientele, as exemplified by one consistently reelected congressman:

In some municipalities he is a generous road-builder, legal counselor, recommendation-maker, job giver, and guardian angel. . . . He has won the loyalty of his sub-leaders and followers by taking care of them whenever they need his advice or help on various matters. He has extended his family through sanguinal, affinal, and *compadrazgo* relationships. He has multiplied his party followers through patronage at the Bureau of Public Works or at the Emergency Employment Agency.[24]

Electoral politics, according to this portrait, consisted of persistently bifactional competition between rival groupings of patron-client clusters:

Competition predictably produces two major groups, each supported by roughly half the population. A group of any significantly smaller proportion of the population would have little chance of victory and, in a society much concerned with winning factional contests, could be expected to fuse with some other group in order to create a larger combination. Conversely, a group supported by much more than half the population would have an excess of votes and, where votes must be obtained through the doing of favors, would be expending its resources needlessly. This functional bifactionalism is not only the predominant pattern in local politics but . . . appears to have been a factor in the persistence of a two-party system during most of the country's recent history.[25]

This pattern of persistent bifactionalism—allegedly reflected in "the unrestrictedness, the closeness, and the intensity of competition for elective office at all levels of government"—guaranteed that politicians were "highly responsive" to their constituents and that ordinary voters exerted "substantial influence . . . upon decision-making."Examining the two-party system that predominated in the pre-martial-law years (before 1972), one scholar concluded: "Each party has had a reasonable chance of winning a good number of elections—and neither party, having won control of a constituency anywhere in the country, has been able to take its continued hegemony for granted."[26]

In the early 1970s, in the context of increasing turbulence in Philippine politics and the declaration of martial law in 1972, scholars variously linked national developments and processes of political change to the putative "transformation" or "breakdown" of patron-client relations. On the one hand, scholars influenced by modernization theory claimed that economic growth and differentiation, urbanization, and the penetration of national bureaucratic institutions into local communities held the potential for "modernizing" Philippine politics, as upwardly mobile "professional politicians" substituted for the previously dominant "avocational" scions of prominent landowning families. These "new men," they argued, would replace traditional patron-client factions with more specialized "political machines," a development that would presage greater rural democratization, party institutionalization, and national integration.[27] Scholars influenced by more economistic approaches claimed that the penetration of capitalism into the Philippine countryside, the commercialization of agriculture, and the resultant trends of increasing landlessness and rising inequalities in income distribution would narrow the scope and effectiveness of clientelistic exchanges, undermine patron-client relations, and pave the way for intensifying factionalism, social unrest, and class conflict.[28]

Viewed from the vantage point of the post-Marcos 1990s, the descriptive and explanatory powers of patron-client relations appear extremely limited. In the 1990s, widespread electoral fraud, vote-buying, and violence combined with high reelection rates for incumbent legislators and local officials to discredit depictions of contemporary politics in terms of bifactional competition between rival patron-client networks. Likewise, the abundance of politicians and political clans who have remained in office for several decades underscores the inaccuracy of accounts that heralded the arrival of "new men" and the fading of "traditional politicians" on the electoral horizon, and scotches predictions that the continuation of secular socioeconomic and demographic trends observed in the 1960s would lead to the unraveling of élite democracy. Finally, scholarly research on the American colonial era and the postwar pre-martial-law period has effectively debunked the nostalgia-driven myth that the unseemly features of contemporary Philippine democracy represent a kind of fall from grace or decline from a lost yesteryear of benign paternalism.[29] The electoral fraud, skulduggery, vote-buying, and violence disparaged today were much in evidence in pre-martial-law—and even prewar—years, and legislators and local officials (and their families) entrenched themselves in various municipalities, districts, and provinces throughout the twentieth century.[30] In short, the notion that patron-client relations ever provided the essential social cement in Philippine life ignores the persistence of coercive pressures and local power monopolies in electoral politics and social relations.

Impressed by these apparent continuities and frustrated by the limitations of the patron-client model, scholars and other researchers have in recent years posed an alternative portrait of the Philippines largely inspired by neo-Marxist discussions of class and state.[31] In the view of these observers, the outcomes of post-Marcos elections have highlighted the persistence or reassertion of direct class rule by a landed élite or oligarchy, which, unique in Southeast Asia, first emerged in the nineteenth century as a nascent bourgeoisie with an economic base independent of the state.[32]

The distinctive feature of the Philippines' response to the expanding demand of the world market was the creation of a substantial indigenous landowning class. Unlike the other states of Southeast Asia where agricultural export crops were grown on land owned by foreign companies, aristocrat-bureaucrats, or small peasants, the commercial revolution in Philippine agriculture gave rise to a new class of commercially oriented landowners who were quite separate from the bureaucracy. It was from the ranks of this class that a new political élite emerged in the late nineteenth century and later, in the twentieth century, a commercial and industrial élite.[33]

Given this oligarchy's early establishment of a solid base in landownership, the state subsequently failed to achieve autonomy from the dominant class in the Philippines. Representatives of the oligarchy continued to be elected to congressional and local office throughout the twentieth century. In the Marxist terminology adopted by some radical intellectuals in the Philippines, the social formation in the archipelago has thus retained significant "feudal" or "semi-feudal" features.[34] In the language of American political science, the Philippines offers a classic case of a postcolonial weak state confronting a strong society dominated by traditional élites and local strongmen.[35]

This depiction of the Philippines as a weak state dominated by an oligarchy with roots in large landholdings, while more politically persuasive and historically grounded than the patron-client model, is nonetheless both descriptively overdrawn and analytically misleading. Revisionist historical scholarship, for example, has highlighted the limitations of the Spanish-era landed élite's wealth, landholdings, and geographical distribution and recast the timing of its emergence as a "national oligarchy" to the twentieth century.[36] In addition, more recent studies of the contributions of forest, mineral, and marine resource exploitation—and public land—to the process of capital accumulation in the Philippines cast considerable doubt on the centrality of private landownership in the generation of wealth in the richly endowed archipelago.[37] Careful research on the role of the Philippine state in the acquisition and maintenance of property and the processing and export of agricultural produce has likewise called into question the extent to which landownership ever provided a truly independent economic base for the exercise of political power,[38] while documentation of massive environmental degradation in the coral reefs, forests, and mineral-rich mountain ridges of the archipelago highlights the role of the state as an instrument—rather than simply an object—of patrimonial plunder.[39] Close analysis of election results and corporation directorates in the 1980s, moreover, has suggested that many of the entrenched politicians and magnates in the country derive their power and wealth not from private landownership but from state resources and foreign (mostly overseas Chinese) commercial capital.[40] Finally, numerous well-documented case studies of entrenched politicians and established "landed élites" have revealed that the accumulation of large landholdings often followed from, rather than preceded, the assumption of political power.[41]

The "strong oligarchy, weak state" thesis also fails to account for variation and change in the course of Philippine history. Concentrations of landownership have not in fact correlated closely with the political longevity of elected officials, and some of the most enduring and notorious politicians and political clans in the archipelago have emerged and prospered in rural bailiwicks notable for an absence of large landholdings and in highly urbanized areas.[42] Ferdinand Marcos, for example, who as three-term congressman (1949–59), senator (1959–65), and the Philippines' longest-reigning president (1966–86) accumulated more power and wealth than any other politician in the nation's history, owed none of his unsurpassed political success to landownership.

Viewed in cross-national comparative perspective, moreover, a portrait of the Philippine state as weak and emasculated by a landed oligarchy fails to illuminate its similarities with and differences from its counterparts in Southeast Asia and elsewhere in the postcolonial world. Among postcolonial plantocracies, for example, the Philippines alone has no history of military rule, while in the context of Southeast Asia its putatively "weak" postcolonial state curiously resembles that of contemporary Thailand, which in the nineteenth century had a monarchical state "strong" enough to avoid direct colonial subjugation.[43] Of all the other countries in Southeast Asia, it is thus striking that only in Thailand have local bosses—called *chao pho* or "godfathers"—achieved such power and prominence in recent years.[44] In short, a depiction of the Philippines as a dominant landed oligarchy and an emasculated weak state clearly leaves a number of important questions unanswered.

Although the scholarly literatures on patron-client relations and oligarchy-state dynamics in the Philippines address different concerns and draw diverging conclusions, their shared assumptions yield common descriptive and analytical limitations. Honing in on the ways and means of electoral politics at the local level, scholars working in the clientelist tradition tend to abstract from the paternalistic veneer of intraclass social relations a model that purports to sketch the structure, and outline the transformation, of Philippine politics writ large. Focusing on the ends and exigencies of political economy at the national level, proponents of the "strong oligarchy, weak state" thesis are inclined to pinpoint the long rule of a dominant social class as the defining feature of the Philippine polity. Taking a more or less essentialized Philippine society as their common point of departure, these two literatures thus downplay the role of state structures and institutions in shaping both the ends and the means of political competition, economic accumulation, and social relations in the archipelago. In examining those elements of the Philippine social formation least convincingly described or explained by patron-client relations or oligarchical domination, such as the tenacity of political bosses and dynasties and the long authoritarian rule of President Ferdinand Marcos, an approach that accords more autonomy and greater causal primacy to the Philippine state may address the shortcomings of the existing scholarly literature.

In contrast with studies that stress clientelism and class domination, this volume takes as its point of departure an analysis of state formation in the Philippines. This approach follows the lead of scholars who have highlighted the distinctive and enduring institutional legacies of American colonial rule in the Philippines and the patrimonial nature of state-oligarchy relations in the archipelago.[45] The myriad manifestations of bossism reflect neither the strength (and subsequent decline) of patron-client relations nor the rule and resilience of a landed oligarchy, but rather the peculiar institutional structures of the Philippine state, whose lineages may be traced over successive phases of state formation. In particular, the subordination of an extremely underdeveloped state apparatus to elected municipal, provincial, and national officials in the American colonial era (and during a phase of what is defined below as "primitive accumulation") proved decisive for facilitating the emergence of bossism in the archipelago.

## Lineages of the Philippine State

In the context of Southeast Asia, state formation in the Philippines has followed a highly distinctive trajectory favorable to the long-term preservation and progressive expansion of "local strongman" power. Precolonial and Spanish colonial state forms in the archipelago were distinguished by the absence of institutionalized supralocal bases for indigenous political authority, and by the availability of state resources and prerogatives for local, personal use. Most distinctive and decisive, however, was the subordination of this relatively underdeveloped state apparatus to elected officials by the American colonial regime; this contrasted sharply with the bureaucratization and insulation of colonial states elsewhere in the region and combined with the onset of "primitive accumulation" to facilitate the emergence of bossism in the Philippines in the early twentieth century.

Before the arrival of the Spanish colonizers in the sixteenth century, "big men" (*datus*) in various parts of the Philippine archipelago strived to maintain local monopolies on coercion and taxation through violence and the accumulation of personal followings. Since residents of these islands lived in dispersed nucleated settlements (*barangay*) clustered along sheltered bays, coastal areas, and river deltas, power rested essentially in control over people rather than land. With kinship reckoned bilaterally, moreover, lineage did not determine succession to political leadership, and authority, in Weberian terms, was essentially "charismatic" rather than "traditional." Local strongmen retained power over their subject populations only insofar as they were able to provide the material resources and project the "prowess," "inner-soul stuff," and capacity for violence that earned them the respect and loyalty of followers.[46] Extracting an economic surplus through compulsory labor services and forced deliveries of agricultural produce, these local strongmen were able to enforce monopolies over—and extract predatory incomes from—trade flows through transportation bottlenecks (e.g., river deltas) and market centers.

Thus the petty "*datu*-ships" of the pre-Hispanic Philippine archipelago were small-scale versions of the "men of prowess" polities found throughout Southeast Asia, as political authority, with few exceptions, remained entirely personal and confined to local settlements.[47] Elsewhere in the region, more extensive and institutionalized political entities emerged, in some cases with elaborate formal hierarchies. Two external factors appear to have been crucial for this regionwide development.[48] First, involvement in, and competition for, long-distance maritime trade stimulated state formation. Second, the penetration of "Great Tradition" religions—Hinduism, Buddhism, and Islam—into Southeast Asian societies provided a set of "languages" that encouraged the development of permanent and suprasettlement political offices or institutions—in other words, "kingship." In the unhispanicized Philippines, which remained relatively untouched by Indic influences and outside certain crucial maritime trade routes,[49] the only instances of political organization observed

above the level of the settlement were found in those few parts of the
archipelago penetrated by Islam and deeply involved in regional and
Asia-wide commerce. In the sixteenth century, the arrival of the Spanish
colonizers impeded the further spread of Islamic influences and initiated
a new phase of state formation in the archipelago.[50]

The distinctive organization of Spanish colonial rule from the late sixteenth to the mid-nineteenth century combined with the virtual absence
of institutionalized, suprasettlement precolonial political formations in
the archipelago to preserve local strongman monopolies over coercion
and taxation. Unlike the Spanish colonies in the Americas, the Philippines
was at the periphery of the empire, relatively insignificant, and under less
vigorous royal control. Spanish economic interests in the archipelago
were restricted to the Manila galleon trade with China, mines and landed
estates were few, and little native produce was extracted from the colony.
Thus the Spanish presence in the Philippines remained minimal and
largely confined to Manila, and the Catholic religious orders, whose friars constituted the most visible manifestation of Spanish power in the
countryside, enjoyed considerable autonomy from the Manila-based secular administration.

   In the colonized areas of the archipelago, local monopolies over coercion and taxation remained in private hands; they derived their force and
legitimacy not from the realm of locally affirmed personal leadership but
from a supralocal, quasi-legalistic political order. First under *encomiendas* (grants) awarded to Spanish *conquistadores* in the sixteenth century
and later under local trade monopolies granted to Spanish *alcaldes mayores* (provincial governors), the *datus* and their descendants gained exemption from tribute and won appointment as village headmen (*cabezas
de barangay*) and town executives (*gobernadorcillos*), collectively known
as *principales*.[51] Hereditary succession governed ascension to these posts
until the late eighteenth century, when the colonial administration initiated a process of municipal elections, restricted to the (entirely male)
*principales* and closely supervised by the meddlesome Spanish parish
priests and *alcaldes mayores*, whose form was "determined by a long series of laws, decrees, and circulars."[52] *Gobernadorcillos* exercised judicial
and executive powers, enforcing Spanish legal statutes, collecting taxes,
administering corvée labor, controlling local police forces, and serving as
the local business agents of the *alcaldes mayores*. As agents of the colonial state, their power rested essentially in law and *puwesto*—position
within the state. Yet their authority advanced only to the *pueblo* (or municipality, composed of several *barangay*), and no circulation of native officials outside or "above" their localities occurred. In short, Spanish colo-

nial-era states preserved indigenous local strongmen as subcontracted agents of the state and introduced derivative and discretionary state power as new bases for local strongman authority.

Under the reign of Charles III (1759–88), Bourbon absolutist reforms in Spain transformed the political economy of the empire, introducing to Philippine society a mechanism through which local strongmen could assume and retain local monopolies over coercion and taxation: private capital. Seeking to improve the fiscal viability of its Asian colony, the Crown established a government monopoly on tobacco in the Philippines in 1766 and eventually abolished the *alcaldes mayores'* exclusive trading licenses. Over the course of the nineteenth century, moreover, the Spanish regime gradually opened Manila and other Philippine ports to foreign trade, stimulating the integration of the Philippines into the world capitalist system. Rising foreign demand for local crops (especially abaca and sugar) and the presence of foreign trading firms in the ports of the archipelago encouraged the commercialization of agriculture and the monetization of the economy. Local merchants began extending credit to cultivators of export crops and, through debt peonage, purchase, and settlement, acquired formal ownership of landholdings.[53]

The resulting transformation of the archipelago's political economy combined with the local structures of colonial authority to generate new forms of private control over the state's monopolies on coercion and taxation. In the municipalities, those who amassed proprietary wealth through moneylending, landownership, and marketing of commercial crops could exercise considerable influence in local elections and over locally elected officials. Numerous accounts of municipal politics in the latter half of the nineteenth century have noted the tendency of wealthy individuals to support proxies as candidates for *gobernadorcillos* and *cabezas de barangay* rather than to seek office themselves. Through their proxies, those local landed or merchant capitalists were able to control tax collection, law enforcement, and the distribution of public works.[54] Meanwhile, the colonial regime's increasing reliance upon tax-farming as a means of generating revenues allowed those with large quantities of cash to purchase local—and supralocal—monopoly franchises on cockfighting and the sale of opium, palm wine, tobacco, and other restricted commodities.[55]

The institutional features of the Spanish colonial state in the Philippines, most notably municipal elections and revenue farms, thus allowed those possessing proprietary wealth—money and land—to control local monopolies on coercion and taxation in the archipelago. In other words, by the end of the nineteenth century, the basis of local strongman rule had shifted from personal martial prowess and armed followings to resources drawn from the colonial state and private capital. Yet this pattern of state formation was hardly exceptional in Southeast Asia during this phase of colonial rule and did not in itself predetermine the nature and extent of local strongman rule in the postindependence Philippines. In fact, it was the peculiar nature of American colonial state-building in the first four decades of the twentieth century, in stark contrast with contemporaneous developments elsewhere in the region, that laid the essential foundations for bossism in the archipelago.

American colonial rule in the Philippines from 1901 until the outbreak of World War II expanded private control over the local coercive and extractive agencies of the state "upward" by subordinating the national state apparatus to provincial- and national-level elected officials. Elections to municipal office, based on highly restricted suffrage and freed from the intervention of ecclesiastical authorities, were first held in 1901, followed by those for provincial governors (1902), representatives to the national Philippine Assembly (1907), an American-style bicameral legislature (1916), and a Commonwealth presidency (1935).[56] Elected municipal mayors retained their Spanish-era discretionary powers over local law enforcement, public works, and taxation, winning complete independence from parish priests and full authority to appoint municipal police forces.[57]

Although elected governors enjoyed similar law-enforcement and taxation powers at the provincial level, representatives to the legislature gained control over a hastily constructed and rapidly "Filipinized" national state apparatus.[58] Within their own districts, legislators exercised effective discretion over the disbursement of pork-barrel funds for public works and the appointment of Constabulary commanders, district engineers, superintendents of schools, provincial fiscals (state prosecutors), treasurers, and assessors, judges of the Court of First Instance, and local agents of the Bureau of Lands.[59] In Manila, meanwhile, these legislators likewise exerted influence over the awarding of contracts, concessions, and monopoly franchises, the appointment of ranking officials in national government agencies (e.g., the Bureau of Customs, the Bureau of Internal Revenue),[60] and the allocation of loans by the Philippine National Bank.[61] Finally, with the election of a Commonwealth president in 1935, a (directly elected) national executive took office, assuming powers far greater than those of his American counterpart, including the authority to disapprove individual items in appropriations bills, discretion over the disbursement of budgeted funds, and supervisory control over local government units.[62] This distinctly American form of late-colonial administration contrasted sharply with the state expansion, bureaucratization, and centralization that proceeded elsewhere in Southeast Asia at the same time.[63]

By the eve of the Japanese invasion in 1941, the American colonial regime and its Commonwealth successor had established the subordination of the state apparatus to a multitiered hierarchy of elected officials. In hundreds of municipalities throughout the archipelago, elected mayors, heading municipal boards composed of elected vice-mayors and several municipal councilors, gained executive control over local state agencies. In more than 50 provinces, governors, presiding over provincial boards composed of elected vice-governors and several other members, likewise assumed authority over provincial offices of various national government departments. Crosscutting this hierarchy of municipal and provincial executive authority, the House of Representatives (a single representative / single district body modeled after its American counterpart) gave more than a hundred congressmen discretion over appointments in their districts as well as influence over the allocation of national state resources. At the national level, a directly elected president shared legislative and executive powers not only with the lower house of Congress but also with 24 members of the Senate, who, after 1939, were nationally elected.

The subordination of municipal, provincial, and national agencies of the state apparatus to elected officials, the onset of primitive capital accumulation, and the expanding role of the colonial state in the economy together facilitated the emergence and entrenchment of colonial-era bosses in a variety of localities and at different levels of state power. American colonial officials noted, for example, that in "a large majority of cases," municipal police forces acted as "the political henchmen, and in too many instances the personal *muchachos* of the *presidentes* and local bosses."[64] In Nueva Ecija, provincial boss Manuel Tinio, a former revolutionary general, used his influence with the Bureau of Lands and his control over the local government machinery—including police forces, justices of the peace, the Court of First Instance, and the Court of Land Registration—to acquire large landholdings.[65] In Negros Occidental, sugar planters seated as congressmen and senators in the legislature similarly expanded their landholdings many times over and, with generous loans from the Philippine National Bank, constructed centrifugal sugar mills to process their cane.[66] In the late 1930s, moreover, Commonwealth president Manuel Quezon gained "near total control" of the legislature, judiciary, and local government[67] and, through government corporations and a close coterie of business cronies (e.g., owners of sugar mills, shipping companies, and banks), exercised considerable control over the "commanding heights"of the Philippine economy.[68] After Liberation in 1945 and independence in 1946, which essentially reconstructed the institutional legacies of American colonial rule, bosses continued to thrive in the Philippines throughout the postwar era.

Thus we see the structural conditions that facilitated the emergence and entrenchment of bosses and bossism in the twentieth-century Philippines. State formation in the Philippines after the precolonial era permitted the survival of private, personal control over the instruments of coercion and taxation. Successive phases of state formation supplanted the charismatic basis of local strongman authority with new bases of local power—derivative and discretionary enforcement of the law and accumulation of land and capital—and, in the American period, extended private control to include the provincial and national agencies of an emerging state apparatus. No phase of "primitive political accumulation," during which the means of coercion and extraction are expropriated from autonomous and private powerholders through their subordination or incorporation into central state bureaucracies and conversion into paid public servants, occurred in the course of Philippine history. Moreover, potentially "state-building" phases of armed mobilization and military consolidation (*caudillismo*), as occurred in many former colonies during national revolutions, were preempted by American intervention (in 1898–1901 and 1945–46).[69]

The form of local strongman rule manifested in the Philippines as "bossism" in fact reflects a common conjuncture in state formation and capitalist development: the subordination of the state apparatus to elected officials against the backdrop of what might loosely be termed "primitive accumulation." "Primitive accumulation" here refers to a phase of capitalist development in which a significant section of the population loses direct control over the means of production and direct access to means of subsistence and is reduced to a state of economic insecurity and dependence on scarce wage labor (before achieving "full" employment and modern welfare capitalism). In these circumstances considerable economic resources and prerogatives remain in the "public" domain and secure (private) property rights have not yet been firmly established by the state. Together, these last two conditions make many voters susceptible to clientelistic, coercive, and monetary pressures and render state offices and state resources central to capital accumulation and control over the "commanding heights" of local economies. From "Old Corruption" England to contemporary India and Russia, the confluence of electoral democracy and primitive accumulation has thus spelled bossism in one form or another. In the Philippine case, it was the American imposition of "colonial democracy" from 1901 onward that determined the nature and extent of local strongman rule in the archipelago.

In conclusion, more than the emergence of a landed élite in the nineteenth century, a distinctive pattern of state formation shaped the processes of twentieth-century capital accumulation in the Philippines, a late, late industrializer whose economy saw considerable colonial and postcolonial state intervention. More than the grip of patron-client relationships, the peculiar institutional legacies of colonial rule facilitated the emergence and entrenchment of small-town bosses, provincial "warlords," and authoritarian presidents by providing mechanisms for private monopolization of the resources and prerogatives of the state. Against the backdrop of these arguments, the following chapters provide case studies of bosses whose careers as local strongmen are highly instructive.

## Case Studies: Cavite and Cebu

The historical processes of state formation in the Philippines are amply documented and easily recounted, but the contours of bossism in the archipelago are more difficult to delineate. The term "bosses" refers to predatory power brokers who achieve monopolistic control over both coercive and economic resources within given territorial jurisdictions or bailiwicks.

"Boss" is a designation at once vague and richly connotative. Although a boss may often function as a patron, the term itself implies (a) that he is the most powerful man in the arena and (b) that his power rests more on inducements and sanctions at his disposal than on affection or status. As distinct from a patron who may or may not be the supreme local leader and whose leadership rests at least partly on rank and affection, the boss is a secular leader par excellence who depends almost entirely on palpable inducements and threats to move people.[70]

In the Philippines, bosses have included small-town mayors, provincial governors, congressmen, and even presidents. "Bossism," in turn, refers to the interlocking, multitiered directorate of bosses who use their control over the state apparatus to exploit the archipelago's human and natural resources.

Neither monolithic nor impervious to transformation, bossism in the Philippines is a social formation whose internal vicissitudes and systemic mutations require comparative analysis. Some bosses succeeded in entrenching themselves in power at certain moments in Philippine history, in some regions of the archipelago, and at various levels of state power, while others have failed. The internal dynamics of domestic capital accumulation and class conflict, moreover, combined with the external pressures of the world capitalist economy and the geopolitical interventions of a global hegemonic power, the United States, to transmute—and occasionally to disequilibrate—the workings of bossism's infernal machinery. To understand the whole from the parts and the parts from the whole is the essential aim of this study.

The following chapters proceed with case studies drawn from two Philippine provinces and include small-town, congressional-district, and provincial bosses. At each level, comparative analysis highlights the structural conditions that allowed a given boss to entrench himself in a given bailiwick, discouraged rivals, and weakened other potential bosses. The dramatic socioeconomic transformation of Cavite and Cebu Provinces over the course of the twentieth century—evidenced in changing patterns of land use, employment, and capital formation—adds a temporal dimension to the study, even as the important structural differences between the two provinces' local political economies allow for traditional paired comparisons. Finally, this multilevel comparative analysis informs a more cursory examination of bosses in other provinces and at the national level, suggesting broader patterns of variation within bossism in the Philippines as a whole.

If "bosses" and "bossism" are merely heuristic terms, the two provinces of Cavite and Cebu, of course, remain two quite real administrative and geographic entities where millions of Filipinos lived, labored, and died during the twentieth century. Beneath the schematic design of this study and its multilevel, cross-case comparisons lies a modest attempt at recounting the social history of two provinces whose rapid industrialization and urbanization are often mystified as entirely benign forms of "progress," even as the wreckage and debris of their recent "development" are conveniently forgotten. Building on the excellent scholarship already available on Cavite and Cebu, this book thus promises new empirical findings and theoretical insights drawn from more than two years of library research, document searches, interviews, and travel in these two provinces, Metro Manila, other parts of the Philippine archipelago, and the United States.[71]

A study of these two provinces, while not necessarily representative of the Philippines as a whole, nonetheless may offer new insights for the understanding of boss rule throughout the archipelago. Unlike such often cited provinces as Negros Occidental and Tarlac, Cavite and Cebu do not possess sizable plantation belts or other large concentrations of landownership, yet both provinces have seen protracted boss rule at the municipal, district, and provincial levels. Closely linked to the Philippines' two key metropoles—Metro Manila and Cebu City—Cavite and Cebu have both undergone dramatic socioeconomic transformation over the course of the twentieth century, and shifting patterns of employment, land use, and capital formation provide the bases for longitudinal comparison of bossism in the two provinces. Finally, the striking contrast between the entrenchment of single-generation gangster-politicians or "mafia bosses" at the municipal and provincial levels in Cavite and the longevity of multigeneration "dynasties" in the small towns, congressional districts, and capital city of Cebu suggests the relevance of the study for comparison of "warlords" and "political clans" elsewhere in the Philippines.

Cavite Province is notable for its contiguity with the Metro Manila area, long sheltered coastline, and diverse topography. Primarily a rice-bowl province, Cavite also has significant zones of banana, coconut, and sugarcane cultivation, and coffee has long been a major cash crop in its southern upland towns. Scattered smallholdings, rather than large latifundia, have been the rule, with farm size in secular decline over the century and share tenancy predominant in the American period but gradually replaced in the postwar era by employment of landless workers, mechanization, and capital-intensive methods and inputs. Since 1900, Cavite's population has grown dramatically, from less than 100,000 at the turn of the twentieth century to more than a million today, and the province's already modest fields, fishing beds, and forests have shrunk considerably over the years as a result of increasing extractive pressures. A massive inflow of foreign and domestic capital into Cavite since the 1970s financed the creation of industrial estates, residential subdivisions, and agribusiness ventures but failed to provide employment for thousands of displaced peasants and marginalized suburban poor in the province. Today, an estimated 40 percent of the predominantly urban population of Cavite lives on or beneath the official poverty line.[72]

Cebu, by contrast, is an island province noteworthy for a mountainous interior and dry, infertile soil, but features a major regional port, entrepôt, and manufacturing center, Cebu City. Virtually unique in the Philippines in its long dependence on corn as the local staple crop,[73] Cebu is also known for its scattered coconut and nipa groves, a small sugar plantation belt, and extensive mining, poultry, and fishing industries. It has more haciendas (especially in sugar and coconuts) than Cavite, but even smaller farms have predominated; share tenancy rose over the years up to the 1970s, when Marcos-era agrarian reform encouraged conversion to cash tenancy and greater reliance on farm workers. Since 1900, Cebu's population has grown dramatically, from roughly 600,000 to nearly 3 million today, even as agricultural involution and environmental degradation reduced corn yields and depleted mangroves and coral reefs around the island province. Since the 1970s, a steady inflow of foreign and domestic capital into Cebu has transformed the regional entrepôt and agricultural processing center of the Visayas and Mindanao into a major location for tourism and manufacturing but today provides low-wage employment for only a small fraction of the swelling ranks of rural and urban poor.[74]

In both Cavite and Cebu, the local manifestations of bossism decisively shaped these briefly sketched processes of primitive capital accumulation. By establishing monopolistic control over coercive and economic resources, town mayors, congressmen, and provincial governors emerged and entrenched themselves as bosses within their respective bailiwicks. The rise, rule, and occasional fall of these bosses is the focus of the following chapters.

# Small-Town Bosses:
# The Mafia-Style Mayors of Cavite

The writings of American and (mostly American-trained) Filipino political scientists of the 1960s and 1970s presented a highly benign image of
local elections and social relations in the rural municipalities of the
Philippines.[1] Elections, it was reported, were eagerly awaited and closely
contested in rural municipalities throughout the archipelago, with a
widespread pattern of bifactionalism and turnover in mayoral races. Local politics, all authors concurred, revolved around rivalries between
élite-led local factions composed of personalistic followings or "patron-
client networks." Stretching from leading town notables to barrio-level
(village) *líders* to the poor farmers, fishermen, and their family dependents who constituted the bulk of the population, these highly fluid factions relied on bonds of consanguinity, affinity, ritual kinship (*compadrazgo*), and personal debts of gratitude (*utang na loób*) that were said
to characterize "traditional Filipino society and values." This pattern of
"premodern" politics thus prevailed thanks to the traditional social structure and political culture.[2]

Going beyond such descriptive assertions, moreover, some scholars
worked within this paradigm to explain patterns of variation and change
in the style and substance of small-town politics in the Philippines. One
study noted marked variations from town to town in patterns of local
factionalism, for example, but designated them inconsequential or inex-
plicable after an inconclusive analysis of election results and census data:
"Local political structure is mainly the product of accidental phenomena

such as local personal and family feuds and alliances, which are but dimly related, if at all, to the ecological features of a town."[3]

More promising, perhaps, was a case study of local politics in two provinces, which presented evidence of varying "modernization" in political leadership at the municipal level. Mayors from old landed families, the author reported, were being replaced by upwardly mobile men from more humble backgrounds, a new breed of professional "machine" politicians. Such changes, it was noted, were more likely to occur in towns where the concentration of land ownership was low and the level of "social mobilization" (measured by literacy, nonagricultural employment, urbanization, and radio and motor vehicle ownership) was high.[4] But the overall trend was clear: "modernization" brought with it "political development" in the form of new types of interest aggregation, articulation, and representation.

Seen from the vantage point of the 1990s, the descriptive and explanatory powers of this literature on municipal politics in the Philippines appear strikingly overdrawn. First, as noted in the previous chapter, press reports and Commission on Elections documents over the years offer ample evidence of widespread use of violence and vote-buying in local elections, thus suggesting the importance of dynamics outside the realm of patron-client relations and "traditional Filipino values" for shaping local politics in the archipelago. Moreover, since the 1970s, detailed research has uncovered—in newspaper articles, election records, court documents, and other archival sources—numerous examples of small-town mayors who used their office, control over state-based coercive and economic resources, and links to provincial and national politicians to perpetuate their own local power monopolies in their respective municipalities. In countless small towns throughout the Philippines, the mayor's political longevity, economic preeminence, and personal control over the local agencies and resources of the state create a degree of monopoly that contrasts starkly with the bifactional competition between rival patron-client networks described in the scholarship of the 1960s and 1970s. In short, such municipalities constituted the bailiwicks for what might be described as small-town bosses.

Evidence of one such small-town boss is found among the presidential papers of longtime senator (1916–35) and Commonwealth President Manuel Quezon (from 1935 until his death in 1944). Two weeks before his election to the Commonwealth presidency in September 1935, Senator Quezon received a letter from Juan Rabellana, a resident of Dolores, a municipality in Tayabas, Quezon's home province. In breathless and long-winded Tagalog prose, Rabellana enumerated a laundry list of grievances against Mauricio Luico, the mayor of the municipality, whom he described as

> an abusive, greedy, and corrupt man who takes bribes for tolerating illegal lotteries and gambling dens; he alone profits from the lottery and gambling den collections and the contracts for the construction of the school and the municipal building. The police—who respect no one but him—are put to work on his coconut lands ... and all the public employees are his relatives: two sons-in-law and one nephew and two second-degree nephews. And he's the head of a gang of cattle rustlers, and the municipal treasurer pockets all sorts of traveling expenses beyond his allowance.[5]

After detailing how Luico had recently won reelection through fraud, vote-buying, and violence, Rabellana noted the complicity of Senator Quezon and other high-ranking government officials in the mayor's predatory behavior since he first assumed office in 1922:

> The town residents are powerless, as you are said to be his close friend and if he goes to see you, he's free to sleep in your bedroom and eat in your kitchen, and so we can't do anything, for he's also said to be a friend of Judge Recto and other judges of the Court of First Instance and especially close to Secretary of Public Works Guinto and Secretary Perez.[6]

Today, some 60 years of "modernization" notwithstanding, shades of Mayor Luico are still visible in contemporary accounts of municipal executives of a distinctly similar ilk. Manila newspapers frequently feature articles implicating town mayors from various parts of the Philippines in murder, extortion, robbery, illegal gambling, illegal logging, and landgrabbing.[7] In July 1993, for example, a barrage of stories appeared in Manila newspapers that focused on the predations of Antonio Sanchez, municipal mayor since 1972 of Calauan, Laguna, a small town only an hour's drive south of the nation's capital.[8] These stories identified two of Sanchez's bodyguards and three Calauan policemen as prime suspects in the brutal murders of two university students the previous month. Subsequent reports linked Sanchez's long tenure as Calauan mayor to his misuse and embezzlement of government funds, landgrabbing, control over illegal gambling operations, and maintenance of a "private army" composed of the town police detachment, members of local civilian militia units, and assorted private bodyguards.[9] The Department of Justice soon reopened an inquiry into Sanchez's role in a series of murders in 1988–89 in Calauan and launched an investigation into the "ill-gotten wealth" that paid for Sanchez's seven matching white Mercedes limousines, a three-story mansion, and education in England for three of his children.[10] Previously "protected" by the provincial governor and other patrons in the Marcos and Aquino regimes, in July 1993 Sanchez found himself suspended from office, arrested, and imprisoned by the less sympathetic Ramos administration.

Inspired in part by the cases of mayors like Luico and Sanchez, this chapter provides an alternative paradigm for the examination of municipal politics in the Philippines. In stark contrast with scholarly analyses of the 1960s and 1970s, the analysis below proceeds not from assumptions or observations about the structure and values of "traditional" Philippine society, but from an appreciation of the resources and prerogatives of municipal state office that facilitated the emergence and entrenchment of small-town bosses in municipalities scattered throughout the archipelago. Moreover, instead of relegating variations in local bossism to the realm of accidental phenomena, this chapter offers an explanation for the different leadership style and longevity of bosses from town to town and province to province that accords greater weight to local "ecological" features. While drawing liberally on insights and methods suggested in other studies of local politics in the Philippines and elsewhere, the bulk of this chapter focuses on Cavite Province, whose small-town bosses provide ample material for both a detailed case study and a comparative analysis.

Small-town bosses have thrived in large part because of the enduring institutional features of the Philippine state, most notably the discretionary powers of elected municipal executives over its local policing and taxing apparatuses. As noted in the previous chapter, by law, since the first years of the twentieth century, elected town mayors have enjoyed considerable control over the appointment and removal of municipal policemen.[11] With the exception of the 1976–86 period, when an Integrated National Police (INP) was established and subordinated to the Philippine Constabulary (PC),[12] since the end of World War II town policemen have depended on municipal funds for their salaries and firearms and on municipal executives for their supervision.[13] Local law enforcement has thus remained in the political realm, subject to the direction and intervention of elected municipal officials.

Along with control over local coercive resources, municipal mayors have enjoyed broad discretion over local finances, through their influence over the appointment of municipal treasurers and assessors, authority to legislate municipal tax ordinances and to set public utility fees, and control over the disbursement of government funds through public works projects and public salaries.[14] While municipal treasurers and assessors have formally served as the local agents of the Department of Finance, appointments, removals, and transfers of these officials have always—

even during the relatively centralized Marcos era—depended to a considerable extent upon the "recommendations" of municipal executives.[15] Municipal mayors have thus retained a significant measure of discretion over the assessment and collection of property taxes and enjoyed manifold opportunities to exploit chronic tax underassessment and delinquency for their personal benefit.[16] Similarly, elected municipal officials have determined the fees for the leasing of public market, wharf, and slaughterhouse concessions, the licensing of cockfighting arenas, ice plants, sawmills, rice mills, fishtraps, jeepneys, and ferries, and the granting of access to municipal fishing grounds, forest lands, mangroves, and quarries.[17] Finally, these same elected officials have wielded significant influence over the allocation and disbursement of government revenues through construction contracts and public sector employment within their respective municipalities. In sum, through their institutionalized control over the local coercive and extractive apparatuses of the state, municipal mayors have exercised considerable regulatory powers over the legal and illegal economies of their municipalities.

However attractive to mayoral aspirants and incumbents, the spoils of municipal office have not in and of themselves guaranteed the entrenchment of small-town bosses in town halls across the Philippines. In fact, as the scholarship of the 1960s and 1970s suggested, closely contested municipal elections and high rates of mayoral turnover, rather than incumbency, do appear to have been the rule in the postwar period.[18] In the seven pre-martial-law mayoral elections in nine provinces examined in one study, for example, almost 65 percent of all mayors served only one term, and the average tenure of a mayor was only six years.[19] In postwar elections in the two provinces discussed in detail in this study, moreover, the rates of electoral victory for incumbent mayors in Cavite and Cebu averaged only 56 percent and 57 percent respectively. Perquisites of office notwithstanding, incumbent mayors frequently fell prey to rival municipal politicians who enjoyed the support of town notables or to hostile provincial politicians who engineered election-day interventions, administrative suspensions, or even assassinations.[20]

In some municipalities, however, small-town bosses have entrenched themselves for decades, consistently winning reelection and establishing monopolistic control over key sectors of the local economy. While the rise of such small-town bosses has typically depended upon the sponsorship and intervention of provincial-level politicians, these bosses' longevity has corresponded closely to the local economic context. In short, small-town bosses have succeeded in entrenching themselves where the local political economy lends itself to enduring monopolistic or oligopolistic control.

Just as the longevity of bosses has varied from one town to the next, so too has the form of monopoly and of boss rule differed according to the "ecological" features of the local political economy. In some cases, the longtime rule of a criminal, predatory boss is associated with monopolistic and heavily coercive control over the "public" or state-regulated sphere of the economy, through discretionary allocation of public resources (e.g., land, personnel, money), selective or extortionary enforcement of laws, self-interested dispensation of contracts, monopoly franchises, and concessions (both legal and illegal), and control over crucial transportation bottlenecks. Some of these gangster-style bosses have resembled mafia: entrepreneurs who rely upon violence as a means of social control and economic accumulation.[21] Others have transformed their bossism into small-town dynasties linked to local patronage networks, to alliances and oligopolistic arrangements with local élite families, and to the accumulation of proprietary wealth within the municipality. In both instances, however, the mayor's office—and the attendant prerogatives over the local agencies of the state apparatus—has proven crucial to the fortunes of the small-town boss or dynasty.

The remainder of this chapter examines the pattern of small-town politics in the province of Cavite, the context underlying the prevalence of predatory mafia bosses, and the limitations on dynasty-building. A case study of the longest-lasting municipal mayor in Cavite highlights how the structure of the local political economy shapes small-town bossism and affects political longevity across the municipalities of this province.

## Municipal Politics in Cavite

Gangster-style competition between rival bosses of the most predatory variety has long characterized small-town politics in Cavite, and elections in the province have resembled nothing if not the mobilization of rival armed camps for guerrilla warfare. Even in the prewar Commonwealth era (1935–41), the rapid expansion of suffrage led to a surge in election-related skulduggery, vote-buying, and intimidation that escalated in the early postwar years into outright political violence following the dispersion of firearms and the formation of armed resistance groups during the Japanese Occupation.[22] After independence in 1946, the armed goons of Caviteño politicians repeatedly intervened in election registration, campaigning, voting, counting, and canvassing, consistently landing the towns of the province on the list of "hot spots" monitored by the Commission on Elections. Killings were not uncommon during early postwar elections, and vote-buying, fraud, and violence still mar these contests in the 1980s and 1990s, especially in the more remote parts of the province.[23] In the January 1988 local elections, for example, the incumbent mayor of one Cavite town sent out teams of armed goons to intimidate election inspectors and poll watchers; they of course facilitated considerable "irregularities" in the counting of votes. The mayor's bodyguards and policemen also drove away an opposing candidate's representative to the Municipal Board of Canvassers and were themselves present for the entire canvassing session.[24] In the 1992 elections, the mayor of another town in the province fielded groups of armed supporters who engaged in widespread vote-buying and intimidation, even as he intrigued to fill the municipal board of canvassers with his sympathizers. Town policemen and the mayor's armed bodyguards allegedly harassed voters believed to be sympathetic to an opposing candidate.[25] In a third town, the mayor, more widely feared than loved, ran unopposed in 1980, 1988, and 1992 and thus did not have to engage in such crude electoral tactics.

Violence has thus long played a crucial role in determining incumbency and turnover in municipal politics in Cavite. Countless election protests document the success of incumbent mayors in using violence to ensure their reelection. In the 1959 municipal elections in Ternate, for example, "the majority of the members of the board of canvassers, including the then incumbent mayor who was disqualified to act as a member of the board for being a candidate, proclaimed the municipal officials elected without canvassing the election returns."[26] Mayoral control over the municipal police has systematically favored the incumbent, as was reported in Magallanes in 1961: "On his way to the polling place [an election watcher] met voters who were told to go home without being able to vote, and . . . upon arriving at the polling place, he saw Councilor Sernat and Chief of Police Sernat of Magallanes voting, together with three (3) small boys who were filling up the ballots."[27]

Violence, including political assassinations, has also featured prominently in the intraelection repertoire of small-town politics in the province. From 1946 to 1972, eight Cavite mayors were killed, as well as ten Cavite town police chiefs and scores of vice-mayors, municipal councilors, barrio captains, policemen, and assorted relatives and political *líders*. Elsewhere in the province, mayors and vice-mayors have been accused of murder, and between 1986 and 1998 five Cavite mayors and at least two municipal councilors lost their lives to assassins' bullets.[28]

Cavite's political economy helps to explain why the spoils of municipal office in the province have been worth killing—or dying—for. First, Cavite's strategic location as a Manila suburb and as the longtime home of the U.S. naval station at Sangley Point encouraged the growth of extensive illegal economies, which local officials monopolized through their police forces. Second, the province's distinctive history of land settlement prevented a local plantocracy from taking hold politically; local politicians used their state offices to accumulate large landholdings, but landownership remained contingent upon continued access to the local agencies of the state.

Enjoying considerable discretion over municipal police forces, Cavite mayors have used violence and selective enforcement of the law to control lucrative illegal activities. In the late Spanish colonial era, the province was already known as "la madre de los ladrones," or "the mother of thieves." Caviteño bandits were known to prey on wealthy families in the lowland towns, rustle cattle in upland pastures, and kidnap sugar merchants en route to nearby Manila. Many of these "outlaw" elements operated in connivance with the local "law-enforcing" agents of the colonial state—cattle-rustling gangs worked in cahoots with local officials who facilitated the approval or forgery of documents required for the sale of livestock. Regularly held elections for the positions of *cabeza de barangay* (village headman) and *gobernadorcillo* (town executive) created a revolving door of sorts, as the newly chosen town executives filled the ranks of the *cuadrilleros* (town policemen) with their flunkies, while those discharged often left their duties as policemen to become *tulisanes* (bandits).[29]

In the American colonial period, Cavite's location continued to ensure that criminal activities in the province flourished. As in many provinces, numerous Cavite mayors had close links with local *jueteng* (illegal lottery) syndicates, which were frequently rigged and generated substantial protection money. Philippine Constabulary sources throughout this period noted the involvement of municipal police in the protection of *jueteng* in Cavite, citing weekly hush payments to mayors and their police forces that dwarfed these officials' government salaries.[30] Moreover, Cavite's proximity to nearby Manila meat markets and slaughterhouses encouraged rampant theft of carabao and cattle in parts of the province. Cavite's provincial fiscal (state prosecutor) noted in 1909 that complainants and witnesses in cattle-rustling cases were frequently threatened by unnamed "influential persons in the province," and as late as 1940 little had changed; cattle thieves still enjoyed protection from municipal officials.[31] Meanwhile, the installation of a U.S. naval station at Sangley Point filled the newly created provincial capital, Cavite City, with brothels, cabarets, and gambling dens catering to American servicemen and facilitated the smuggling of American-made firearms into the province. Gangsters preyed upon Cavite City's seedy establishments, but only at the discretion of the local authorities.[32]

In the early postwar era (1946–72), an increasingly suburban Cavite continued to earn a reputation for rampant criminality. Cavite town mayors and their policemen were frequently implicated not only in *jueteng* rackets and cattle rustling but also in banditry, highway robbery, carnapping, and smuggling and in the protection of such activities as gun-running, prostitution, illegal fishing, and marijuana cultivation.[33] In the 1950s, Cavite became a major base for carnapping operations in nearby Manila: "syndicates" maintained repair shops where jeepneys stolen in Manila were overhauled for resale.[34] Over the years, these syndicates moved upmarket, from passenger jeepneys to luxury cars, while other groups responded to the growing demand for marijuana by establishing clandestine plantations to grow the illegal crop. Meanwhile, rival gangs in Cavite City battled over the protection rackets connected with the U.S. naval station located at Sangley Point. Prostitution, smuggling, and gambling earned the province's most urban town the nickname "Little Chicago." Finally, coastal towns in Cavite—most notably Tanza—emerged in the 1960s as major transshipment points for foreign cigarettes smuggled from Borneo and bound for nearby Manila. According to government documents that surfaced in 1964, an average of 2,400 cases of smuggled cigarettes—yielding 600,000 pesos in profits (at P3.9 to the dollar, more than U.S.$150,000)—arrived monthly on Tanza's shores, along with large quantities of firearms, ammunition, and other valuable contraband.[35]

Beginning in the 1970s, the closer integration of Cavite with Metro Manila drew the province into the orbit of criminal syndicates operating in the nation's capital. More recently, local officials in Cavite have taken their cut from illegal gambling and narcotics smuggling syndicates based in southern areas of Metro Manila (e.g., Pasay City, Las Piñas), big-time fishing magnates from Navotas (Manila's fishing port) engaged in illegal trawling, and illegal recruiters of overseas contract workers (e.g., female "hostesses, dancers, and entertainers") with headquarters in Makati, the capital's financial district.[36] Flanked by armed bodyguards, "protected" by relatives in the ranks of the police and the military, implicated in murders, and hardened by their guerrilla experiences in World War II or their jobs as policemen or nightclub bouncers in Manila, Cavite's town mayors typically styled themselves in mafioso—rather than gentry—fashion.

Aside from illegal activities, Cavite town mayors have used their political positions to acquire and expand landholdings in their municipalities, a pattern established during the settlement of Cavite Province in the Spanish colonial period. Under the Spanish regime, Cavite was the site of several large friar estates, which totaled well over 35,000 hectares of prime land and encompassed virtually all of the province.[37] The size and economic significance of these friar estates effectively precluded the emergence in Cavite of a dominant class of Chinese mestizo landowners as occurred elsewhere in the archipelago in the nineteenth century.[38] Rather, the ascendant nineteenth-century élites in the towns of the province consisted of *inquilino* tenants who subleased the friars' lands to subtenant-cultivators and thereby garnered substantial rentier profits.[39] The position of the *inquilinos* depended heavily on the favor they enjoyed with the friars who administered the estates. The friars "rewarded the sycophants, their own paramours, and the latter's kin with good lands,"[40] while "those whom they hated were dispossessed of lands through mere whispers of servants, paramours and relatives."[41] As generation succeeded generation, loyal families needed to continue currying the friars' favor in order to renew and expand their *inquilino* contracts for the cultivation of rice and sugar.[42] The scions of leading *inquilino* families married among themselves, competed in highly restricted elections for local offices,[43] and formed the upper ranks of the insurrectionary leadership in Cavite during the revolution against the Spanish.

With suffrage severely limited by the American colonial regime, members of the emerging *inquilino* dynasties triumphed easily in the municipal elections held in 1901 and worked thereafter to convert their small-town political power into a means of securing property rights over the lands their forefathers had leased from the Spanish friars.[44] Indeed, after the American government's purchase of the friar estates and their subsequent sale to "previous tenants" by the notoriously corrupt Bureau of Lands, many Cavite town notables acquired ownership of the same tracts on which their families had previously served as *inquilinos* for the religious orders.[45] These purchases were typically made on highly concessional, long-term installment payment schedules and were financed by government loans, which more often than not were never paid off.[46] Thanks to the leniency of friends in the Bureau of Lands and the Philippine National Bank and the intercession of friendly legislators, many Cavite town notables held on to lands they never paid for, and by 1934 the accounts for nearly 12,000 hectares remained in arrears.[47]

In subsequent years, however, the descendants of Cavite's *inquilinos* failed to establish secure property rights over their landholdings, and landownership in the province remains to this day highly contingent upon the ebbs and flows of local politics. In 1936, for example, hostilities between prominent Cavite politicians and President Quezon led to confiscation of the largest estate in the province and to legislation mandating the subdivision and resale of all portions of the former friar lands "remaining undisposed of" and disqualifying as purchasers those previously delinquent in their mortgage payments.[48] As noted in the following chapter, the pattern of subsequent land sales during the Commonwealth period reflected the continuing discretion of elected officials over landownership in Cavite, as local notables linked to newly elected congressman Justiniano Montano reaped the rewards of his intimacy with Benigno S. Aquino Sr., who as secretary of agriculture and commerce oversaw the Bureau of Lands.

Throughout the postwar period, landownership remained heavily dependent upon political power. Land tax assessments and decisions regarding the construction of roads, bridges, and irrigation facilities fell under local elected officials' discretion.[49] In the 1950s, land reform legislation imposed restrictions on the division of the harvest between landlords and share tenants and permitted the subdivision of large estates through expropriation, provisions that were enforced "selectively" by various Cavite mayors. In Naic, for example, longtime town mayor Macario Peña built up a local following by expropriating and subdividing several large haciendas and stringently enforcing land reform legislation that mandated a 70–30 division of the harvest between share tenants and landlords.[50] Mayoral discretion over large tracts of public land also proved politically and economically advantageous: in Bacoor, for example, Mayor Benigno Guinto oversaw the redistribution of some 2,000 hectares of expropriated land.[51]

Finally, since the 1970s, the transformation of many Cavite towns into suburban clusters of residential subdivisions, golf courses, and industrial estates has subjected landowners to new forms of regulation. Elected municipal officials control the awarding of building permits, the passage of municipal zoning ordinances, the use of government-owned land, the allocation of public works, the approval of reclamation projects, and, most important, the implementation of agrarian reform.[52] By selectively revising municipal land-use plans and applying pressure on municipal agrarian reform offices and tenant-cultivators (i.e., potential beneficiaries of agrarian reform), local officials facilitated the "conversion" of land to industrial, commercial, or residential use, exploiting a key loophole in the agrarian reform legislation that exempts nonagricultural land from expropriation and redistribution.[53] With such mechanisms of land-use regulation at their disposal, Cavite's municipal mayors became the province's leading real-estate agents and brokers.

In addition to discretionary powers over land use, the holders of local political office control the awarding of petty monopoly franchises and concessions. Licenses for fishtraps, market stalls, ice plants, rice mills, copra bodegas, and cockpits have ultimately depended upon the mayor's patronage or percentage.[54] Special municipal ordinances have facilitated punishment of political rivals through taxes on their businesses.[55] Contracts for the construction of roads, bridges, buildings, and other local government facilities have provided ample opportunities for patronage, pilferage, and profit. Favoritism and kickbacks have guided mayors' awarding of contracts, and many mayors have owned construction companies themselves.[56]

Thus has the economic transformation of Cavite increased the spoils of local office in the province. As billions of pesos of investment flooded into the province in the 1980s and 1990s, a massive construction boom lined the pockets of favored contractors and local officials alike, much as planned reclamation projects promise to do in years to come. Meanwhile, many Cavite mayors have set up their own businesses—savings banks, recruitment agencies, import-export firms, customs brokerages—in Manila.[57] In particular, the large number of Caviteño employees in the Bureau of Customs has encouraged many politicians from the province to participate in what is often described as "monkey business" at Manila's notoriously corruption-ridden port area.[58]

Though economic and political power has remained closely fused in Cavite throughout the postwar era, small-town politics in the province were not the exclusive domain of an established local landed or "commercial élite."[59] In every Cavite town, a few families do stand out as identifiably landowning political clans: typically they are the descendants of Chinese mestizo *inquilino* dynasties from the late Spanish era, and they own substantial properties and play a dominant role in the local economy as moneylenders, rural bankers, agricultural input suppliers, coffee or coconut traders, fish dealers, rice mill operators, and owners of cockpits, movie houses, ice plants, fishing boats, gasoline stations, and construction companies. Evolving over the years from their early base in large landholdings into a commercial élite, these intermarried clans have dominated municipal politics in Cavite. Their family names are prominent among the lists of municipal councilors elected every four years in various towns in the province. A few of these prominent families, moreover, claim province-wide landholdings and commercial networks, namely those who trace their roots back to *inquilino* clans in the northern towns of Cavite, which historically formed the core of the friar estates, possessed the most fertile rice-growing tracts, and were near Manila markets. In the southern coastal and upland towns of the province, large landholdings, substantial shares in rural banks, and dominant roles in trading networks remain in the hands of families from Bacoor, General Trias, Imus, Kawit, and Rosario, whose descendants have figured prominently over the years among the candidates for the provincial board. Yet these established landed families—whose properties rarely exceeded a few hundred hectares—by no means reigned supreme in Cavite politics.

Indeed, in the early postwar period some of the prominent landed families that had dominated town politics before the war were eclipsed politically or displaced: the Bayots of Amadeo (who owned 200 hectares), the Camposes of Dasmariñas (150 hectares), the De Leons of Ternate (350 hectares), the Espinelis of Magallanes (300 hectares), the Ferrers of General Trias (500 hectares), the Nazareños of Naic (250 hectares), the Kiamzons of Silang (200 hectares), and the Riego de Dioses of Maragondon (100 hectares). The Rojases of Cavite City, who owned nearly 700 hectares of prime land in Silang, were similarly on the outs.[60] These families had enjoyed close links to the leading provincial politicians in the prewar years but lost influence once their common patron, Governor (1946–54) Dominador Camerino, fell out of favor in Manila, faced suspension and criminal charges, and lost a reelection bid in the mid-1950s. By contrast, the landed Trias clan retained its prominence—with scion Ernesto Trias Genuino serving three terms as mayor of General Trias municipality (named after the revolutionary general Mariano Trias)—through close links with the dominant postwar politician in Cavite, long-time congressman Justiniano Montano, whose influence made the family's construction business the most favored in the province in the postwar period.[61]

Though in some cases intermarried or otherwise allied with prominent landed families, most postwar Cavite mayors were "new men" whose careers began in the state apparatus and depended heavily on the support of Montano, their common political patron. For just as Congressman Montano fed public works contracts to the mayor of General Trias, Ernesto Genuino, so he boosted the careers of Dasmariñas mayor Carungcong's brothers in the Constabulary and the Cavite Electricity and Development Authority and installed numerous other protégés in the Bureau of Customs and other government agencies. In fact, the longest-serving Cavite mayors before the onset of martial law were Montano's "creations": Santos Ambagan of Amadeo (1952–68), whom Montano had earlier promoted to provincial jail warden; Rafael Dalusag of Bailen (1956–60, 1964–72) whom Montano had defended against charges of wartime "guerrilla" atrocities; Cesar Casal of Carmona (1956–72), whose rise from the municipal treasurer's office to the mayorship Montano engineered; Telesforo Unas of Maragondon (1956–72), whose college education Montano supposedly paid for out of his own pocket; and Macario Peña of Naic (1955–72), whom Montano plucked from the Pasay City police force to run for mayor in his hometown.

Thus the political fortunes of Cavite town mayors were closely linked

Longtime Cavite congressman Justiniano S. Montano Sr. delivering a speech in the House of Representatives. Over the years, Montano used his position in the House to bolster his position in Cavite. (Lopez Museum Library)

TABLE I
*Administration During the Montano Era, 1947–71*

| Year | Administration | Montano | Montano Mayors Elected |
|------|----------------|---------|------------------------|
| 1947 | Liberal | Nacionalista* | 2 |
| 1951 | Liberal | Nacionalista* | 3 |
| 1955 | Nacionalista | Nacionalista | 12 |
| 1959 | Nacionalista | Nacionalista | 12 |
| 1963 | Liberal | Liberal | 16 |
| 1967 | Nacionalista | Liberal | 12 |
| 1971 | Nacionalista | Liberal | 9 |

*Though officially a Liberal, Montano supported Nacionalista candidates in the 1947 and 1951 elections while his rivals in Cavite constituted the Liberal slate.

to those of their patron in the provincial arena rather than to some stable base in the local economy outside of state control. Through his own machinations and his position as Cavite's provincial kingpin, Montano had substantial funds to dispense for essential election expenses: the fielding of *líders*, the buying of votes, the hiring of goons, and the bribing of officials. Moreover, as provincial chairman of one of the two recognized political parties, Montano controlled the appointment of election inspectors, whose cooperation was crucial for both defending against and engaging in the fraud and manipulation necessary for electoral victory. Finally, Montano's standing in Manila influenced the dispatching of Philippine Constabulary troops, the enforcement of Commission on Elections rulings, and the settlement of electoral protests in the courts. Unsurprisingly, local election results closely followed—rather than preceded—his political rise and fall (see Table 1).

During the Montano era, the close link between municipal and provincial politics was also evident in the intensity of small-town rivalries: four mayors were assassinated during Montano's ascendance in 1949–54, and three mayors died in 1972, the year of his political downfall.[62]

As in the era dominated by Montano, from the late 1970s through the mid-1990s most Cavite mayors relied on a powerful patron, Juanito ("Johnny") Remulla, longtime governor of Cavite (1979–86, 1988–95). With close allies in the national legislature and government agencies, Remulla was able to assign officials and distribute public works in Cavite and to facilitate business for his "boys" in Manila. Moreover, in addition to a considerable personal fortune and access to government funds, Remulla received generous campaign financing from interested *jueteng*

Longtime Cavite congressman Justiniano
S. Montano Sr. (at left) and his perennial
provincial foe, Dominador Camerino.
(Lopez Museum Library)

Cavite governor Delfin Montano and Dominador Camerino shaking hands under the watchful eye of Brigadier General Manuel Yan of the Philippine Constabulary. Despite such "truces" between rival factions in Cavite, elections in the province during the pre-martial-law period were always violent and regularly left large numbers of casualties. (Lopez Museum Library)

operators, construction companies, factory owners, and Manila-based politicians. Remulla's opponent in the 1992 election estimated that the governor spent over 200 million pesos (US$8 million) to guarantee his re-election and that of his protégés. Indeed, in the local elections of 1980, 1988, and 1992, only a handful of Remulla's candidates for mayor failed to win.[63] Moreover, all five of the Cavite mayors who were killed during this period had somehow "crossed" the governor.

In sum, the municipal mayors of Cavite have been mafia-style, small-town bosses deeply involved in criminal activities and heavily dependent upon violence both for purposes of reelection and for economic accumulation. Rather than the leading members of an established local oligarchy of landed families, most of these small-town bosses were "new men," political operators whose close links to provincial politicians initially catapulted them into office and whose control over the local state apparatus—rather than an independent economic base in landownership—remained the centerpiece of their small-town empires.

Yet some of these small-town bosses in Cavite were more successful

Gaming and Amusements Board chairman Justiniano N. Montano Jr. This son of the longtime Cavite congressman was accused of using his office for match-rigging, race-fixing, protection of illegal betting operations, and the management of boxers through "dummies" for his own personal profit. (Lopez Museum Library)

Political poster for Cavite provincial board member Cesar E. Casal. Casal served as Carmona town mayor from 1955 through 1979, after which he took a seat on the provincial board. Casal used the town mayor's office to acquire large landholdings and a key role in the local economy over the years.

**LDP-PARTIDO MAGDALO KANDIDATO OPISYAL**

## CESAR E. CASAL
**CPA-LAWYER**
Sa Pagka (BOKAL) BOARD MEMBER
24 na taon - Alkalde ng Carmona
9 na taon - Kagawad, Sangguniang
Panlalawigan - Cavite

ANG KARANASAN, KATAPATAN
AT KATARUNGAN AY GANAP NA
SANDATA NG ISANG LINGKOD BAYAN

than others in entrenching themselves in power. In many towns, factional competition between rival clans possessing land and local commercial networks opposing provincial-level politicians prevented the emergence of a longtime mayor with monopolistic claims on political and economic power. In a few towns, however, mayors have held power for many years by seizing control of the "commanding heights" of the local economy. Among such longtime Cavite mayors, Cesar Casal of Carmona has been the most successful small-town boss in the province in the postwar period.

## Lotteries and Land Deals:
## Mayor Cesar Casal of Carmona

Before Cesar Casal's ascendance to the mayorship of Carmona in 1955, no single boss had dominated the political and economic life of this inland eastern Cavite town. The largest landed estates in the municipality belonged to wealthy families residing outside Carmona, in the neighboring market town of Biñan, Laguna. Carmona-based landowning families such as the Baylons, Carillos, Ermitaños, Manarins, Medinas, and Zamoras were active in municipal politics, but no one clan had achieved lasting preeminence in the town's economic and political life.[64]

A series of developments in provincial and national politics paved the way for Cesar Casal's successful candidacy in the election of November 1955. From 1946 through 1954, the mayor of Carmona was Bernardo Hebron, a protégé of Cavite governor Dominador Camerino, a Liberal Party stalwart. After Nacionalista Ramon Magsaysay was elected president in 1953, Liberal Party members in Cavite came under attack for their opposition to Magsaysay. In 1954, Magsaysay suspended Camerino and replaced him with a protégé of (Nacionalista) Senator Justiniano Montano Sr., Camerino's archrival in Cavite, who had supported Magsaysay in the previous election. The new governor proceeded to dismiss 300 "provincial guards" and "special agents" previously appointed by Camerino and to harass recalcitrant pro-Camerino mayors with suspensions and court cases, a campaign designed to weaken Camerino before the 1955 local elections, in which Senator Montano's son, Delfin, ran for the provincial governorship.[65] Among five Liberal, pro-Camerino mayors suspended was Carmona mayor Bernardo Hebron, who was charged with a minor infraction of the election law in 1953.[66]

Additional assistance from the Magsaysay administration helped to ensure a sweeping victory for Montano's emerging political machine in the November 1955 local elections in Cavite. Malacañang released 2 million pesos in pork-barrel funds for improvements to government highways and waterworks in Cavite in the summer of 1955, thus providing substantial money for vote-buying and other campaign expenses.[67] The Commission on Elections (Comelec), moreover, placed the municipal police forces of sixteen of Cavite's nineteen towns—including Carmona—under the control of the Philippine Constabulary (PC), thus conveniently leaving only Montano's strongholds free from supervision on election day.[68] Benefiting from tremendous advantages in financial and coercive resources, Delfin Montano easily won the Cavite governorship in November 1955, and close Montano protégés—including several political neophytes—captured the mayorships of fourteen Cavite towns.

Among the neophyte mayors elected on the Montanos' coattails was Cesar Casal of Carmona, whose Nacionalista slate—selected by Montano—won the vice-mayorship and all eight seats on the town's municipal board. Aside from close personal ties to the Montanos, Casal enjoyed four distinct advantages as a mayoral candidate in his hometown. First, his mother belonged to the landed Ermitaño clan,[69] whose scions had long been active in politics and whose tenants and dependents constituted a significant local following in an electorate of fewer than 2,000 voters. Second, Casal had married a member of the prominent Paular family, whose wealth and influence in Carmona provided additional assets for his campaign. Third, Casal, a certified public accountant, had served for several years as a clerk in the municipal treasurer's office in Carmona, a position in which he enjoyed discretion over the assessment and collection of property taxes from landowners (i.e., potential key campaign supporters) in the municipality. Fourth, Cesar Casal's brother, Alfredo Casal, served as the chief of the licensing division of Manila City Hall, a government position even more useful than Cesar's for raising campaign funds.

More than any of the other neophyte municipal executives elected in 1955 in Cavite, Cesar Casal occupied a mayoral office from which he could control key sectors of the local economy in his municipality. Fortuitously for Casal, the passage of the Land Reform Act of 1955 (Republic Act 1400) provided for landed estates of more than 300 hectares to be expropriated and redistributed among tenant-cultivators upon petition of the majority of the tenants or under conditions of "justified agrarian unrest,"[70] but left considerable room for political intervention in the implementation of the law:[71]

The best advertised and most acceptable is the espousal of the tenant petitioners' cause by a Congressman, a governor, or most frequently, a municipal council. This brings faster and more favorable administrative consideration for the tenants. Or, a quiet word in the right place by a politically potent individual may cause indefinite postponement of plans to expropriate some reluctant landlords.

The most insidious result of political influence is that estates are sometimes bought at too high a price without strong tenant interest.[72]

In Carmona, efforts exerted by Mayor Casal and Senator Montano led to the expropriation of several large estates in the neighboring town of Biñan, Laguna, most notably that of the Yaptinchays, who owned 350 hectares of prime rice and sugar land in the Cavite municipality.[73] Following the expropriations, Mayor Casal won appointment by the Land Tenure Administration (LTA) as the administrator of these properties, a position that allowed him considerable leverage over the tenant-cultivators, who were still obliged to make onerous amortization payments before acquiring legal title to the land.[74] Over the years, through a combination of legal maneuvers, debt peonage, and intimidation, Casal gradually secured ownership of large tracts of the former Yaptinchay estate.

A distinctive feature of Carmona's local economy also provided Mayor Casal with discretionary powers over another large tract of prime irrigated land in the town. Since the signing of a royal decree by the Spanish monarch in 1859, more than 300 hectares of land in the town had been declared communally owned by the residents of the municipality of Carmona, with cultivation rights to an assortment of 180 plots awarded to local residents in a triennial lottery known as the *sorteo*. The original decree stipulated:

These agricultural lands shall be divided into lots that shall be distributed every three years among all residents, household heads who live separately from their parents, and others who pay the proper annual fees into the Ways and Means accounts of Carmona . . . who will be selected in the said council through a public auction in cases of competition for the usufruct of some of the said lots.[75]

Although the closely scrutinized *sorteo*—held in the municipal plaza under the vigilant gaze of the assembled town residents—remained free from manipulation, those Carmona residents fortunate enough to "win" parcels of communal land found themselves effectively subordinated and indebted to Mayor Casal once they began to exercise the three-year cultivating rights awarded them in the lottery. Discretion over the irrigation of the communal lands, for example, lay in the hands of a "water tender" appointed by Mayor Casal, whose favorable treatment could considerably raise the yields from wet-rice cultivation on a communal plot. *Sorteo* winners' lack of sufficient capital, moreover, frequently forced them into relationships of indebtedness to and dependence upon Mayor Casal, who assumed proprietary rights over their plots in exchange for cash payments and labor services or offered credit and agricultural inputs in exchange for a share of their harvests.

As owner of the expropriated Yaptinchay estate and "landlord" of the communal land, Casal combined his official powers in Carmona and his connections outside the municipality to expand his control over the town's agricultural economy. Over the years, he became the proprietor of one of Carmona's four rice mills and the sole franchise dealer of fertilizers in the municipality for the Manila-based Atlas Fertilizer Corporation. Together with his brother, Casal came to hold a major share of stock in Carmona's rural bank. In addition, supposedly through his brother's Manila City Hall connections, Casal obtained milling contracts—and joined the planters' association—at the sugar central located on the wealthy Yulo family's 7,000-hectare Canlubang Estate in nearby Laguna.[76] (The family patriarch, José Yulo, who served as secretary of justice in the 1930s and remained prominent in politics in the postwar era, acquired the Canlubang Estate through a series of financial maneuvers involving the government-owned Philippine National Bank and the Rehabilitation Finance Corporation.)[77] Finally, using both legal maneuvers and violence, Casal acquired additional properties in Carmona; his methods earned him the epithet "landgrabber" among town residents and left him accused of sponsoring intimidation and murder.[78]

His vast landholdings, control over communal land, and central role in the processing of rice and sugar cultivated in Carmona, brought Casal not only enormous wealth but also a considerable following of dependents. Casal enjoyed claims on Montano's pork-barrel funds, inclusion in the Montanos' party slates, control of the municipal policy force and other state agencies, and influence over the dispensing of public employees in Carmona. Thus Casal won reelection to the mayorship in 1959, 1963, 1967, and 1971 and delivered consistent majorities to the Montanos in consecutive congressional and gubernatorial elections in Carmona, through a combination of machine mobilization, vote-buying, fraud, and intimidation.[79] Even as the voting population in Carmona expanded from roughly 2,000 in 1955 to more than 10,000 in 1992, these tactics remained effective in the municipality.[80] Once entrenched as town mayor, Casal no longer depended on the backing of local élite families, as is suggested by the low rate of incumbency among the municipal councilors on his ticket over the years. From his days as a lowly clerk in the municipal treasurer's office, Casal had used his control over local state resources to transform himself from small-time political operator into a wealthy *hacendado* and an entrenched local boss.

Over the years, however, Carmona's proximity to Metro Manila set in motion the economic transformation of the municipality, a process that increasingly intruded on Casal's local fiefdom. In 1961, for example, the People's Homesite and Housing Corporation, a national government agency, bought up more than 900 hectares of idle land in a rugged, hilly area of Carmona to use for the resettlement of "squatters" living in Metro Manila.[81] Eight years later, the Marcos administration began to relocate more than 3,000 families from various urban squatter sites in Metro Manila to this Carmona Resettlement Project, promising homes, electricity, artesian wells, and jobs. Upon arrival, however, the families found an inadequate water supply, poor sanitation facilities, no electricity, and few local employment opportunities.[82] Government agencies, moreover, refused to give the relocated families full title to their assigned lots on the resettlement site until they had lived there for five consecutive years, thus leaving them vulnerable to a lot-grabbing syndicate that operated with the blessings of local officials.[83] Disheartened by these squalid conditions, many families returned to Metro Manila, even as the government continued to "resettle" thousands of squatter families to Carmona throughout the 1970s. In 1980 the resettlement area, now supervised by the National Housing Authority, was formally separated from Carmona and renamed General Mariano Alvarez.

Meanwhile, by the late 1970s, the construction of a major highway, whose four lanes cut right through Carmona, had rendered the suburban municipality a choice site for real-estate "development."[84] In the early 1980s, for example, José Yao Campos, the Marcos front man and pharmaceuticals magnate, bought up millions of pesos worth of property in Carmona where he planned to build a golf course and residential subdivision.[85] Following the ouster of President Marcos in 1986, the Presidential Commission on Good Government (PCGG) sequestered Campos's properties in Carmona and eventually sold them to a Manila-based real-estate firm, the Fil-Estate Realty Corporation. Fil-Estate subsequently began construction in Carmona on the 430-hectare Manila Southwoods Residential Estates and Golf and Country Club, which by 1993 featured a 36-hole Masters and Legends golf course designed by Jack Nicklaus, a residential subdivision, and plans for a commercial center within the complex. Today Fil-Estate's Manila Southwoods is the single largest employer and landowner in the municipality.[86]

In the early 1980s, at the urging of Cavite provincial governor Johnny Remulla, the municipality of Carmona redesignated more than 100 hectares of communal land as the Cavite-Carmona Development Project and sold off plots to various manufacturing concerns for "industrial development." The Technology Resource Center (TRC), a government corporation under Imelda Marcos's Ministry of Human Settlements, purchased more than 50 hectares for resale or leasing to small and medium-sized industries. Many of the companies that bought lots were of murky origin and reputation and enjoyed close ties to the Marcos family. One company connected to the Enriquez-Panlilio clan, for example, re-

ceived a 6-million-peso loan from the TRC, as did another company controlled by Governor Remulla's family members and close associates;
Marcos crony Ricardo Silverio bought a ten-hectare plot. Yet by the late
1980s, Filipino, Japanese, Korean, and Taiwanese companies had invested hundreds of millions of pesos in the Cavite-Carmona Industrial
Estate and employed several thousand workers in more than 30 factories.
Today, Carmona's once bucolic landscape stands significantly transformed, with a four-lane highway, a golf course, and an industrial estate
as its most visible landmarks.

To a considerable extent, the transformation of Carmona into a suburban "development" community eroded Casal's seemingly monolithic
control over the town's (once largely agricultural) economy. Thanks to
the highway, many Carmona residents today commute to jobs in Metro
Manila and thus are able to support their families outside the realm of
Casal's rice and sugar empire. Thanks to the industrial estate and the golf
course, other Carmona residents have found nonagricultural employment
in their hometown. Finally, thanks to the profits to be made on Carmona
real estate, powerful outsiders like Governor Remulla and Manila-based
real-estate moguls have begun to play active roles in the "development"
of the municipality.

Faced with these impingements and intrusions upon his fiefdom, Casal
gracefully shifted into semiretirement while guarding his economic interests in Carmona. Following the political demise of the Montanos in
1972, Casal reached a modus vivendi with Provincial Governor Camerino and, after the latter's death in 1979, with his successor, Johnny
Remulla. In 1979, anticipating the first local elections held since martial
law, Casal agreed to step down as municipal mayor in favor of a
Remulla-backed candidate and in exchange for inclusion on the governor's slate for the provincial board.[87] In 1980, 1988, 1992, and 1995,
Casal won election to the provincial board on the Remulla ticket, and in
1992 the *engkargado* (overseer) of his sugar plantation was elected vice-
mayor of Carmona.[88]

Considering Casal's options and his advanced age (he was born in
1914), it was appropriate for Casal to take a back-bench seat on the
provincial board rather than retain the high-profile mayorship of a busy
town. As a provincial board member with a lower profile, he avoided implication in the controversies that accompanied Carmona's "development" in the 1990s. When residents protested the sale of Carmona's communal land by building homes on the parcels in question and filing suit
against the mayor and the governor, Casal was noticeably silent.[89] When
armed goons burned down these squatters' homes and killed a leading
plaintiff in the lawsuit, he remained similarly aloof. In local gossip about

the assassination of Mayor Felino Maquinay in 1990, rumors about the "disappearance" of a local labor activist, and protests against the planned relocation of a Manila dumpsite in Carmona,[90] Casal's name almost never cropped up. With his protégés installed in office in Carmona and his own seat on the Cavite provincial board, however, Casal was able to retain a significant measure of influence over local affairs in the municipality.

In effect, Casal's continued involvement in politics became a kind of insurance policy for his properties in Carmona. In theory, his extensive landholdings could be redistributed according to the terms of the Comprehensive Agrarian Reform of 1988, but provincial land-use plans and municipal zoning ordinances have conveniently designated his lands as nonagricultural, a ruse that exploits a key loophole in the legislation and effectively exempts the land from land-reform coverage. In fact, Casal sold off some of his properties to the Manila Southwoods (and is reported to have bought up condominiums in Quezon City) and may continue to do so as real-estate prices in Carmona rise even higher, but in the meantime his sugarcane plantation remains decidedly agricultural. If Casal were to lose his political clout, however, local Agrarian Reform officials might someday take a more active interest in his extensive properties in Carmona.

In sum, Cesar Casal's political longevity marks him as the most successful small-town boss in the province. From his relatively modest origins as a small-time political operator and Montano protégé, Casal gained nearly monolithic control over key sectors of Carmona's local economy by skillfully exploiting his mayoral powers. Through his control over public land, connections to agribusiness concerns outside Carmona, and prominent role in the supply of credit, inputs, and processing facilities, Casal came to dominate the agricultural economy of the municipality. Combined with his access to state patronage and supervisory powers over the local police forces, Casal's accumulation of wealth and personal dependents virtually guaranteed his reelection and self-perpetuation in power. Even as Carmona's electorate expanded fivefold and its landscape underwent manifold transformations, Casal remained entrenched in the municipality.

As the exemplary municipal boss of postwar Cavite, Casal demonstrated both the possibilities for predatory economic accumulation and the limitations on the security of property that have long distinguished small-town politics in the province. More than his counterparts in other Cavite municipalities, Casal found a local economy peculiarly subject to mayoral regulation and thus available for mayoral monopolization and "privatization." Yet Casal's success at landgrabbing in the 1950s perhaps foretold the later uncertainty surrounding the future of his properties. Childless and lacking a political heir apparent (e.g., a favored niece or nephew), Casal will not be able to protect the security of his estate beyond his lifetime. Upon his death, lawsuits by the descendants of former Yaptinchay tenants will be more likely to prosper, and the Department of Agrarian Reform may finally take an interest in his considerable landholdings. In both his success as a boss and his failure to establish a dynasty, Casal thus exemplifies the small-town politicians of Cavite, whose heavy reliance on elective office for capital accumulation limited the possibilities for passing on political and economic power over the generations.

## Conclusion

Small-town politics in the province of Cavite has not closely conformed to the standard portrait of bifactional competition between rival patron-client networks in the Philippines. While mayoral aspirants in the municipalities of this province have clearly relied on personal relationships to mobilize the local electorate, these ties appear to have been neither as crucial nor as reciprocal as typically assumed. In Cavite, vote-buying, violence, and fraud have been persistent and prominent features of municipal elections since at least 1946 and today remain essential ingredients of local political success. In Cavite municipalities, moreover, relationships of personal dependence and indebtedness typically have produced such gross disparities in access to scarce resources, coercive pressures, and possibilities for monopoly that "clients" have suffered from hopelessly unequal terms of exchange and "patrons" evolved into local bosses. Political competition between these small-town bosses has thus focused not so much on the cultivation of patron-client relationships as on the acquisition and retention of monopolistic or oligopolistic control over scarce resources, the assumption of coercive and regulatory powers, and the production and reproduction of conditions of scarcity and insecurity for the broad mass of the local population.

In this context, postwar changes in small-town politics in Cavite unfolded not through the breakdown or transformation of patron-client relations but in response to shifting patterns of capital accumulation and state intervention in the local economy. In municipalities in the province, large landowners evolved both into providers of agricultural inputs, credit, marketing, and processing, and more recently into construction magnates, real-estate brokers, and "developers," whose local commercial success today depends as much as ever upon the favor of elected officials. However, with interests in customs brokerage firms, real-estate holdings, savings banks, security and overseas workers' recruitment agencies, and trading companies in Metro Manila, the commercial élite of Cavite also shifted into urban entrepreneurial activities outside the purview of local political protection and sponsorship. Meanwhile, the closer integration of Cavite with nearby Metro Manila and with the world economy more generally recast small-town bosses in the province as brokers, gatekeepers, and facilitators for major corporations (and criminal syndicates) in Manila, Hong Kong, and Tokyo. As industrial estates, golf courses, and residential subdivisions intruded upon the landscape of the province in the 1980s and 1990s, municipal mayors found themselves increasingly at the service of outside capital.

In the municipalities of Cavite, the historical link between landownership and access to the state, as well as the geographically prefigured role of illegal activities in this suburban province's economy, have undermined oligopolistic arrangements among local élite landowning families and encouraged the rise of small-time political operators to positions of local political and economic supremacy. Relying heavily on the use of violence and the protection and patronage of provincial politicians, these gangster-politicians have evolved into small-town mafia-style bosses, using the discretionary powers of elected municipal offices to assume monopolistic control over key sectors and strategic chokepoints of their respective local economies but failing to translate their essentially state-based empires into enduring legacies for dynastic self-perpetuation.

The longevity of small-town bosses in Cavite has been rooted in the local political economies. In Cavite Province, the most enduring twentieth-century small-town boss operated in the municipality whose local economy was most readily available for regulation or appropriation by the town mayor. Thus in Carmona, the government's expropriation of large landed estates and the centrality of the communal lands to the local economy facilitated the entrenchment of longtime mayor Cesar Casal. In Carmona, close links to markets, production sites, and processing centers outside Cavite allowed the municipal mayor to assume a monopolistic brokerage position in the local economy.

Although perhaps an administrative "outlier" in the province of Cavite, Carmona by no means constitutes an outlying case. Casal's mayoral longevity in Carmona is fairly matched by that of longtime mayor (1955–86), provincial board member (1988–92), and congressman (1992–95) Telesforo Unas of Maragondon, a town noteworthy for its lack of large landowners, extensive public forests, pastures, and quarry and its proximity to market towns in the neighboring province of Batangas. Moreover, this case study of Carmona suggests a pattern of variation in the longevity of small-town bosses and dynasties that may be applicable elsewhere in the Philippines. In short, long-term bosses survive and prosper in municipalities whose local economies lend themselves to monopolistic control. In some such municipalities, where the "public" or state-regulated sphere of the economy dwarfs local concentrations of private capital, criminal and predatory mafia-style bosses depend heavily on violence and access to state offices and resources for political self-perpetuation and capital accumulation.

Mafia-style bosses are also entrenched in other congressional districts and provinces throughout the archipelago. Like their counterparts at the municipal level, these provincial warlords have used violence, discretionary powers, and state patronage to hold on to power. However, these congressional/provincial bosses have accumulated many more resources and privileges than the small-town bosses and have established empires that cover entire congressional districts and provinces. The next chapter discusses the district- and province-wide empires built up by successive bosses in twentieth-century Cavite.

# The Provincial Warlords of Cavite, 1896–1995

Early on the afternoon of March 3, 1992, a light-green Toyota Corolla pulled up in front of the municipal hall of Ternate, Cavite, a town just two hours' drive from Manila. According to eyewitnesses, five men alit with drawn M-16 armalite rifles and approached Ternate mayor Octavio Velasco, who was standing outside the building together with his two bodyguards and the town police chief.[1] First saluting Velasco and assuring him "we just need to talk" (May pag-uusapan lang tayo), the armed men suddenly opened fire, pumping several rounds of bullets into the mayor and his three companions. Jumping back into their car, the five sped off in the direction of nearby Maragondon, Cavite, leaving Velasco, his two bodyguards, and the Ternate police chief to die. An autopsy revealed that Velasco had received at least nineteen gunshot wounds.[2]

Following Malacañang's demand for a "crackdown on private armies," Cavite's provincial police superintendent directed a series of raids on local officials' residences and confiscated numerous weapons, while the Commission on Elections considered placing Cavite under its direct control.[3] Within a few days, the head of the Criminal Investigation Service of the Philippine National Police (PNP) had filed murder charges against five suspects, all of whom were police officers detailed as bodyguards of Cavite congressman Jorge Nuñez, whose rivalry with Velasco in Ternate was well established.[4] In subsequent weeks, Congressman Nuñez emerged from hiding to answer charges that he had ordered the killings and withdrew his candidacy for reelection. Meanwhile, evidence linking

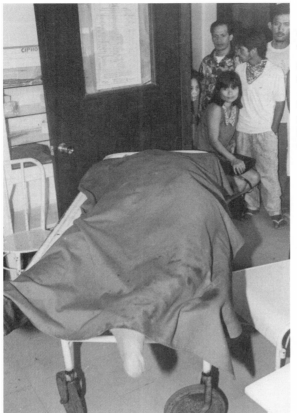

The corpse of Octavio Velasco, mayor of Ternate, Cavite, after his assassination in early 1992. A close ally of Governor Remulla was accused of masterminding the killing. (*Manila Chronicle*)

The municipal hall of Ternate, Cavite, where mayor Octavio Velasco, his two bodyguards, and the Ternate chief of police were killed. Note the blood and bullet marks on the wall. (*Manila Chronicle*)

Cavite governor Juanito ("Johnny") Remulla, Nuñez's longtime ally and patron, to the Velasco assassination faded from the newspaper accounts and failed to resurface in the police investigation and trial. Knowledgeable observers in Cavite, however, noted that Velasco was the fifth mayor in the province since 1986 to fall to assassins' bullets after coming into conflict with Governor Remulla.

For observers familiar with Cavite history, moreover, the Velasco assassination recalled political killings in the province from 40 and 95 years earlier, killings remarkably similar to those of March 1992 in Ternate, both in their geographic location and in their role in the struggles of successive bosses to capture and preserve province-wide power in Cavite. In the famous "Maragondon Massacre" of 1952, the mayor and police chief of Maragondon (a neighboring town of Ternate) were kidnapped and murdered by a band of hired killers and local officials allegedly enlisted by then senator Justiniano Montano. After several powerful political allies (including Manila mayor Arsenio Lacson) vouched for Montano's whereabouts on the night when he was said to have called a meeting to plot the Maragondon murders, the senator went free, while some of the less powerful defendants—most notably famed Cavite bandit Nardong Putik (Leonardo Manecio)—earned prison sentences for the crime. As discussed below, the "Maragondon Massacre" came at the height of Montano's rivalry with Governor Dominador Camerino (1946–55) for supremacy in Cavite, a rivalry that led to the violent deaths of four town mayors and countless other local *líders* in the years from 1946 to 1955. In an even more famous episode in May 1897, revolutionary *supremo* Andres Bonifacio and his brother, Procopio, were executed in Maragondon, following court-martial proceedings (for their "treason against the Revolution") approved by revolutionary general Emilio Aguinaldo. Although Aguinaldo had formally commuted the Bonifacio brothers' death sentences to indefinite exile, their deaths at the hands of his men effectively resolved the contest between Aguinaldo and a rival faction closely linked to Bonifacio for leadership of the Revolution in Cavite.[5]

In short, the 1897, 1952, and 1992 killings in Maragondon and Ternate highlight the crucial role of violence in the efforts of successive bosses to achieve and maintain province-wide supremacy in Cavite. Throughout the twentieth century, aspirants to—and wielders of—provincial power in Cavite mobilized armed followers and employed violence to intimidate and eliminate their opponents. Despite the dramatic economic transformation of the province, a distinct pattern has continued to structure politics in Cavite at the provincial level: single bosses have dominated the province for decades, subordinating town mayors and other local *líders* to their rule through coercion and control but failing to pass on this political and economic preeminence to their progeny.

To some extent, the longevity of successive bosses in this single-congressional-district province has rested upon the extensive prerogatives enjoyed by governors and members of the House of Representatives. Provincial governors, while possessing few formal powers of taxation, licensing, or regulation,[6] have had considerable discretion over the local coercive and law-enforcement agencies of the state apparatus: direct control over special agents, provincial guards, and jail wardens; supervisory and disciplinary authority over both municipal police forces and Constabulary detachments;[7] and decisive input in the appointment, transfer, removal, and promotion of Philippine Constabulary provincial and company commanders (and today's provincial police superintendents).[8] Thus, as one provincial governor from northern Luzon noted in a 1971 interview:

A governor could use strong-arm tactics. . . . He could use a private army to dominate and control the local officials in his province. . . . He doesn't have to worry about the authority given to his office or about his performance. . . . This kind of governor can become a political kingpin who imposes his will on the people."[9]

Congressmen, who possess no formal authority in the realm of law-enforcement, hold tremendous sway over the flow of pork-barrel funds to their districts.[10] Through membership in House committees, intimacy with the president, and representation in the powerful Commission on Appointments, moreover, congressmen also maintain broad influence over personnel in the myriad agencies of the state apparatus, including those assigned to their home districts. In comparison with the regular turnover observed in most municipal mayorships, the high rates of incumbency for provincial governors and congressmen in both the pre-martial-law and the post-Marcos eras suggest that control over state resources and powers encourages the entrenchment of district- and provincial-level bosses throughout the archipelago.[11]

To a considerable extent, moreover, the distinctive features of Cavite's political economy prefigured this pattern of provincial boss rule. As noted in Chapter 2, since the earliest phases of primitive capital accumulation in the Spanish colonial era under the auspices of the religious orders, control over land in Cavite has depended largely on access to the local agencies of the state, and land settlement patterns have not led to the concentration of land in vast haciendas. Moreover, the suburban province's proximity to the national capital has stimulated the growth of extensive illegal economies—cattle rustling, highway robbery, car theft, and smuggling—available for regulation, exploitation, and monopolization by those in charge of the law-enforcement agencies of the state in Cavite. Three successive provincial bosses—Emilio Aguinaldo (1901–35), Justiniano S. Montano Sr. (1935–72), and Juanito Remulla (1979–95)—dominated Cavite in the twentieth century. The remainder of this chapter compares their respective province-wide empires and discusses the relevance of enduring boss rule in Cavite for an understanding of provincial warlords elsewhere in the Philippines.

## Cavite's Caudillo, 1901–35: General Emilio Aguinaldo

Under the Spanish colonial regime, Cavite was the site of several large friar estates, which totaled well over 35,000 hectares of prime land and encompassed virtually all of the settled and cultivated area of the province.[12] As explained in the previous chapter, the large landholdings of the religious orders prevented the emergence of a local landowning class in Cavite, but the friars granted a favored few—known as *inquilinos*—leaseholds on large tracts of land, for subleasing to subtenant-cultivators and substantial rentier profits.[13] These *inquilinos*, who depended heavily upon the favor of the friars for their leasehold privileges, evolved into the local élite of Cavite; their scions came to dominate the ranks of the *gobernadorcillos* (town executives) and *cabezas de barangay* (village headmen) in various towns of the province. Members of these *inquilino* dynasties, moreover, later formed the upper echelons of the insurrectionary leadership in Cavite during the Revolution.[14]

In the insurrection of 1896, Emilio Aguinaldo emerged from one of the *inquilino* élite dynasties to make the first bid by a Caviteño for supramunicipal power. Aguinaldo's family had long held leaseholds on friar land in Cavite Viejo (today's Kawit), and both his father and his older brother had served as *gobernadorcillo* of the town. In 1895, Emilio himself had been elected *capitan municipal* (the new Spanish title for the *gobernadorcillo*) after serving for eight years as a *cabeza de barangay* in one barrio of Kawit.[15] It was from this vantage point of small-town political and economic power and prominence that he emerged at the forefront of the revolutionaries' recruitment drive in Kawit at the outbreak of the Philippine Revolution.

When the Spanish colonial regime executed thirteen wealthy residents of Cavite El Puerto in September 1896 in retaliation for their Masonic and Katipunan affiliations, Aguinaldo began to form a "revolutionary government" in Imus from the ranks of Cavite's small-town élite clans, drawing *inquilinos* and *tulisanes* (bandits) alike into his following. In Kawit, he patched up feuds between rival *inquilino* clans, rallied the 40 *cuadrilleros* (town policemen) under his command, and invited the *tuli-sanes* who had long preyed upon the town to join his cause.[16] In order to expand his political base, Aguinaldo filled his Cabinet with relatives, friends, and Masonic brothers from the prominent families of the northern towns that comprised the Recollects' Hacienda de Imus and with scions of local *inquilino* clans from other parts of the province.[17] These subordinates, who held municipal offices and long-standing leaseholds on friar lands, provided an ample base for further recruitment from among their client *cuadrilleros*, affiliated *tulisanes*, and subtenant farmers of more modest means and status.[18]

Although the complex history of the Philippine Revolution is beyond the scope of this study, the pattern of armed conflict and political competition in Cavite that emerged with the breakdown of Spanish authority at the turn of the century would endure in the province for decades to come. Bifactional competition between rival claimants to revolutionary leadership counterposed Aguinaldo's *Sangguniang Magdalo* (Magdalo Council), centered in Imus and Kawit, against the Alvarez clan's *Sangguniang Magdiwang* (Magdiwang Council), centered in the nearby coastal town of Noveleta. Mariano Alvarez, *capitan municipal* of Noveleta and a relative by marriage of Katipunan *supremo* Andres Bonifacio, drew upon his own network of friends and relatives among Cavite's small-town élite clans to challenge the hegemony of Aguinaldo and the Sangguniang Magdalo in the province. Thus, at the outbreak of the first phase of the Revolution, the Sangguniang Magdiwang claimed jurisdiction over the towns belonging to the Dominican and Augustinian estates that stretched along the coast below Kawit and inland to the upland towns in the remote southern reaches of the province. Aguinaldo's Sangguniang Magdalo, by contrast, had a solid base on the Recollects' vast haciendas, which encompassed populous Kawit and Imus in the north as well as a broad swath of territory that extended east to Carmona and south toward Tagaytay Ridge and included Dasmariñas, Silang, and Mendez. In the course of the Revolution, however, the Magdalo subordinated the Magdiwang to its rule, as Aguinaldo eliminated Bonifacio and established himself, however briefly, as the supreme revolutionary *caudillo* throughout Cavite and, more tenuously, elsewhere in Luzon.[19]

Aguinaldo surrendered to the Americans in 1901, but the network of alliances between *inquilino* clans in Cavite towns that he had mobilized during the Revolution survived intact and, with the immediate imposition of American "colonial democracy," provided the basis for a province-wide political machine.[20] In the highly restricted municipal elections held by the American colonial regime in 1901, scions of these small-town Cavite dynasties, whose forefathers had served as *inquilinos* and *gober-*

*nadorcillos* in the nineteenth century, triumphed easily and assumed office as municipal mayors throughout the province.[21] Moreover, the Americans' transfer of provincial powers to local hands linked the fortunes of Aguinaldo's nascent political machine to the forces of the national state in nearby Manila. General Mariano Trias, a close associate of Aguinaldo, was in 1901 appointed and, with American support, elected by Cavite's municipal executives to the provincial governorship the following year.[22] Although the declaration of martial law in Cavite in January 1904 led to the replacement of Trias with an American governor and the postponement of subsequent gubernatorial elections until 1907, the provincial treasurer, Daniel Tirona, the second Magdalo minister of war and younger sibling of Aguinaldo's "cherished compadre" (*minamahal na kumpare*) and brother-in-law, Candido Tirona, remained the highest-ranking Caviteño official in the province.[23]

As in most of the Philippines, the elections of 1907 for governorships and seats in the Philippine Assembly marked the historic linking of Cavite's municipal and provincial politics with Manila-centered national government patronage and tied the fortunes of Caviteño revolutionary veteran-politicos to the ebbs and flows of national politics.[24] The ex-revolutionaries entrenched in provincial towns were quite willing to engage in vote-buying, fraud, and intimidation on behalf of their revolutionary leader.[25] In the September 1935 election, for example, Aguinaldo's opponents complained to the Constabulary authorities in Manila:

We have received confidential reports that the Aguinaldistas will force voters in the said towns [Kawit, Bacoor, Imus, Noveleta, Alfonso, Gen. Trias, and Rosario] to vote for General Aguinaldo, and that during the counting the same Aguinaldistas will compel election inspectors to read ballots in favor of General Aguinaldo.[26]

Backed by such a machine, Aguinaldo and his brother-in-law soon emerged as the acknowledged masters of politics in Cavite and as leading opponents of the Nacionalista regime. Serving three terms as lone Cavite representative to the national legislature and two additional terms as senator from the 4th senatorial district, Tirona emerged as one of the ranking leaders of the Democrata Party, which, though a small minority in opposition to the Nacionalista regime, at times controlled crucial swing votes when the faction-ridden majority party was split.[27] Despite the Nacionalista Party's virtual monopoly on patronage, splits within the ruling bloc allowed Tirona and his Democrata machine to survive in Cavite. In 1922, 1931, and 1934, for example, when the Nacionalistas were most divided, Democratas won both the Cavite governorship and the province's lone seat in the lower house of the legislature. Tirona's most successful protégé, Pedro Espiritu, was elected twice to the legislature and twice as provincial governor. Espiritu, whose Imus-based family subsequently won the franchise to supply electricity to Cavite's northern towns, served also as personal secretary to Tirona's brother-in-law and close associate, General Emilio Aguinaldo.

Tirona's political fortunes were closely intertwined with—and highly dependent upon—the privileged position of Aguinaldo in the national political arena. As the preeminent *caudillo* of the Revolution, Aguinaldo commanded considerable public attention, and through leadership of the Association of the Veterans of the Philippine Revolution he maintained a following among some 50,000 war veterans, whose ranks included prominent political figures scattered throughout central and southern Luzon.[28] In the 1920s, moreover, Aguinaldo's close relationship with American governor-general Leonard Wood afforded him considerable influence over executive appointments. For example, José P. Melencio, the general's son-in-law, was named the appointive representative for Cotabato in the national legislature, and his law partner, A. G. Escamilla, the appointive delegate for Nueva Vizcaya. As one commentator noted:

> From the mere clerk job to the exalted office of appointive representative, the Veterans' president had always utilized his influence to [sic] the Governor General. He was virtually responsible for the appointments of Christian Filipino representatives for non-Christian provinces. These were his own men. In the municipal board of the city of Manila, Aguinaldo has always a look. In fact he has succeeded more than once in having some of his aides and trusted subordinates filled [sic] unoccupied seats in the council.[29]

Aguinaldo's relationship with longtime Senate president and Partido Nacionalista leader Manuel Quezon also worked to their mutual personal advantage. In 1920, for example, Quezon arranged for the passage of a bill providing the retired general with a generous pension of 1,000 pesos per month.[30] More important, with Quezon's connivance Aguinaldo as early as 1908 occupied a broad swath of former friar land in the town of Dasmariñas without any contract and finally purchased the tract in a public auction in 1927. Amounting to 1,185 hectares of prime sugar land, the estate was divided into 69 lots in order to facilitate circumvention of the limitation on individual purchases of public land to 144 hectares, through the use of various Aguinaldo children and grandchildren as "dummies" in the sale.[31] Moreover, Aguinaldo's purchase was made on an installment basis, and over the years he consistently failed to make payments to the government, such that by 1934 he had paid less than 10 percent of the purchase price and an even smaller portion of the accumulating interest.[32] Bureau of Lands officials calculated that the aging *caudillo* had managed to avoid paying well over half a million pesos by squatting on the land since 1908 and still owed more than half that amount in debts to government lending agencies.[33] While Quezon facilitated both legislative approval of the original transaction and executive leniency in the collection of Aguinaldo's interest payments, the general expressed his gratitude at crucial times, supporting Quezon in his formation of the Partido Nacionalista-Colectivista in 1922 and in his opposition to the Hare-Hawes-Cutting Act in 1933.[34]

Aside from privileged access to state sinecures, patronage, and public lands and loans, Aguinaldo enjoyed considerable power as a broker with Manila for his followers in Cavite. For example, with Aguinaldo's assistance, families who had held *inquilino* leaseholds on monastic lands in the province acquired ownership rights to the same tracts they had subleased from the religious orders, after the corrupt Bureau of Lands purchased the friar estates and then sold them to "previous tenants." Some families closely linked to Aguinaldo and based in northern rice-bowl towns such as Imus and Kawit, moreover, acquired landholdings in the southern upland towns of the province through these sales, thus establishing an enduring pattern of economic domination within the province. Through the intercession of Aguinaldo and his minions in the legislature and the bureaucracy, many Cavite families retained ownership rights to lands they never paid for. Similarly, during the American colonial period Cavite mayors profited by providing "protection" to local cattle rustlers and selectively enforcing statutes prohibiting *jueteng* (illegal and frequently rigged lotteries). With discretion over the assignment of Constabulary officers to Cavite through his personal contacts in Manila and his protégés' positions in the national legislature, Aguinaldo could ensure the cooperation of provincial law-enforcement authorities with the local cattle-rustling and *jueteng* syndicates.

Yet the dominant figure in national politics during this period, Senate President Manuel Quezon, was not content to rely on General Aguinaldo as his "man in Cavite" and in fact worked to build up his own close friend and fellow Nacionalista Antero Soriano as a latter-day Magdiwang counterforce to Aguinaldo's Magdalo machine. Soriano, a big-time gambler and Quezon crony who hailed from the southern Cavite coastal town of Tanza, thus won a seat on the board of directors of the Manila Railroad Company and through rigged auctions and two dummy corporations acquired from the Bureau of Lands extensive tracts of former friar-owned rice land in his hometown and in neighboring Naic.[35] In 1912, Soriano won the Cavite governorship and was reelected in 1916, beating Tirona in 1919 for the 5th district senatorial seat. In 1925 he won the special election for Cavite's seat in the House of Representatives after the death by natural causes of his protégé, Augusto Reyes. By 1926, Manila journalists wrote of a "Soriano bloc" in the lower chamber of the legislature, a force that remained powerful until Soriano's death in 1929 after a prolonged illness.[36] Although Soriano's protégés as Cavite's governor and congressman were voted out in 1931, his choice for Cavite City mayor, Ramon Samonte, remained in this appointed post for several years after his mentor's death.

Overall, the electoral system installed by the American colonial regime transformed Aguinaldo's "army" of *inquilinos, gobernadorcillos, cuadrilleros,* and *tulisanes* into the basis for a provincial boss's political machine. His closest followers, drawn primarily from among the Spanish-era small-town élite clans, were quick to reassert their control over the local tentacles of the colonial state apparatus, winning the highly restricted mayoral elections in various municipalities of the province in the early years of American rule. With Aguinaldo's blessings and assistance, they used their political influence to secure land rights and, through mayoral control over municipal police, often supported such criminal activities as cattle rustling and banditry. Moreover, with the watchful friars gone, mayors and their minions were free to act as the financiers, operators, and protectors of *jueteng* operations in their towns, as long as they enjoyed friendly relations with Aguinaldo and the provincial authorities.

With the removal of the friars and the linking of municipal, provincial, and national politics in 1907, a new, previously unattainable niche of provincial power was created, promising considerable control over the "commanding heights" of Cavite's economy. With his Magdalo machine in place, Aguinaldo and his well-heeled sidekick Tirona were perfectly positioned to seize this niche and make it their own. For more than three decades they used their influence over the expanding Cavite electorate to establish ties with national politicians in Manila such as Leonard Wood and Manuel Quezon, ties that in turn strengthened their hold over the province. Aguinaldo secured himself a fat monthly pension, the largest and richest tract of land in Cavite, and extensive privileges and patronage plums in Manila. Meanwhile, his protégés as congressmen and governors controlled Cavite-bound pork-barrel and handsome shares of the daily *jueteng* take even as they pampered their client town mayors with whispered asides to the provincial fiscal and carefully penned notes to the director of the Bureau of Lands.

Yet this happy state of affairs depended heavily on the maintenance of reciprocal—if not genuinely friendly—ties with powerful patrons in Manila. Following the reconsolidation of the Partido Nacionalista in 1934, the Bureau of Lands issued an executive order revoking the sale of the lands in Dasmariñas to Aguinaldo and confiscating the estate in its entirety.[37] Enraged, Aguinaldo announced his intention to run against Quezon in September 1935 for the presidency of the Commonwealth. Exploiting his hold on key levers in the election machinery, Senate President Quezon decided to create real trouble for the general in his own bailiwick. With generous support from the Partido Nacionalista, partisan elements in the provincial Constabulary command, and Soriano protégé Ramon Samonte seated as governor, Quezon's candidate, Justiniano Montano, defeated Aguinaldo's sidekick Tirona for Cavite's seat in the Assembly, while Quezon won a landslide victory over the aging general.[38] Soon after assuming his seat, Montano engineered the passage of a bill that provided for the subdivision and sale of all portions of the former friar estates "remaining undisposed of" and disqualified as purchasers all those who—like Aguinaldo and his many cronies—had previously been delinquent in payments. Montano's bill, which Quezon approved in 1936, facilitated the transfer of Cavite lands from Aguinaldista to Montanista hands by retaining the original prices fixed when the plots were first offered for sale, by providing highly concessional installment schedules, and by offering preference to "bona fide occupants" at the discretion of Secretary of Agriculture and Commerce Benigno S. Aquino Sr., who had taken Montano under his wing.[39]

This course of events established a pattern for turnover in provincial leadership in Cavite that continued to regulate politics in the province throughout the postwar period. Once a Cavite provincial boss challenged or otherwise antagonized the national powers-that-be, funds for road construction would dry up, lands acquired through dubious means would be confiscated and redistributed, unsympathetic Constabulary officers and provincial fiscals would be rotated to Cavite, and the loyalty of town mayors and other local *líders* would fall into doubt. Such was the dynamic that unraveled Aguinaldo and Tirona's machine in 1935, and that in the postwar period spurred the rise and fall of a second provincial boss, longtime Cavite congressman Justiniano S. Montano Sr.

## Cavite's First Warlord, 1935–72: Justiniano Montano Sr.

Three external conditions shaped Cavite politics from the inauguration of the Commonwealth in 1935 until the declaration of martial law in 1972, a period dominated by Justiniano Montano. First, the endurance of formal democratic institutions in the Philippines entailed regular presidential elections, continued dependence of rival candidates on votes controlled by provincial bosses, and considerable congressional influence over pork barrel, bureaucratic appointments, and disbursement of government franchises and contracts.[40] Second, the onset of import-substitution industrialization in the late 1940s encouraged new forms of legal and illegal economic activity in Cavite that were flourishing by the mid-1960s.[41] Third, the rapid growth of Metro Manila spilled over into adjacent Cavite, stimulating a distinctly suburban pattern of "development."[42]

Overall, the early postwar years (1946–72) witnessed dramatic socioeconomic transformation in Cavite. The population doubled, from around 260,000 in 1948 to over 520,000 in 1970, nearly half of which was classified as urban.[43] At the same time, agricultural production expanded and intensified in response to rising demand in nearby Manila and abroad. Wet-rice cultivation continued to predominate, but export crops such as sugarcane, coffee, and coconuts increasingly supplemented rice as the mainstay of Cavite's agricultural economy. Agriculture grew increasingly capital-intensive, with farmers relying more and more on irrigation, fertilizers, pesticides, hand tractors, and threshers.[44]

Landownership in Cavite Province became increasingly concentrated in the hands of families based in the northern, more urbanized towns of Imus, Kawit, and Cavite City, as well as in marketing centers in neighboring Laguna and Batangas. Significantly, local capitalists continued to dominate in Cavite without much competition from Manila-based magnates or foreign firms. Yet political power at the provincial level rested not in the hands of the local landowning élite, but in those of a provincial boss whose economic base lay in the state apparatus itself.

Like Emilio Aguinaldo before him, Cavite's premier postwar provincial warlord, longtime congressman Justiniano Montano, owed his political ascendancy and longevity to the skillful deployment of violence and state resources rather than to an independent base in land or proprietary wealth. Though related by blood and marriage to landowning families in two Cavite towns, Montano's political emergence stemmed primarily from the favor he enjoyed from Manuel Quezon's Nacionalista Party machine in the prewar period. Fresh out of the University of the Philippines College of Law, he placed second in the bar examinations of 1929 and was immediately rewarded by Cavite governor Fabian Pugeda (a Nacionalista and a Soriano protégé) with appointment as assistant provincial fiscal in his home province, an office created by Pugeda after Montano declined the position of justice of the peace in the southern Cavite town of Silang.[45] As provincial fiscal, Montano joined the selective and discretionary law enforcement long central to Cavite politics and established throughout Cavite a lasting reputation for his considerable legal skills.[46] He resigned in 1932, however, after Pugeda lost the governorship to Democrata Pedro Espiritu, the protégé of Aguinaldo and Tirona.

Despite this apparent setback, local political developments in Cavite worked in Montano's favor. Since his election in 1931, Governor Espiritu had waged a highly publicized yet selective campaign against *jueteng* operations in the province; its purpose was to dismantle his predecessor's machine and prevent the *jueteng* scandal (which implicated the governor of neighboring Laguna Province) from spreading to Cavite.[47] Taking full advantage of his gubernatorial powers, Espiritu added a large number of "special agents" to the provincial payroll, suspended several hostile town mayors, and closed down small-time *jueteng* dens so that his wealthy ally, the notorious Cavite City "*jueteng* king," Honorio Rojas, could expand his operations.[48] Meanwhile, Montano opened a private law practice, defending the suspended mayors against Espiritu's accusations and taking on the election protest cases of Nacionalista candidates who had lost in the 1931 municipal contests.[49] In May 1935, moreover, Espiritu's death left the governorship in the hands of provincial board member Ramon Samonte, a Nacionalista and Montano supporter. Thus in his 1935 election campaign, Montano was supported by several incumbent or former town mayors and had an ally in the provincial capital, as well as a modest base in Tanza, where his mother's family had substantial landholdings, and in Naic, where his wife's clan, the Nazarenos, had long held sway. These factors no doubt helped Montano to win Quezon's endorsement and to defeat Tirona by a respectable margin for the lone Cavite seat in the national legislature.

In 1935, as in subsequent elections, Montano relied heavily on nefarious tactics to guarantee his reelection and to advance the political fortunes of his protégés in Cavite. In the 1935 and 1938 elections, for example, Montano evidently manipulated voter-registration lists and intimidated voters, election inspectors, and members of the provincial board of canvassers on election day.[50] In the early postwar period, moreover, Montano engaged in bloody confrontation with Cavite governor Dominador Camerino.[51] All told, between 1946 and 1954 four Cavite town mayors and eight municipal police chiefs lost their lives to assassins' bullets as a result of the Montano-Camerino rivalry.[52] Though Montano's son Delfin replaced Camerino as governor in 1955, warlord tactics continued to play a key role in Cavite elections. On election day in 1961, for example, Governor Montano unleashed over 400 armed "special agents,"[53] who, along with the Montanos' protégé mayors and their armed henchmen in precincts throughout Cavite allegedly "accompanied, followed, watched, assisted and/or prepared the ballots of the registered

TABLE 2
*Cavite Politics and Presidential Elections, 1946–69*

|      | President Elected | Cavite Margin | Cavite Backer |
|------|-------------------|---------------|---------------|
| 1946 | Manuel Roxas (LP) | +27,000 | Camerino (LP) |
| 1949 | Elpidio Quirino (LP) | +38,000 | Camerino (LP) |
| 1953 | Ramon Magsaysay (NP) | +10,000 | Montano (NP) |
| 1957 | Carlos Garcia (NP) | +14,000 | Montano (NP) |
| 1961 | Diosdado Macapagal (LP) | +33,000 | Montano (LP) |
| 1965 | Ferdinand Marcos (NP) | -27,000 | Camerino (NP) |
| 1969 | Ferdinand Marcos (NP) | +16,000 | Camerino (NP) |

voters inside the voting booths during the voting." A handwriting expert later testified that over 8,800 ballots had been "prepared in groups, each group by one hand, or ballots each written by two or more persons."[54]

Montano also used electoral fraud and violence to deliver votes to patrons in Malacañang (see Table 2). Successive presidents amply rewarded these two rival Cavite kingpins' services on their behalf with patronage and special favors. The impact of national realignments on provincial politics in Cavite is abundantly clear (see Table 3).

Montano owed his success in demolishing Camerino's machine in the mid-1950s, for example, largely to the patronage of Nacionalista president Ramon Magsaysay, who received 10,000 more votes in Cavite in 1953 than incumbent president Elpidio Quirino.[55] In 1954 the Nacionalista-controlled House Electoral Tribunal awarded Cavite's congressional seat to a Montano protégé, and Malacañang suspended Governor Camerino in favor of a Montano man who fired the governor's 300 provincial guards and special agents and harassed recalcitrant pro-Camerino mayors with suspensions and court cases.[56] Montano's protégés also won appointment to the Tagaytay City mayorship and to the positions of mayor, chief of police, and city fiscal in Cavite City. Well-publicized closings of brothels, raids on illegal gambling dens, roundups of unregistered jeepneys, and "mass screenings" of resident Chinese followed in Cavite City; these were thinly veiled mechanisms for extorting higher rates of protection money for Montano's machine.[57]

Other Magsaysay moves strengthened Montano's hold over Cavite. In the summer of 1955, Malacañang released 2 million pesos in pork-barrel funds for improvements to government highways and waterworks, thus providing substantial liquid funds for vote-buying and other expenses for Delfin Montano's successful gubernatorial campaign in November of that year.[58] Magsaysay also signed into law a bill sponsored by Montano that

TABLE 3
*National Realignments and Provincial Politics, 1947–71*

| Year | Administration | Election of Palace Favorite |
|------|----------------|------------------------------|
| 1947 | Roxas (LP) | Camerino (LP) elected governor |
| 1951 | Quirino (LP) | Camerino (LP) reelected governor |
| 1955 | Magsaysay (NP) | Delfin Montano (NP) elected governor |
| 1959 | Garcia (NP) | Montano (NP) reelected governor |
| 1963 | Macapagal (LP) | Montano (LP) reelected governor |
| 1967 | Marcos (NP) | Montano (LP) reelected governor |
| 1971 | Marcos (NP) | Lino Bocalan (NP) elected governor |

transferred the provincial capital from Cavite City to the newly created Trece Martires City, formerly a sleepy inland barrio in Tanza largely owned by the Montano family.[59] According to the bill's provisions, newly elected governor Montano henceforth served as ex-officio mayor of Trece Martires, thus enjoying complete discretion over the appointment of the municipal police force and considerable insulation from public scrutiny in his administration of the province's affairs.

Finally, in Magsaysay's last year in office a Montano-sponsored bill created the Cavite Electricity Development Authority (CEDA) and placed control over electric power in the province in the hands of the governor. The publicly owned and operated CEDA proved a veritable cash cow for rampant overcharging, profit-siphoning, and payroll-padding of almost 1,000 Montano ward leaders officially serving as CEDA inspectors and collectors. Control over electric power buttressed the Montanos' leverage over the owners of various businesses emerging in Cavite. Proprietors of ice plants along the Cavite coastline and rice mills in inland towns had to deal with the Montanos in order to obtain electricity.

President Diosdado Macapagal (1962–65) supplemented these provincial perks by advancing Montano's fortunes in Manila, amply rewarding the Cavite kingpin for delivering a 33,000-vote margin of victory in the province over incumbent Carlos Garcia in the November 1961 elections. With Macapagal's support, Montano won election in 1962 as House Majority floor leader, thus increasing his stake in pork-barrel allocations, allotment of appointees, and cut of grease money from lobbyists interested in the success or demise of certain bills under consideration by the legislature. The new president also appointed Montano's youngest son, Justiniano Jr.—a boxing enthusiast and horsebreeder—chairman of the powerful Game and Amusements Board (GAB), the government agency tasked with the supervision of horse-racing, jai alai, and boxing. As GAB chairman, the younger Montano was later implicated in match-rigging, race-fixing, illegal betting, and the management of boxers through "dummies" for his own personal profit.[60]

Over the years, the long tenure of Justiniano Montano Sr. in the national legislature (1935–39, 1946–56, 1958–72) advanced his position in Cavite in a number of ways. First, Montano's influence on the allocation of pork barrel to the province's nineteen municipalities and three chartered cities provided him with a loyal following among the province's mayors. Second, his seat in Congress guaranteed him a measure of discretion over the assignment of national government agency officials to Cavite—the provincial Constabulary commander, the judge of the Court of First Instance, the provincial fiscal, the provincial treasurer, the district engineer, and the division superintendent of schools—which buttressed his command over municipal mayors and other local power brokers. In addition, Montano was able to install numerous protégés in strategic positions within the national bureaucracy (e.g., the Bureau of Customs, Social Security System, Government Service Insurance System, and Bureau of Internal Revenue). Finally, Montano's seat in Congress offered opportunities for personal economic advancement through horse-trading and lobbying in the legislature.

Exploiting his privileges, Montano constructed a political machine of considerable strength in the province. By 1956, twelve of the nineteen municipalities were in the hands of Montano mayors, along with the appointive mayorships of Tagaytay City and Cavite City; by 1964, only three municipalities remained in non-Montano hands. He used his position in the Nacionalista and Liberal Parties to control the appointment of election inspectors throughout Cavite, and selected slates for municipal councilors, vice-mayors, and mayors in all Cavite towns, typically favoring his close associates over landowning families. Working against the élite clans in northern towns like Imus and Kawit who consistently supported the Magdalo machine, Montano entrenched his protégés in the upland towns of Amadeo, Bailen, Magallanes, Maragondon, and Silang and installed other allies in coastal and inland rice-bowl towns such as Bacoor, Carmona, General Trias, Naic, and Tanza.

Moreover, by the late 1950s, Montano had converted the bulk of state coercive resources in Cavite into a "private army" that buttressed his hold over the province. Following the election of his son Delfin to the governorship in 1955, he could command provincial guards, special agents, and prisoners under the provincial jail warden, along with the municipal police forces who operated under pro-Montano mayors.[61]

With the provincial Constabulary commander and other officers in his pocket, Montano was by the early 1960s in a position not only to guar-

Lino Bocalan, reputed "smuggling lord" of Cavite and long-time close associate of Congressman Montano. President Marcos's success in forging an alliance with Bocalan was crucial to Montano's downfall in the early 1970s. (Lopez Museum Library)

antee overwhelmingly favorable election results in Cavite for himself and his patrons in Malacañang, but also to control the booming illegal economy along the extensive coastline of Manila Bay. For by the late 1950s, Tanza, Montano's hometown and stronghold, had emerged as the key port for the smuggling of foreign cigarettes and other goods from Borneo, thanks to the town's location and superior natural anchorage facilities.[62] According to government documents that surfaced in 1964, an average of 2,400 cases of smuggled foreign cigarettes—yielding 600,000 pesos in profits—arrived monthly on Tanza's shores, along with firearms and other contraband.[63] In this way, Tanza benefited handsomely from the Philippine government's efforts, beginning in the 1950s, to promote the domestic tobacco industry through subsidies and restrictions on the import of foreign cigarettes.[64] Capipisa, one of the town's coastal barrios, earned fame for its plush residences and its paved streets, which were sponsored largely by barrio resident Lino Bocalan, a "modest fisherman" turned millionaire who came to own homes in Makati's exclusive Urdaneta Village and in San Francisco, California, and enjoyed police escort when he drove through Cavite in his Mercedes Benz.[65]

Based in Tanza, these smuggling operations evolved into an economy of considerable scale, a veritable octopus of transportation routes to and from Cavite as well as distribution and marketing channels in Manila; his operations were supported by officials at all levels of the government.[66] A syndicate of smugglers in Cavite, Sulu, and Zamboanga financed and provided transportation for the shipment of the contraband cigarettes, and local procurers handled distribution in Manila, but "protection" rested essentially in Montano hands. The Montanos enforced highly selective antismuggling efforts on Cavite's shores and roads, secured the release of confiscated contraband goods, and apprehended syndicate members. Position within the state apparatus determined the division of labor between father and son: Cavite governor Delfin Montano ensured local police cooperation, while his father as House Majority floor leader, Macapagal ally, and longtime chum of Defense Secretary Macario Peralta Jr. enjoyed ample access to the military establishment and considerable discretion over the assignment of Constabulary officers to his home province. Hush money supplemented career concerns to guarantee military cooperation: the smuggling syndicate's payroll included substantial monthly "salaries" for the relevant Constabulary officers.[67] In exchange for such compensation, various military units turned a blind eye to the syndicate's smuggling operations and even helped police to enforce the syndicate's monopoly against potential competitors.

The Montanos' political preeminence in Cavite also offered them unprecedented opportunities for more legitimate economic advancement in the early 1960s, as nearby Manila's industrial and demographic growth increased the value of Cavite property. In particular, the Montanos' landownership and real-estate development positions in Cavite brought them enormous profits. With the provincial government under Delfin's thumb and congressional pork-barrel allocations for Cavite in his own hands, Justiniano Montano literally paved the way for his family's expanding real-estate investments in Cavite.[68] The Montano family investments in Cavite were generously supported by such government agencies as the Home Financing Corporation[69] and bankrolled by laundered profits from smuggling operations. Montano-controlled companies developed real estate for subdivisions in northern towns in the suburbs of the expanding Manila metropolis[70] and bought up hundreds of hectares in the south for conversion to agribusiness ventures, including a piggery and 2,000 hectares of sugar land.[71] Congressman Montano and his son the governor pushed the selective expansion of roads and public works in the province, ensuring the rapid appreciation in value of these properties.

Financed with smuggling profits and dependent upon state largesse and leverage, these investments failed to provide Montano a permanent base in landholdings that would render him invulnerable to the ebbs and flows of national politics and allow him to pass on his provincial bailiwick to

Justiniano S. Montano Sr. in the Philippines in the late 1980s after more than a decade of exile in the United States. The former Cavite congressman and onetime senator was unable to resurrect his once seemingly impregnable political machine in the province. (*Manila Chronicle*)

his sons in classic dynastic fashion. Thus Montano's antagonistic relationship with president Ferdinand Marcos in the late 1960s and early 1970s led to his early political demise. In 1965, Montano had delivered the Cavite vote to Macapagal by a margin of nearly 28,000 votes, so when Marcos emerged victorious in the national count, Montano's Cavite became prime opposition country.

Marcos henceforth worked to undermine Montano's position: Constabulary campaigns against smuggling, Commission on Elections crackdowns on election anomalies, and congressional intrigues to undermine Montano's influence and resources considerably weakened Montano's hold on Cavite. In 1966, for example, Marcos's allies in the House of Representatives launched an exposé on smuggling in Cavite, naming Lino Bocalan and the Montanos as the leaders of a major syndicate in the province.[72] A carrot-and-stick courtship of Bocalan proceeded, with Malacañang first threatening, then rewarding, the notorious smuggling lord through court cases and disruption of his operations.[73] Thus Marcos demonstrated to Bocalan that business as usual required direct relations with Malacañang, rendering Montano's protection and brokerage services redundant.

Marcos also attacked Montano in the local and congressional elections

Cavite governor Juanito ("Johnny") Remulla (1979–95), seen here eating clams in a coastal Cavite town to disprove reports that a "red tide" had poisoned the local fishermen's catch. (*Manila Chronicle*)

of 1967 and 1969, backing Camerino's machine with the full array of national state resources at his disposal. For example, the Commission on Elections assumed control over all towns and cities of the province, deputizing the Constabulary to oversee the municipal and city police, provincial guards, and special agents of the governor on whom the Montanos' electoral fortunes heavily depended.[74] In 1967, moreover, selectively implementing a Malacañang-imposed firearms ban, the Constabulary disarmed pro-Montano mayors and policemen before the elections while allegedly allowing Camerino's henchmen to hold on to their guns.[75] Moreover, Marcos worked to prevent pro-Montano interference in the canvassing of election returns in Cavite by removing Montano supporters from the provincial board of canvassers in 1967.[76] With his election machinery thus seriously impaired, Montano lost several municipalities to pro-Camerino mayors in 1967, and, failing to deliver a majority in Cavite for Liberal Party presidential candidate Serging Osmeña in 1969, only won reelection to the province's lone seat in Congress by a plurality, as two pro-Marcos candidates split the Nacionalista vote.

By early 1971, Montano had lost his position as House Minority floor leader,[77] and Lino Bocalan had defected to the Marcos camp. The 1971 elections thus saw Lino Bocalan—whose smuggling operations had gained high-level protection that bypassed Montano—defeat Delfin Montano for the Cavite governorship with generous support from Malacañang.[78] Though a Liberal victory in the presidential elections of 1973 would certainly have revitalized Montano's machine in Cavite, Marcos's declaration of martial law and closing of Congress in September 1972 dashed whatever hopes the Cavite warlord had entertained for a comeback. Having flown to the United States for a visit in early September, Montano was—by coincidence or design—absent when martial law was proclaimed, and he remained abroad for the duration of Marcos's reign. When Montano returned to the Philippines in 1986, he found his family's properties—and political influence—in Cavite considerably diminished and a new boss, Cavite governor Johnny Remulla, already entrenched in the province.

## Cavite's Industrial Warlord, 1979–95: Juanito ("Johnny") Remulla

The Marcos regime's impact on events in the province was unprecedented. Indeed, until his ouster in 1986, Marcos halted the consistent turnover of national patrons that had fueled provincial rivalries in Cavite in the early postwar years. Moreover, the abolition of Congress, expansion of national state agencies, and empowerment of the military establishment carried the ominous threat of intrusion and centralization, especially for a province so near to Manila. Similarly, the explosive growth of Manila in the 1970s and 1980s further impinged upon neighboring Cavite. Meanwhile, the evolution of an avowedly export-led industrialization strategy had important implications for the suburban province, as the establishment of the Cavite Export Processing Zone and major tourist resorts in the province during the Marcos period amply attested. Finally, continuing industrialization in the Philippines and rapid economic growth in nearby Hong Kong, Taiwan, and Japan set the stage for a massive influx of investment into Cavite from Manila-based magnates and foreign firms.[79]

The socioeconomic transformation of Cavite after the declaration of martial law in 1972 was indeed dramatic. The population nearly doubled in 20 years, from 520,000 in 1970 to over 1.1 million in 1990, the majority of which is now urban and dependent upon employment in industries and services.[80] The highways linking Cavite to Metro Manila are jammed with commuter buses, jeepneys, commercial vans, and cargo-laden trucks. While industrial estates, residential subdivisions, and golf courses supplant rice fields and fishponds in more and more Cavite municipalities,[81] agribusiness thrives elsewhere in the province. Thousands of hectares planted with coconut, coffee, and sugarcane link Cavite to nearby mills and processing plants, even as pineapples, peanuts, avocados, and ornamental flowers tie entrepreneurs in the province to select Manila markets.[82] Huge signboards at entrances to the province proudly advertise "Cavite's 2nd Revolution," featuring "Industrialization, Agricultural Modernization, Tourism Development, and Rapid Urbanization." The champion of this rapid economic transformation was provincial governor Johnny Remulla (1979–86, 1988–95).

During Remulla's tenure as Cavite governor he was clearly as ruthless as his warlord predecessor Montano. In May 1984, for example, Remulla's goons reportedly harassed schoolteachers and opposition leaders in the weeks preceding the elections to the Batasang Pambansa (National Assembly), while on election day his armed bodyguards drove election observers and opposition representatives away from the provincial capital where the election results were canvassed. Scattered election-day reports from various parts of the province detailed massive vote-buying, ballot-stuffing, missing election returns, and disenfranchisement through intimidation.[83] When the votes were tabulated, close Remulla associates had won seats in the Assembly. In the February 1986 "snap" presidential elections, Remulla's armed bodyguards once again drove opposition representatives and NAMFREL (the National Citizens Movement for Free Elections) volunteers from the provincial capital where the votes for Cavite were canvassed. Reports from around the province spoke of massive vote-buying, flying voters (those who cast ballots in multiple precincts), harassment of opposition and NAMFREL observers by armed goons, policemen, and military officials, and the release of prisoners from Cavite jails on "special furlough." Complaints about missing ballot boxes, election returns prepared in advance by local officials, and systematic disenfranchisement were legion.[84] According to NAMFREL's subsequent report:

In Cavite, armed goons, local officials together with other KBL partisans harassed NAMFREL volunteers all over the province. The NAMFREL was denied entry in 164 precincts and KBL partisans roamed around poll precincts intimidating voters, NAMFREL volunteers, and opposition workers. Flying voters were prolific and vote buying was massive. There were suspicions concerning fake ballots, especially in Trece Martires City. Tampering of election returns may have been rampant, as all election returns had erasures while some did not bear the total number of votes in words and figures as required. Ghost precincts may have been used as reinforcement as shown by the more than 100% coverage by the Batasan count.[85]

When the votes were published, Remulla's machine had delivered more than 240,000 votes for Marcos, handing him an 80,000-vote victory in a region (Southern Tagalog) that Aquino otherwise carried.

In other elections, Remulla refrained from using such crude tactics, in large part because they were unnecessary. He was elected governor three times—in 1980, 1988, and 1992—by more than 100,000 votes. In those three contests, vote-buying, the support of numerous local elected and appointed government officials, and the bloc-voting of the Iglesia Ni Cristo guaranteed Remulla's victory without bloodshed.[86]

Once installed as governor in 1979, Remulla began to construct a considerable political machine in Cavite. With close allies in the national legislature and government agencies, Remulla was able to assign officials to jobs and allocate public works in Cavite, as well as facilitate business for his followers in Manila. For example, Renato Dragon, Remulla's fraternity brother and close associate, who served as assemblyman (1984–86) and congressman from Cavite's 2nd district (1987–98) in the House of Representatives, used his seat in the national legislature to advance various business interests inside and outside the province: a controversial savings bank, a recruitment agency for overseas contract workers, various real-estate ventures, and a logging concession in Mindanao.[87] To deliver votes to Dragon and other protégés, Remulla had at his disposal generous campaign financing from interested Manila-based *jueteng* operators, construction companies, factory owners, and politicians.[88] In the local elections of 1980, 1988, and 1992, only a handful of Remulla's candidates for mayor failed to win.[89] Meanwhile, five mayors who had antagonized Remulla lost their lives to assassins' bullets. With his protégés filling municipal positions in various towns and on the provincial board, as well as Cavite's three seats in Congress, by the early 1990s the governor's political machine appeared even more solid than those of his two predecessors.

Like Montano before him, Remulla owed his rise to provincial kingpin status less to landownership and small-town political followers than to his links with powerful patrons and his control of the key sectors of the provincial economy. In 1963, Remulla, then a young attorney fresh out of the University of the Philippines School of Law, convinced Montano to "carry" him on the Liberal slate of candidates for Cavite's provincial board, presenting himself as a convenient foil to longtime Montano foe Dominador Camerino, who also hailed from Remulla's hometown of Imus. Along with numerous other Montano protégés, Remulla won election in 1963 and was reelected to the provincial board as a Montano Liberal in 1967. Yet the proddings of Remulla's Upsilonian fraternity brother, then president Ferdinand Marcos, eventually encouraged him to break with his former patron and ally himself with the Nacionalista administration in Manila. With Marcos's encouragement and support, he ran unsuccessfully—as a Nacionalista—against Montano for Cavite's lone congressional seat in 1969. In 1970 he won election as one of Cavite's two delegates to the Constitutional Convention, and the following year he recaptured his seat on the provincial board. After the suspension of Governor Bocalan in 1972, Vice-Governor Camerino assumed the provincial executive's office, and Remulla took Camerino's seat; after Camerino's death in 1979, Remulla assumed the governorship, to which he won reelection in 1980, 1988, and 1992.

Aside from this familiar series of successful provincial political intrigues, Remulla's early career featured an element new to Cavite politics—close links with a major Manila-based oligarchic family, the powerful Puyat clan. The Puyat dynasty owed its immense fortune to the success in the 1930s and 1940s of forefather Gonzalo Puyat (1910–67), who had parlayed scrap-iron and furniture businesses into lucrative government construction contracts and extensive lumber concessions in Mindoro and Surigao.[90] By the 1950s, Gonzalo Puyat & Sons included a steel plant; by the 1960s, the company had three manufacturing divisions—furniture, galvanized iron sheets, and flour—and the family had founded a major commercial bank, the Manila Banking Corporation.[91]

Unsurprisingly, the Puyats' economic success was matched by and intertwined with dynastic forays into politics. Gonzalo Puyat himself enjoyed a close friendship with Commonwealth President Manuel L. Quezon,[92] and his son Gil served as director of the Philippine National Bank from 1945 to 1949 and then ran successfully for the Senate as a Nacionalista in 1951. As president and major financier of the Nacionalista Party in the 1950s and 1960s, Gil Puyat won reelection to the Senate in 1957, 1963, and 1969; he even ran unsuccessfully for vice-president as Carlos Garcia's running mate in 1961. Though the Puyats evidently retained political clout with Marcos in the martial-law years, their influence with the Palace waned in the early 1980s. Their flagship, the Manila Banking Corporation (MBC), was one of the favored commercial banks during the 1970s, but by the time of Marcos's ouster MBC was teetering on the verge of bankruptcy due to bad loans extended to agribusiness affiliates and other nonperforming accounts.[93] Meanwhile Remulla, who had served faithfully as the Puyats' legal counsel in the 1960s, helped the family acquire properties in Cavite in the 1970s and then mortgaged to the Manila Bank hundreds of hectares of prime land that he had acquired in the province in the early 1980s.[94]

Remulla had also graciously facilitated the entry of Marcos's "crony capitalists" into Cavite even before he became provincial governor. Rodolfo Cuenca, Marcos's golfing partner and favored construction magnate, won multimillion-peso government contracts for Manila's South Expressway and the Manila–Cavite Coastal Road and Reclamation Project, while the government-owned National Development Corporation formed a joint venture with a Cuenca company to develop several hundred hectares of prime land in Cavite for an industrial estate.[95] Marcos associate Ricardo C. Silverio and front man José Yao Campos acquired extensive properties in the province whose values appreciated rapidly after the government constructed highways and main roads nearby.[96] The Enriquez and Panlilio families, who were among the First Lady's closest friends, developed the famous Puerto Azul beach resort in Ternate, Cavite, with multimillion-peso loans from government financial institutions, specially converted public lands, and exclusive expropriation rights over extensive tracts of beachfront and inland property.[97]

Even electricity, formerly a franchise reserved for local control, fell into the hands of Marcos cronies with Remulla's assistance. Following the proclamation of martial law, a group of well-to-do Cavite residents with close links to then governor Dominador Camerino had formed the First Cavite Electric Cooperative Inc. (FCECI), taking advantage of Marcos's rural electrification program and widespread dissatisfaction with the Montanos' use of the Cavite Electricity Development Authority (CEDA) as a cash cow.[98] Within a few years, FCECI had supplanted CEDA as the supplier of electricity to seven of the most "progressive" municipalities in the province. Yet by the early 1980s, Benjamin ("Kokoy") Romualdez, the brother of First Lady Imelda R. Marcos, had other plans for electricity in Cavite. With the Marcoses' assistance, Kokoy had seized the Manila Electric Company (Meralco) from the Lopez family in the early years of martial law; with Imelda chairing the Board of Administrators of the National Electrification Administration (NEA), he had engineered the increase of Meralco's rates and the reduction of its franchise tax. Soft loans from the NEA helped Meralco to finance the appropriation of electric cooperatives in provinces surrounding Metro Manila so that the company could expand its franchise area.[99] In Cavite, Governor Remulla helped Meralco through various legal maneuvers and encouraged a wave of negative publicity against FCECI. In 1984 he organized a referendum of FCECI subscribers that resulted in a "popular decision" to waive the cooperative's franchise and sell off its assets to Meralco. Critics alleged that Remulla spent some P4.6 million on vote-buying and other referendum-related expenses and that his ward leaders manufactured fraudulent votes in order to produce the desired results.

More generally, from Remulla's first term as governor of Cavite (1979–86), he used strongarm tactics to establish himself as the "godfather" of the province's industrial revolution. In numerous documented cases, he dispatched armed goons, ordered the bulldozing of homes, and engineered the destruction of irrigation canals to expedite the departure of "squatters" and tenant farmers who were demanding compensation for their removal from lands designated for sale to Manila-based or foreign companies for "development" into industrial estates.[100] Though Remulla typically tempered such hardball tactics with offers for a "settlement," the "carrot" was never as impressive as the "stick." As one peasant leader noted:

> If your Barangay captain, the police, your mayor, your governor make you a request, and if you have not yet acceded to the request, you can expect that next if your *carabao* does not disappear, or your tools, then maybe you will next disappear yourself; if you don't wind up among the unsolved cases, then for sure you will be ambushed. There's a lot of that here in Cavite, but it mostly doesn't come out in the newspapers.[101]

Despite widespread dissatisfaction, Remulla—through municipal and provincial board resolutions and personal lobbying with various government agencies—pushed through the conversion to industrial and residential use of massive tracts of land in Cavite to facilitate their exemption from agrarian reform.[102] The log books of various Municipal Agrarian Reform offices in Cavite testify to frequent visits by one of Remulla's sons, and files bulge with local officials' recommendations in favor of land conversion. In Dasmariñas, for example, the Municipal Agrarian Reform officer processed applications for the conversion of more than 2,300 hectares from March 1988 to July 1992.[103] By all estimates, in the early 1990s Cavite became the leading province in land conversion, and Remulla deserved much of the "credit."[104] Indeed, various knowledgeable sources in the province estimate that the governor received a "fee" of ten pesos for every square meter of land converted to industrial use.

Finally, Remulla effectively enforced the province's unofficial but as yet unchallenged designation as a "no-strike zone." Under Remulla's reign as governor, a large percentage of jobs in Cavite-based manufacturing establishments had been "reserved" for members of the Iglesia Ni Cristo that did not allow its followers to join labor unions. In general, factories in Cavite required prospective employees to provide letters of recom-

mendation from the town mayor or the governor attesting to their relia-
bility. Moreover, the Industrial Security Action Group, a special police
unit directly responsible to the governor, made its presence felt at industrial estates throughout the province. Finally, persistent rumors and stories about the "salvaging" and "disappearance" of would-be Cavite labor
leaders discouraged even the most powerful labor union federations in
the country from attempting to organize workers in the province of "industrial peace and productivity."[105] Overall, Remulla's "industrial relations policies" made Cavite an attractive site for investors and allowed
his political machine to keep pace with the province's industrialization.[106]

While servicing the expanding interests of big business in Cavite,
Remulla, like Montano before him, attempted to shore up his position as
provincial warlord by amassing proprietary wealth commensurate with
his political position. Indeed, the juiciest construction contracts in Cavite
were supposedly reserved for companies in which the governor had a
special interest.[107] Moreover, like Montano in the 1960s, Remulla had by
the 1980s become by far the biggest landowner in Cavite, thanks to the
multi-million-peso behest loans he received from government financial
institutions in the Marcos era, the pressures he put on landowners reluctant to sell and tenants slow to vacate properties he coveted, and the success he enjoyed in delaying the implementation of agrarian reform on
land under his name or those of his dummies. All told, Remulla came to
own more than 1,000 hectares of prime land in various parts of Cavite.
Cavite's real-estate boom and Remulla's discretionary allocation of new
roads and electricity and irrigation facilities dramatically increased the
value of his properties over the years.[108] Thus, while depositing kickbacks, protection payments, and purloined government funds into the
war chest of his political machine, Remulla tried to establish a permanent economic base in the province independent of his grip on the state
apparatus.[109]

Yet Remulla was destined to go the way of Montano. For although
Remulla established close links with major power brokers in the Aquino
administration (most notably Jose "Peping" Cojuangco Jr., the president's brother) soon after Imelda Marcos's downfall, he failed to reach a
similar accommodation with her successor, President Fidel Ramos. Indeed, while Remulla won reelection to the governorship in 1992 by an
enormous margin and "carried" numerous protégés into local office
throughout the province, he misjudged the likely outcome of the presidential contest. After initially throwing his support behind Ramon
"Monching" Mitra Jr., Remulla ended up hedging his bets, dividing up
his machine's Cavite vote between Mitra and his rival, Eduardo "Dand-

ing" Cojuangco Jr. After the election, both losing presidential candidates expressed their displeasure with Remulla's "betrayal" in classic mafioso style, sending miniature coffins as gifts on his birthday.[110]

Against this backdrop, the 1995 elections saw the culmination of a determined effort by President Ramos to dislodge Remulla from the governorship of Cavite. Cesar Sarino, a key player in the Ramos presidential campaign in Cavite,[111] used his position as chairman of the Government Service Insurance System, a notorious cash cow, to amass a substantial anti-Remulla war chest. The owner of the rural bank in Silang, a construction contractor from Kawit, the mayors of Naic, Rosario, and Bacoor, and the representative of Cavite's 3rd district in Congress played complementary roles in an evolving anti-Remulla conspiracy. The prominent Campos clan of Dasmariñas was likewise represented in the Department of Defense and the Supreme Court. Early on in the Ramos administration, this cabal installed a sympathetic provincial police superintendent, a like-minded provincial fiscal, and a set of pliable regional trial court judges in Cavite. Selective "crackdowns," contracts, and customs assignments followed shortly thereafter. Moreover, Remulla's properties, previously released from government sequestration through Peping Cojuangco's intercession, were once again placed in the hands of the Presidential Commission on Good Government.

By the eve of the May 1995 local elections, Ramos and his allies in Cavite had already recruited key former Remulla backers to help demolish his province-wide machine. Former National Bureau of Investigation director Epimaco Velasco, a native of Tanza, Cavite, was drafted as the administration's candidate for governor, while Senator Ramon Revilla, a Caviteño action film star and chairman of the powerful Senate Committee on Public Works, fielded his *artista* son "Bong" as vice-governor on a Ramos-backed slate against Revilla's old cockfighting chum Johnny Remulla. With numerous Cavite town mayors and other key local *líders* around Cavite pressured into switching their loyalties, and generous supplies of money and PNP troops sent from Manila to neutralize the incumbent's monetary and coercive inducements, Velasco beat Remulla easily, removing from Cavite the previously unbeatable "machine" that had ruled the province since the late 1970s.[112]

## Conclusion

From the dawning of Aguinaldo's revolutionary leadership in 1896 to the twilight of Johnny Remulla's career in 1995, the evolution of metropolitan Manila spurred changes in employment, land use, and capital formation in Cavite. Agribusiness ventures, residential subdivisions, golf courses, and industrial estates came to overshadow rice fields, pastures, fishponds, sugar plantations, and coconut and coffee groves as the mainstays of the Cavite economy. Population growth and the extension of suffrage expanded the Cavite electorate from some 7,000 voters in 1912 to more than 27,000 in 1934, 82,000 in 1957, 133,000 in 1969, and nearly 400,000 in 1992, according to the records of the Commission on Elections. Yet in spite of these dramatic socioeconomic developments, certain political patterns persisted in the province.

Over the course of the twentieth century three successive bosses achieved entrenchment in political office and control over the "commanding heights" of the economy in Cavite. Emerging from small-town obscurity by dint of their prowess and—in the cases of Montano and Remulla—the patronage of national politicians, these three bosses used their mastery over state resources to construct province-wide political machines and economic empires. Exploiting their access to government financial institutions and pork-barrel funds, their ability to appoint government personnel, and their control over who received legal and illegal contracts and monopoly franchises in Cavite, these three bosses amassed extensive regulatory powers over the provincial economy, "private armies" from among the ranks of the provincial and municipal police forces, and vast landholdings. They relied heavily on state office for electoral self-perpetuation and capital accumulation and neglected to establish bases in proprietary wealth outside the realm of state regulation. Like Emilio Aguinaldo and Justiniano Montano before him, Johnny Remulla lost his provincial empire when a hostile national politician intervened.

The preceding analysis has noted both continuity and change in the successive reigns of these three provincial bosses in Cavite. All three succeeded in entrenching themselves for decades at a time by seizing control over the most strategic and lucrative sectors of the provincial economy and acquiring the largest landholdings in the province. Yet they all relied heavily on state office and violence rather than an independent base in land ownership or proprietary wealth and failed to pass on their province-wide empires to their progeny in dynastic fashion.

Nonetheless, shifting patterns of employment, land use, and capital formation gradually transformed the role of these provincial bosses in the political economy of Cavite. Relevant changes included the passing of control over electric power in the province—from Aguinaldo's Imus-based cronies in the American period to the Montano-run public authority in the postwar era to the Manila Electric Company (Meralco) in the 1980s and 1990s. By the mid-1990s, the penetration of Cavite by foreign and Filipino manufacturing firms and Manila-based banks, construction companies, and real-estate moguls had recast Remulla as a facilitator, gatekeeper, and broker for big business (and big crime) interests with solid economic bases and political contacts outside Cavite.[113] For the foreseeable future, control over Cavite's economy will lie in the hands of Manila-based and foreign corporations serviced by Governor Remulla's successors.

This pattern of protracted rule over entire provinces by predatory mafia-style bosses has parallels elsewhere in the Philippine archipelago. In general, provincial bosses have entrenched themselves in provinces where illegal activities, transportation chokepoints, or heavily state-regulated industries and agricultural sectors dwarf concentrations of land and capital and are available for privatization and monopolization through coercion and control over the agencies of the state. As in Cavite, provincial bosses in such provinces have entrenched themselves for decades at a time but have failed to pass on these provincial empires to their children in dynastic fashion. As in Cavite, moreover, the penetration of some such provinces by foreign and Manila-based corporations in recent years has begun to subordinate provincial bosses to the national and international interests and logic of capital.

The careers of provincial bosses Aguinaldo, Montano, and Remulla are instructive for their limitations as well as their longevity. When compared to established dynasties in other congressional districts and provinces in the Philippines, these bosses' inability to pass on the provincial mantle to their progeny appears as noteworthy as their success in entrenching themselves in power for decades at a time. Their failures to establish enduring footholds outside the state machinery reflect distinctive features of the local landscape and reveal the importance of state power at the provincial level for control over the commanding heights of the provincial economy.

In this regard, the mafia-style municipal and provincial bosses of Cavite have differed sharply from the dynasties entrenched in the municipalities and congressional districts, and also at the provincial level, in Cebu. The following three chapters focus on the most successful and enduring municipal, congressional, and provincial dynasties of Cebu Province.

# The Small-Town Dynasties of Cebu

The preceding two chapters described a mafia-style form of bossism in Cavite that thrived throughout the twentieth century on the lucrative illegal economies afforded by suburban Cavite's proximity to Metro Manila and the insecure property rights associated with landholdings in the province. Municipal and provincial bosses used their elective state offices to control key sectors of local economies and to construct local political machines. Yet the same features of Cavite's political economy that have facilitated mafia-style bossism in the province have similarly inhibited dynasty-building; bosses have remained entrenched for decades but were unable to establish a solid base in proprietary wealth independent from the state that was invulnerable to political manipulation and inheritable from one generation to the next. Thus they remained heavily dependent on state resources and private violence for both capital accumulation and electoral competition. Instead of passing their small-town or provincial empires to their children they rose and fell through the interventions of more powerful politicians outside their local bailiwicks.

By contrast, this chapter and the two that follow describe a distinctively dissimilar form of bossism in the small towns, congressional districts, and capital of Cebu Province. In this province, interfamilial economic and political competition was the pattern over the course of the twentieth century, and it was dramatically less violent and decidedly more paternalistic than that in Cavite. In several small towns and con-

gressional districts and at the provincial level as well, entrenched dynasties have enjoyed enduring monopolies over economic activities and political offices within their respective bailiwicks. This dynastic form of
bossism in Cebu has operated in a local political economy far more hos-
pitable than Cavite's to the accumulation of proprietary wealth independent of state office, secured from political intervention and intrigue, and
easily transferred from one generation to the next.

Cebu's municipal, district, and provincial dynasties contrast starkly
with the mafia-style, single-generation bosses of Cavite, and they appear,
at first glance, to exemplify the "political clans" and "political dynasties"
discussed in recent scholarship on local politics in the Philippines.[1] However, the enduring dynasties of Cebu have relied far less on landownership and patron-client ties to retain control over their localities than has
previously been assumed. The case studies here provide ample evidence
that the emergence, entrenchment, and endurance of such dynasties often
rested instead on the skillful use of state office and the construction of political machines.[2]

In the 50 or so municipalities of Cebu Province there has been a distinctive pattern of electoral competition and capital accumulation among
a Chinese mestizo élite. This pattern owes much to the history of land settlement and class formation in Cebu Province. A case study of the Escario
clan of Bantayan highlights the structural features of the local political
economy that facilitated the entrenchment of this single most enduring
small-town dynasty in Cebu Province. The contrast between municipal
politics in Cebu and Cavite suggests some conclusions about small-town
bossism throughout the Philippines, which are offered at the end of the
chapter.

## The Political Clans of Rural Cebu

As in Cavite, intense competition between local factions has long characterized small-town politics in Cebu Province, and skulduggery, vote-
buying, and violence have persistently intruded upon municipal elections. According to one leading scholar of Cebu's history, even in
pre–World War II electoral contests, when suffrage restrictions limited
the size of the electorate, "such practices as *hakot* (ferrying voters in
hired trucks or rigs to public rallies and polling centers), *pakaon* (feed-
ing the voters), and *panghulga* (intimidation) were already common."[3]
Violent incidents also occasionally flared up during prewar election
campaigns.[4] In the postwar era, the expansion of the electorate only
made politicians more reliant on vote-buying, fraud, and violence. An

election protest filed in 1947 before the Cebu Court of First Instance, for example, described the following election "anomalies" in the municipality of Pinamungahan:

(1) Some ballots written in favor of Nemenzo were written by persons other than the electors themselves; (2) the presence of heavily armed policemen and special policemen who intimidated voters to vote for the respondent; (3) the opening and grabbing of ballots; (4) absence of lights in voting booths forcing electors to fill ballots in the presence of inspectors' table[s] and dictated by a policeman; (5) that 50 ballots cast in favor of the petitioner were [intentionally] marked with ink and invalidated; (6) ballots bearing the name Piczon Carlos and Carlos were not read in favor of Piczon; (7) searching of Nacionalista voters and changing the sample ballots with sample ballots of the Liberal candidates.[5]

Moreover, such electoral tactics have remained in use in Cebu Province throughout the postwar period. A lawsuit cited the following allegations of "massive fraud and irregularities" in the 1992 election in the municipality of Ginatilan:

The ballot boxes were stuffed with manufactured and/or fake ballots. . . . The ballot boxes were opened by members of the Board of Election Inspectors even after they had been closed and sealed. . . . There was massive vote buying and intimidation of voters to coerce them to vote for certain candidates. . . . Votes for the petitioner/protestant were not counted in his favor. In certain precincts petitioner/protestant's watchers were not allowed to observe the proceedings of the Board of Election Inspectors. . . . Election returns were "doctored" or tampered with to favor the respondent/protestee. . . . Members of the Board of Canvassers who were highly partisan in favor of respondent/protestee manipulated the canvass of election returns to favor the respondent/protestee.[6]

In fact, the "anomalies" and "irregularities" cited in these election-protest cases were by no means anomalous or irregular: in every postwar election up to 1998, the Commission on Elections (Comelec) listed several Cebu municipalities among the "critical areas" meriting Comelec and Constabulary intervention.

However, small-town politics in Cebu has been considerably less violent than in Cavite. Election-related killings have been extremely rare, and Cebu town mayors have been more sparing in their use of violence.[7] Whereas all 21 Cavite towns have had a municipal mayor or chief of police who was either murdered or accused of murder, in the entire postwar period and in all 52 towns of Cebu, only three town mayors have lost their lives to assassins' bullets, and only a few municipal executives have been accused of murder in court.[8]

As in Cavite, town mayors in Cebu used their control over municipal police forces as a means of regulating and monopolizing illegal activities.

For example, mayors have long been involved in *jueteng* (illegal lotteries), and syndicates organized by town mayors have used the province's insular geography and Cebu City's role as the premier interisland port of the Visayas and Mindanao to smuggle contraband (e.g., American cigarettes, Japanese motorbikes) from passing foreign vessels.[9] In 1990 the killing of a Constabulary informer brought to light the smuggling activities of the municipal mayor of Argao, a town located on Cebu's southeast coast.[10] In addition to smuggling, Cebu town mayors have used the municipal police forces to engage in selective and extortionary enforcement of laws that prohibit dynamite fishing in their municipal waters. Mayoral involvement in illegal fishing has assumed various forms: imposition of "protection" payments on local fishermen, intercession on behalf of fishermen apprehended for illegal fishing, and connivance in the marketing of explosive materials used in so-called blast-fishing.[11] In more than a dozen Cebu towns where fishing is a mainstay of the local economy, fishermen use dynamite every day, with which they are said to have destroyed 86 percent of the province's original coral reefs.[12]

Along with regulatory powers over these illegal activities, Cebu town mayors have enjoyed enormous discretion over key contracts, concessions, and monopoly franchises in their towns. As in Cavite, municipal executives in Cebu have been known to manipulate the dispensing of government funds within their municipalities by influencing the location of construction projects (e.g., paved roads, public markets, schoolhouses), fixing the employment of workers and the awarding of contracts, and skimming off funds allocated for public works through overpricing, ghost projects, and padded payrolls. In this regard, it is perhaps worth recalling that Cebu was the site of one of the biggest public works scandals in recent Philippine history, involving the embezzlement—through falsification of public documents—of millions of pesos allocated for the construction of a paved highway linking the southern towns of the province to Cebu City.[13]

In addition, Cebu town mayors control mining and quarry concessions within their municipalities.[14] In Argao in 1991, the mayor awarded his own brother a permit to quarry sand and gravel in the Argao River. While the mayor's brother raked in hundreds of thousands of pesos by selling the sand and gravel to a local construction company contracted by the provincial government to pave a road through the town, local farmers found their irrigation facilities and farm lands disrupted by the excavation.[15] Moreover, mayors also have the authority to award (and to terminate) monopoly franchises for ice plants, gasoline stations, and cockpits.[16] In particular, Cebu's cockfighting arenas—the least capital-intensive and most lucrative monopoly franchises awarded by municipalities—have served as focal points for small-town political battles and as prizes for the winners of mayoral elections and their local allies.[17] Finally, since the 1970s, Cebu's town mayors have profited from the construction of golf courses, residential subdivisions, and industrial estates in the municipalities immediately north and south of Cebu City. In a pattern reminiscent of that in Cavite, they dispensed building permits, passed municipal zoning ordinances, approved reclamation projects, and used government-owned land selectively to further their own interests.

In postwar Cebu, however, more of the small-town mayors have been products of the entrenched landed dynasties of the province, whose bases in corn, coconut, and sugar holdings have remained relatively independent of state power over the years. Perhaps the best example of such small-town political dynasties is the Villacarlos family, whose members occupied the mayorship of Madridejos town from the end of World War II through 1986, and who have owned more than 500 hectares of land planted with coconut and corn. Other cases abound: the Pepitos, whose scions have served as municipal mayor of Consolacion since 1955 and whose land holdings in the town have amounted to nearly 300 hectares; the Almagros, with nearly 600 hectares of corn fields and a long history of political prominence in Dalaguete; the landed Ursals, who have ruled San Remigio with few interruptions since 1946. The Gantuangcos of Carcar and Aloguinsan, the Barbas of Toledo City, and the Tumulaks of Oslob have similarly combined large landholdings with long-term mayorships in their respective municipalities.[18]

Along with these large landowners, other long-time mayors emerged out of the local commercial élite, whose control over the links between their municipalities and Cebu City complemented their small-town political power. The To-ongs of Asturias, for example, long prominent in the copra (dried coconut meat) trade in the municipality, have held the town mayorship since 1967. Municipal heads of the Philippine Coconut Producers' Federation COCOFED in Cebu have included Benito Aller (Alegria mayor, 1951–86), Sergio Baguio (Cordova mayor, 1959–76), Pedro Cabaron (Moalboal mayor, 1955–63, 1976–86), Elpidio de Dios (Carmen mayor, 1947–80), Librada Pace (Barili mayor, 1959–76, 1988–95), José Tumulak (Oslob mayor, 1963–80), and a member of the Binghay clan, whose members held the mayorship of Balamban from 1955 to 1967 and from 1988 to the present.[19] Politically successful owners of bus companies have included Geronimo Estimo, onetime mayor of Moalboal, and the Cerna family, whose members served four terms as mayor of Pinamungahan and were succeeded in 1986 by another bus-company clan, the Yaphas (three terms to date). Other bus-line owners have preferred to back entrenched town mayors, such as the Librandos of Badian, who long supported five-term mayor Januario B. Agravante Jr. (whose family owns extensive coconut lands), and the Bendebels of Balamban, who forged an alliance with the Binghay clan, whose scions have held the town mayorship for four terms.[20]

In contrast with the gangster-politicians of Cavite, the small-town bosses of Cebu have ruled as representatives of local élite families, whose properties and commercial interests have not depended so heavily upon the ebbs and flows of municipal politics. Only two women have served as municipal mayors in Cavite; thirteen women have held town mayorships in Cebu, including longtimers Librada Pace of Barili (1959–76, 1988–95), Beatriz Calderon of Samboan (1967–86), Beatriz Durano of Danao (1955–71), and Remedios Escario of Bantayan (1959–67, 1992–95). Whereas in Cavite most postwar mayors were essentially "new *men*," numerous Cebu mayors since 1946 have been the sons or daughters of prominent prewar landowner-politicians.[21]

The political preeminence of these landed dynasties in the small-towns of Cebu reflects a provincial political economy that historically fell largely outside the purview of state control and remained in the hands of private capitalists with roots in Cebu City. As they did in Spanish colonial Cavite, the religious orders established landed estates in Cebu (in Mandaue-Banilad, Cebu City, and the Talisay-Minglanilla area), but these so-called friar lands amounted to no more than 10,000 hectares and comprised less than 10 percent of the arable land in the province.[22] Commercialization of agriculture in Cebu during the nineteenth century followed a pattern not unlike that observed in the hinterlands of Manila and Iloilo, wherein the opening of Philippine ports to foreign trade led urban merchants to encourage the cultivation of commercial crops in demand in world markets. Following the opening of Manila's port in 1834 and the abolition of Spanish provincial governors' trading monopolies in 1844, Cebu emerged as a major entrepôt for export crops—most notably sugar—from the Visayas and northern Mindanao, which were shipped to European and American markets via Manila. In Cebu Province itself, this development led to the rapid expansion of sugar cultivation:

During the 1840s, Cebu's hinterland and most of the lowland plains along the east coast were turned over to sugar cultivation, crude milling devices were erected, and sugar was shipped to Manila for export. By mid-century Cebu province had become one of the Philippines' leading sugar producers and Cebu City was well on its way to becoming a major centre of commerce.[23]

The primary beneficiaries of Cebu's emergence in the 1840s and 1850s as a regional emporium were Chinese mestizo merchants based in Cebu City. Descendants of immigrant men from Fujian Province who had converted to Catholicism and married Cebuana women (*indias*) in church ceremonies, Chinese mestizos inherited the capital and cash-economy experience of their *sangley* (trader) forefathers, while enjoying less onerous tax burdens, freedom of mobility, and rights to own property and participate in town government, according to Spanish colonial tax classification and legal restrictions.[24] Already dominant in interisland, retail, and wholesale trade, Chinese mestizo merchants in Cebu City became the primary lenders to farmers in need of cash to expand their sugar cultivation. By extending credit, they gained control of the sugar trade and, through purchases and *pacto de retroventa* (mortgage) agreements, acquired landholdings in the east coast towns where sugar cultivation had expanded. Dispossessed of their land and lacking capital and commercial networks of their own, Cebuano smallholders in these towns thus became tenants of urban-based Chinese mestizo merchant-moneylender-landlords.[25]

Following the opening of Cebu's port to world trade in 1860, the increasing availability of credit in the Visayan entrepôt accelerated capitalist penetration of the countryside and further concentrated landownership in the hands of urban-based Chinese mestizo merchants. Beginning in the 1860s, American and British commercial houses based in Manila established permanent offices in Cebu City and started to finance local entrepreneurs. Commercial opportunities also attracted Spanish and Chinese immigrants. The increased availability of capital stimulated cultivation and land speculation in Cebu Province such that "towns located on the northeast and western coasts of the island, previously of peripheral importance as producers of agricultural export crops, quickly became major centers of sugar, tobacco, and abaca cultivation."[26] In contrast with their scattered holdings in the eastern towns in the 1840–60 period, Cebu's now more fully capitalized urban merchant-moneylender-landlords amassed large estates or haciendas throughout the province in the two decades following the opening of the city's port, through purchases and *pacto de retroventa* mortgage agreements, while dispossessed Cebuano smallholders fell into tenancy in greater numbers.[27] In the 1880s, a crisis in the world sugar market, induced by competition from the European sugar beet industry, led to a reduction in the demand for—and price of—Philippine sugar. As the price and volume of sugar declined, owners of sugar land in towns of Cebu Province fell into bankruptcy and gave up their estates to urban creditors. The result was a further concentration of landholdings in the hands of Cebu City-based merchant-moneylender-landlords.[28]

By the turn of the century, this mostly Chinese mestizo commercial-landowning élite had crystallized into a Cebuano oligarchy with roots in both town and country. Today their scions dominate small-town politics

in Cebu. One scholar has noted that in nearby Bohol and Leyte and in
northern Mindanao,

The acquisition of provincial lands led to an elite emigration from Cebu. Most of
these elite families, however, did not wholly uproot themselves; on the contrary,
most left behind parents or siblings and retained their urban property. A number
of brothers, cousins, or in-laws of the leading merchants established themselves
in the municipalities and fed business into the family's ventures in Cebu, often obtaining loans from their wealthy merchant relatives. Of the original 30 or so principal families of the mestizo *gremio* in the early 1850s, most had clearly established branches of their family in the provinces by the 1890s. There were very few
Parian [city-based] mestizo families who did not have links with one or more
prominent provincial families by this time; for some the links were substantial.
The expansion of the urban elite into the city's widening hinterland was the beginning of the formation of a province- and region-wide elite.[29]

Since its formation at the turn of the century, this largely Chinese mestizo
élite has adapted to changing market conditions by diversifying and spe-
cializing production in Cebu Province. Today, plantations in several
northern towns furnish cane to two sugar centrals, cattle pastures in several towns on the southeast coast provide meat for Cebu City slaughterhouses, and poultry farms on Bantayan island off the northwest coast
supply chickens, eggs, and dung (for fertilizer) to markets throughout the
Visayas. More generally, coconut groves and cornfields throughout the
province supply the warehouses of major milling corporations in Cebu
City through networks of small-time corn millers and copra traders,
while fish and seafood from Cebu's coastal waters flow into Pasil market
on trawlers, pumpboats, and trucks.

In these increasingly capital-intensive commercial networks, as in the
residential subdivisions, factories, and tourist resorts concentrated in
Metro Cebu but also scattered throughout the province, descendants of
Cebu's nineteenth-century Chinese mestizo dynasties have by and large
preserved and expanded their families' properties and commercial interests, while newcomers—especially Hokkien-speaking immigrants from
China's Fujian Province—have made significant inroads.[30] At the same
time, the twentieth century witnessed the further immiseration of the
broad mass of Cebu Province's population; increasing land scarcity has
led to agricultural "involution" on marginally productive corn lands, environmental degradation of the remaining forest cover, mangroves, and
fishing beds, and migration to the swelling slums of Cebu City.

Over the course of the twentieth century, Chinese mestizo élite families
of nineteenth-century vintage parlayed their predominance in landownership and commercial networks in Cebu Province into commensurate
preeminence in municipal politics. With suffrage severely restricted by the

TABLE 4
*Correlation Between Manila Administration and Cebu Mayors, 1955–80*

| Local Election | Administration Party | Mayors Elected |
| --- | --- | --- |
| 1955 | Nacionalista | 52 Nacionalistas |
| 1959 | Nacionalista | 52 Nacionalistas |
| 1963 | Liberal | 46 Liberals |
| 1967 | Nacionalista | 48 Nacionalistas |
| 1971 | Nacionalista | 46 Nacionalistas |
| 1980 | KBL | 50 Nacionalistas |

American colonial regime, members of élite families of Cebu Province dominated the municipal elections held in 1901 and—through patronage networks, vote-buying, electoral fraud, and violence—largely retained their preeminence throughout the century as the electorate expanded.[31] Unlike in Cavite, in Cebu Province a landed-commercial élite with a solid economic base independent of the state has persistently dominated small-town politics.

Nonetheless, state patronage has also proved decisive in many municipal election contests between rival élite families. During the Liberal Party administrations of Manuel Roxas and Elpidio Quirino, for example, 51 Liberal mayors were appointed by Liberal governor Manuel Cuenco (who had been appointed by President Roxas) in 1946 and Liberal Cuenco protégés won 48 (of 51) mayorships in the elections of 1947. But when President Quirino supported Nacionalista gubernatorial candidate Sergio "Serging" Osmeña Jr. four years later in 1951, only 33 Cuencista Liberals won reelection.[32] Subsequent elections evidenced a similarly close and consistent correlation between the party of the incumbent administration in Manila and the affiliation of mayors elected in the small towns of Cebu (see Table 4).[33]

Unlike in Cavite, however, where the province-level rivalry between Montano and Camerino in the early postwar period and the entrenchment of Governor Remulla in the 1980s and 1990s were decisive in small-town political contests, in Cebu the representatives of the province's seven congressional districts were key players in municipal elections over the same periods. For example, longtime congressman Ramon M. Durano Sr. of Cebu's 1st district (1949–72) assisted in the installation and reelection of such protégés as Pedro Monsanto (mayor of Catmon, 1959–86), Tiburcio Donaire (mayor of Poro, 1967–80), and Margarito Maningo (mayor of San Francisco, 1946–63 and 1967–86). Before the imposition of martial law, the Cuencos similarly promoted mayors in the family bailiwick—the 5th district—while longtime congressman Manuel

Zosa (1949–65, 1969–72) likewise provided for his allies in the municipalities of the 6th district.[34] In the post-Marcos era, Congressman Celestino E. Martinez Jr. swept in protégés in all nine municipalities in his
(4th) district in 1992, while his counterpart in the 2nd district, Congressman Crisologo Abines, "carried" (*nagdala*) eleven associates to mayoral
victories, including two siblings and a close business crony.

In sum, the municipal mayors of Cebu have been members of small-
town dynasties with extensive landholdings and commercial interests.
While not averse to using coercion and profiting from illegal activities,
Cebu town mayors have depended less on violence in election contests
and relied less on "rackets" for capital accumulation than their counterparts in Cavite. Although they did not hesitate to exploit their discretionary powers over the local economy and were vulnerable to the interventions of political enemies, town mayors in Cebu have typically
represented élite families whose economic bases in landownership and
commerce lay largely outside the realm of political regulation, manipulation, and intrigue.

Like the municipal bosses of Cavite, some of the small-town dynasties
of Cebu were more successful than others in entrenching themselves in
power, as suggested by the above-noted high level of turnover in mayorships in the province. In many towns, competition between rival clans together with the machinations of congressional and provincial opponents
prevented dynasties from establishing themselves. In other towns, however, small-town dynasties entrenched themselves for many years by using their proprietary wealth, the discretionary powers of the mayor's office, and state patronage to control key sectors and nodal chokepoints of
the local economy. Among such longtime Cebu clans, the Escario family
of Bantayan was the most successful twentieth-century small-town
dynasty, ruling their municipality with only one brief interruption
(1986–88) from 1937 to this writing in 1999.

## Chicken Dung, Coconuts, and Crabs:
### The Escarios of Bantayan

In the three and a half decades of the twentieth century before a member
of the Escario family was elected mayor, no single "dynasty" dominated
the political and economic life of Bantayan, a coconut, corn, fishing, and
poultry town on the island of the same name off the northwest coast of
Cebu. Instead, large landowning families of Chinese mestizo ancestry
such as the Abellos, Arcenases, Causings, Escarios, Lozadas, Roskas, Ru-

bios, and Ybañezes were active and dominant in municipal politics, but no one clan dominated the town's economic and political life.

Residing in Spanish colonial-style houses around the town plaza, these landowning families formed a close-knit small-town oligarchy, whose members not only intermarried but in many cases also claimed a common ancestor, Manuel Rubio, who emigrated from Capiz Province (on the nearby island of Iloilo) to Bantayan early in the nineteenth century. Availing himself of the commercial opportunities of the period, Rubio acquired large landholdings on Bantayan island. As one of his ancestors noted many years later: "This Manuel Rubio came to own very many large landholdings which he planted with coconut and corn. He had land in almost all of the barrios or barangays in the three municipalities of Bantayan, Madridejos, and Santa Fe."[35]

Much of Rubio's land was passed on to his daughter, Maria Rubio, and her children, who married into the Escario and Arcenas families. Yet much of Rubio's inheritance went to an "illegitimate" son (*anak sa gawas*), Benigno Causing, whom Rubio had fathered during an extramarital affair with the daughter of a prominent Chinese merchant (Kao Sing) who is believed to have held the opium franchise for northern Cebu for some period during the late nineteenth century. Assuming ownership of many of his father's properties after his death, Causing married an Escalona and fathered daughters who were betrothed to Abellos, Arcenases, and Roskas. Early postwar land tax records suggest how these clans divided up their common forefather's properties: Abellos: 158 hectares; Causings: 470 hectares; Escarios: 405 hectares; Lozadas: 617 hectares; Rubios: 125 hectares. Competing in highly restricted municipal elections beginning in 1901, scions of these landowning families and their allies took turns occupying the mayor's office of Bantayan (see Table 5).

A set of fortuitous circumstances facilitated the successful Bantayan mayoral candidacy in 1937 of Isidro Escario, whose family subsequently broke this pattern of intra-oligarchy competition and established firm political and economic control over the municipality. In 1934, Mayor Pedro Lozada appointed Isidro, the son of former mayor Felixberto Escario, as a land tax collector in the office of the municipal treasurer, a consolation prize to his father who had lost the mayoral race to Lozada. When Lozada, an aging and inattentive mayor, ran for reelection in 1937, he found himself opposed by his erstwhile tax collector, who had begun to campaign "while in the field" and had earned the support of important landowners (e.g., the Rubio family) through his sympathetic property tax assessment and collection practices. Moreover, Escario was married to the former Remedios Abello, whose father, a retired schoolteacher, was a municipal councilor, and whose mother was a Causing with extensive

TABLE 5
*Bantayan Mayors, 1901–37*

| Term | Mayor |
|------|-------|
| 1901–1908 | Gregorio Escario |
| 1908–1910 | Margarito Escario |
| 1910–1912 | Gregorio Escario |
| 1912–1916 | Roque Villacin |
| 1916–1919 | Pedro Lozada |
| 1919–1922 | Roque Villacin |
| 1922–1928 | Felixberto Escario |
| 1928–1931 | Mariano Causing |
| 1931–1934 | Jose Ybañez |
| 1934–1937 | Pedro Lozada |

landholdings.[36] In addition, Escario demonstrated a willingness to use violence and intimidation to win the mayorship: today Escario's friends and foes alike recall that Lozada was afraid to leave his home to campaign on election day. Finally, Escario no doubt benefited from the intensification of political rivalries at the provincial level, between longtime Cebu kingpin Sergio Osmeña Sr. and the up-and-coming Mariano J. Cuenco. In 1935, President Quezon had appointed Cuenco to the patronage-rich position of secretary of public works and communications, a ruse designed to undermine Quezon's longtime rival for national dominance, Vice-President Osmeña. Thus, unlike in previously Osmeña-dominated elections, Escario could avail himself of generous campaign support from provincial rivals eager to secure a base in the municipality.[37] Drawing strength from his discretionary use of municipal offices, his alliance with local landed families, his willingness to employ violence, and his access to state patronage, Isidro Escario went on to defeat Lozada in the municipal elections and assumed the mayorship in 1937.

In subsequent years, the Escario family employed these same tools to retain their hold over Bantayan; first Isidro (1937–59), then his wife, Remedios (1959–67), and eventually their sons Jesus (1967–86) and Rex (1988–92) assumed the mayorship.[38] As in other towns in Cebu, the Escarios have used the town's police force to profit from illegal activities in the municipality.[39] Bantayan's rich fishing grounds—known for a plentiful supply of crabs and other marine delicacies—are a major source of livelihood for a few thousand town residents.[40] The selective enforcement of regulations prohibiting dynamite and purse-seine trawl fishing in municipal waters has proven a useful mechanism for extortion and patronage and has allegedly allowed Escario cronies to monopolize the sale of explosive materials in the town.[41] Moreover, as in other towns in Cebu, the Escarios have evidently engaged in the protection of illegal lotteries known as *jueteng* in Bantayan, which in recent years have operated out of the residence of a barangay councilman in the *poblacion*, less than 100 meters from the church.[42] In addition, the Escarios maintained close relations throughout the 1960s with the famed Cebuano pirate Isabelo "Beloy" Montemayor, who often spent time with his relatives on the islet of Botiguis, which lay within Bantayan's municipal boundaries and fell well within the Escario family's domain.[43] The Escarios not only engaged in blue-seal cigarette smuggling and gun-running with Montemayor but also protected and profited from his frequent acts of "piracy."[44] Finally, as suggested by the recent indictment of Rex Escario (Isidro's son and Bantayan mayor, 1988–92) for his role in a 1990 bank robbery in Mandaue City, members of the Escario family have also been involved in other illegal activities in Bantayan and elsewhere in Cebu Province.[45]

Aside from these illegal activities, the Escarios have used the mayor's office to facilitate their seizure of monopoly privileges in Bantayan's economy. For example, Isidro Escario emerged in the postwar period as the

Rex Escario, mayor of Bantayan, Cebu (1988–92), accused of election-related violence and involvement in a major Cebu City bank robbery.

sole *contratista* or labor broker and recruiter in Bantayan for sugar plantations on the nearby island of Negros Occidental that required seasonal
migrant workers (*sacadas*). Over the years, hundreds of *sacadas* from
among poor Bantayan residents came to depend on Escario for cash ad-
vances, known as *anticipo*, especially during the lean months:

> The people of Bantayan in particular suffer severe food shortages resulting from
> the monsoon rains which hinder them from regularly pursuing their main source
> of subsistence—fishing. With their corn still growing, and fish supply rather
> scarce, food prices soar, forcing sacada households to fall back on cash advances
> from the *contratista*. The earnings to be had from cane-cutting are so little that
> the *contratista*'s cash advance cannot be done without, and in this way a large
> section of this assetless rural poor is condemned to migrate every season as the
> monsoon rain comes.[46]

By advancing credit at high interest rates to the *sacadas* during the mon-
soon season in Bantayan and primary commodities at inflated prices during the milling season in Negros, Escario came to maintain his captive
following of poor dependents in a state of permanent indebtedness. As
town mayor, Escario possessed the authority to prevent Bantayan *sacadas*
from reneging on their work contracts; as *contratista*, he received payment directly from the plantation owners for the work of the laborers he
had recruited and supervised.[47]

Along with this monopoly on labor contracting, the Escarios controlled commercial activity going into and out of Bantayan. In the 1960s,
the Escarios built a private port in the coastal barrio of Baigad that was
said to be capable of accommodating two vessels easily and of storing
more than 2,000 sacks of rice. With boats carrying San Miguel beer and
Coca-Cola arriving twice weekly in Baigad, the Escarios, according to the
records of the Philippine Ports Authority (PPA), earned more than 3 million pesos in *arrastre* (stevedoring) fees in 1991 alone.[48] At the public
port in the *poblacion* of Bantayan, meanwhile, the family of Isidro Escario's brother Epifanio has long held the lucrative *arrastre* contract,
earning hundreds of thousands of pesos in annual fees while, according
to PPA officials, pocketing deductions from their poorly paid workers'
salaries that were supposed to be invested in the government social security system. In addition, the Escarios engineered the passage of a municipal ordinance in the 1980s that prohibited the ferry linking Bantayan
with nearby Cadiz, Negros Occidental, from docking at the pier, ostensibly to prevent damage to the vessels during low tides along Bantayan's
shore. Instead, the daily ferry—which services a lively trade in eggs and
chicken dung as well as a steady flow of human traffic—was forced to an-
chor a few hundred meters away from the pier, leaving ferry passengers

and cargo at the mercy of an Escario-operated dock-to-ferry shuttle service that charged exorbitant rates.[49]

In contrast with the more brazenly predatory, land-grabbing, and monopolistic tendencies of longtime mayor Cesar Casal of Carmona, Cavite, however, the Escarios have always shared control over the Bantayan economy with relatives and allied families in the town. Escario cousins have held the franchises to operate the sole ice plant and *sabongan* (cockfighting arena), the Abello clan has maintained the only (movie) theater, and the closely allied Mercado family has operated the one bus company on the island, linking Bantayan not only to Madridejos but also to Santa Fe, where Bantayan-bound passengers and cargo arrive daily on the ferry from Cebu. Moreover, while the Escarios have played prominent roles in both the fishing industry and the copra trade over the years, they never succeeded in driving out the other owners of large coconut groves and fishing boats in the town.[50] The family has refrained from assuming a role in Bantayan's rural bank or in the electric cooperative that distributes electricity to the three municipalities of Bantayan island.

The Escarios have maintained close alliances with commercially prominent immigrant Chinese families in Bantayan, whose uncertain citizenship status and dependence upon municipal monopoly franchises necessitated mayoral protection and favor. The patriarch of one of these clans, Ho Laysan, was an immigrant from Amoy (Xiamen), Fujian Province, who arrived in Bantayan in 1938 but did not obtain Philippine citizenship for himself and his family until 1980. His family established the town's general store, selling everything from hardware to dry goods to beer. According to some Bantayan residents, the Laysans have always enjoyed lenient regulatory treatment in their business: sugar stolen from passing Victorias Sugar Mill barges and lumber bought from illegal loggers on Leyte, for example, are sold without police intervention. Moreover, when cans of kerosene at the Laysans' store started a fire in April 1973 that burned down the municipal hall, hospital, public market, and numerous houses, causing nearly 20 million pesos in damage and rendering 5,000 families homeless, Mayor Jesus Escario and the town police force allegedly protected the Laysans from an angry mob of Bantayan *poblacion* residents who sought violent retribution.[51] After the fire, the Laysans moved their general store to a slightly less central location and opened a separate gasoline station (with a municipal franchise) that services all the fishing boats and motorized "tricycles" in the town. For these privileges and protection services, the Laysans have rewarded the Escarios with generous financial support during elections, as has Noe Quiamco, the Chinese immigrant businessman (now a Philippine citizen) who owns the ferry servicing the Bantayan-Cadiz route.

The Escarios also benefited over the years from mutually beneficial ties with successive congressmen, from whom they extracted generous state patronage in exchange for electoral support (votes) in Bantayan. In the 1950s, for example, Isidro Escario enjoyed close relations with his distant relative Nicolas G. Escario, representative of Cebu's 7th district (1949–57), who had married into a wealthy Negros-based family of sugar barons and founded the Cebu Institute of Technology in Cebu City.[52] In the 1960s, with patriarch Isidro elevated to a seat on the Cebu Provincial Board and then briefly to the vice-governorship, the Escarios likewise supported the successful candidacies of Tereso Dumon for the 7th district congressional seat (1961–69), and in the 1970s they cultivated a warm relationship with longtime 1st district representative Ramon M. Durano Sr., whose influence had expanded throughout Cebu Province during the decade before martial law and survived the abolition of Congress in 1972. In the post-Marcos period, the Escarios similarly affiliated themselves with Congressman Celestino ("Junie") Martinez Jr., who won successive elections in the 4th district (comprising much of the pre-martial-law 7th district, including Bantayan) by massive margins in 1987, 1992, and 1995. Although ex-mayor Rex Escario was convicted for awarding in 1990 a 400,000-peso public works project without public bidding, the Escarios assumed considerable discretion over the pork barrel delivered to Bantayan by their successive patron-saint congressmen.[53]

Over the years, even as the local electorate swelled from fewer than 23,000 voters during the Commonwealth era to more than 300,000 in 1992, the Escarios' control over much of the local economy virtually guaranteed consistent electoral successes in Bantayan for the family. Flush with funds from their various family businesses and illegal activities, the Escarios have always amassed considerable war chests for election-campaign expenses such as payments to voters, *líders*, poll-watchers, election inspectors, and vote counters and canvassers. Enlisting members of prominent allied families as candidates for the municipal council, the Escarios cobbled together election slates representing key factions of the local oligarchy. By mobilizing tenant farmers and workers on their extensive landholdings, *sacadas* from their work as *contratistas*, employees in their assorted businesses, and beneficiaries of their patronage, the Escarios also built up a large network of dependents.

The Escarios undoubtedly also benefited from a widely acknowledged reputation as generous patrons and providers to the poor and downtrodden folk of Bantayan. Isidro Escario, who passed away in the 1970s, served as the sponsor of countless weddings and baptisms in Bantayan, while his wife Remedios, popularly known as "Ma Mediong," remained—even in the eyes of her most hardened political enemies—the unsurpassed "Santa Claus" of the town.[54] In fact, many Bantayan residents claim that the Escarios provided assistance of various kinds to town residents of modest means and no known affiliation with their municipality's most prominent family. Over the years, all these acts of generosity supposedly bound countless members of the voting public to the Escarios through bonds of fictive kinship (*compadrazgo*) and obligation that proved enduring. Some were even provided burial places in the family-owned cemetery, Bantayan's Eternal Gardens.

Nonetheless, the family has consistently resorted to violence, intimidation, and electoral fraud to guarantee the reelection of successive Escario mayors and their allies. Beginning with his first election in 1937, Isidro Escario relied not only on the threat of violence to defeat his rivals for the mayorship, but also on the illicit election-day assistance of sympathetic schoolteachers, who by law have been tasked with receiving and counting election ballots.[55] In the 1960s and early 1970s, incidents of political violence appear to have escalated in Bantayan. Escario henchmen (including Police Chief Salvador Abello, the brother of Remedios Escario) intimidated voters and killed off a few of the family's enemies, and Constabulary troops assumed control of the town police force for protracted periods.[56] Moreover, in the late 1980s and early 1990s, the Escarios continued to rely on such hardball tactics to win elections: in early 1988 Rex Escario and five armed companions barged into the home of an opposition sympathizer (the son of a barangay captain) one night, beat him up, and nearly shot him dead with an M-16.[57] In the midst of the attack, the future mayor of Bantayan is said to have vented his rage against the unreliability of his family's supposed "clients": "What offenses have the Escarios committed that you can call us thieves and hustlers, when you don't even pay rent for your shed on our land?"[58] Finally, after the May 1992 elections, among the most closely contested in the postwar history of Bantayan, opponents claimed that Remedios Escario won election through the introduction in many precincts of fake ballots by sympathetic (and/or paid-off) schoolteachers serving as election inspectors, backed up by a campaign of harassment and intimidation perpetrated in part by some 80 "goons" imported from the nearby provinces of Negros Occidental and Masbate.[59]

The past few elections, it might be argued, were the most closely contested in Bantayan, not only because province-level rivals of Congressman Martinez supported the Escarios' foes, but also because economic growth in the town had allowed many local residents to outgrow their dependence on the goodwill of Bantayan's most powerful clan. Encouraged by the extremely hot and arid climate and the low costs of sand and fishmeat on the island, local élite families have since at least the 1970s invested heavily in poultry farms, which supply the three Visayan metropoles of Bacolod City, Ilolio City, and Cebu City with millions of eggs and thousands of bags of chicken dung.[60] While roughly a third of these products are exported via the Escarios' private port in Baigad, the bulk of this brisk trade flows out through the public ports of Bantayan and Santa Fe, bringing massive profits and commercial links to poultry farmers that weaken their dependence on the Escarios.[61] The rich fishing beds off the coast of Bantayan, moreover, are an enormous source of wealth for families who own large fishing vessels (*kubkub* and *basnigan*);[62] in the late 1980s an American company established a crab meat processing plant in the town and bought its fresh crabs directly from local fishermen.[63] Similarly, Bantayan island's beautiful white-sand beaches attract tourists, and the small airport in Santa Fe may someday service resorts owned by local families (e.g., the decidedly anti-Escario Hubahib/Ybañez clan) with connections to travel agencies and Philippine Tourism Authority offices in Cebu City. Finally, the close connections between Bantayan and Cebu City allow members of wealthy families in the town to strike their fortunes in construction, port services, and real estate in the province's booming urban center or to rise to prominent positions (such as a Regional Trial Court judgeship) in the government, even as less fortunate Bantayanons head off to work as factory laborers, itinerant peddlers, domestic servants, construction workers, and seamen in Cebu City, Manila, and such distant destinations as Hong Kong and Saudi Arabia. All these developments gradually undermined the Escario family's once virtually monolithic control over the Bantayan economy.

Nonetheless, the Escarios remain the masters of Bantayan for the foreseeable future. Through bonds of affinity, consanguinity, and fictive kinship, the family is still central to all political alliances among the town's most prominent families. Through years of control over the mayor's office and the economy, moreover, at the beginning of the twenty-first century the Escarios retain significant regulatory and proprietary powers in local commerce. Finally, its links to powerful patrons in Congress and in the provincial capital as well as its sizable following of dependents in Bantayan give the clan distinctive advantages over potential political rivals. Thus, although Isidro is dead, and two of the couple's sons excused themselves from politics, the aging Remedios has served as mayor since 1992, with her daughter—Geralyn Escario Cañares—as vice-mayor, and various nephews and cousins wait in the wings to follow in her footsteps. In short, unlike longtime mayor Cesar Casal of Carmona, Cavite, the Escarios of Bantayan constructed a small-town empire of dynastic proportions that has endured for nearly 60 years and promises to outlive, in some form, its original progenitors.

## Conclusion

This chapter has contrasted the mafia-style municipal bosses of Cavite with the conditions that allowed a dynastic version of bossism to flourish in the small towns of Cebu. In Cebu, the commercialization of agriculture in the nineteenth century under the auspices of Cebu City–based Chinese mestizo merchant capital presaged the political entrenchment in the American colonial period of landed-commercial élite families in the small towns of the province. Less reliant on violence and illegal activities for electoral success and capital accumulation than their counterparts in Cavite, municipal mayors in Cebu have represented élite families whose economic bases in landownership and commerce have remained relatively independent of political intervention and permitted political succession over the generations in the manner of small-town dynasties.

Despite the different manifestations of bossism in Cebu and Cavite, the pattern of variation in the longevity of small-town bosses and dynasties in the two provinces has depended upon virtually identical contextual factors rooted in the local political economies. In both Cavite and Cebu, the most enduring small-town boss or dynasty of the province operated in the municipality where the local economy was most susceptible to regulation and/or appropriation by the town mayor. While in the case of Carmona, the government's expropriation of large landed estates and the centrality of the communal lands to the local economy facilitated the entrenchment of longtime mayor Cesar Casal, in Bantayan the flow of commerce through transportation bottlenecks and the importance of municipal regulations and franchises for the local fishing industry likewise prefigured the Escarios' enduring hold over political and economic power in the town. In both Carmona and Bantayan, moreover, close links to markets, production sites, and processing centers outside Cavite and Cebu allowed the municipal mayor to assume a monopolistic brokerage position in the local economy.

Although these two municipalities may have been administrative "outliers" in the provinces of Cavite and Cebu, they are by no means outlying cases. In Cavite, Casal's mayoral longevity in Carmona was fairly matched by that of Telesforo Unas, longtime mayor (1955–86), provincial board member (1988–92), and congressman (1992–95) of Maragondon, a town noteworthy for its lack of large landowners, its extensive public forests, pastures, and quarry, and its proximity to market towns in the neighboring province of Batangas. In Cebu, the Escarios' long reign over Bantayan is replicated today by the Abines clan on the southern tip of the province, who control the ferry route to nearby Negros Oriental, the bus franchise to Cebu City, and the local fishing industry, courtesy of Abines scions in the mayorships of Oslob and Santander and in Cebu's 2nd district congressional seat (see Chapter 5).

Moreover, the two small towns discussed in this chapter and Chapter 2 suggest patterns of variation in the longevity of small-town bosses and dynasties elsewhere in the Philippines. In short, long-term bosses and dynasties survive and prosper in municipalities whose economies lend themselves most readily and most fully to monopolistic or oligopolistic control. In some such municipalities, where the public or state-regulated sphere of the economy dwarfs locally available concentrations of private capital, notoriously criminal, predatory, mafia-style bosses depend heavily on violence and access to state offices and resources for political self-perpetuation and capital accumulation. In other municipalities, by contrast, where proprietary wealth is more concentrated and more secure, local dynasties combine the discretionary powers of the mayor's office, alliances, and oligopolistic arrangements with other élite families, local and extra-local patronage networks, and private capital accumulation to entrench themselves over successive generations. In both instances, however, control over the mayor's office—and over the local agencies of the state apparatus—has bolstered the fortunes of the small-town boss or dynasty.

# The District-Level Dynasties of Cebu

In contrast to Cavite, where there has been a succession of entrenched provincial bosses, in Cebu, family dynasties have constructed political machines and economic empires at both the congressional district and the provincial level. This two-tiered pattern reflects the distinct political economy of town and countryside in the island province. In the six rural congressional districts of Cebu, supramunicipal dynasties emerged and flourished, achieving domination over large population centers, control of nodal commercial and transportation chokepoints, and/or command over concentrations of private capital in the local economy. At the provincial level, a single dynasty based in Cebu City retained preeminence for most of the twentieth century by allying itself with urban merchant capitalists and by building a political machine centered in the Visayan entrepôt but radiating out into the province as well.

This chapter examines the pattern of dynastic bossism in the congressional districts of Cebu Province. An examination of the single most enduring district-level dynasty in the province underscores the role of state-based resources and prerogatives for the construction of a supramunicipal empire and political machine capable of withstanding both the problems of dynastic succession and the ebbs and flows of national politics. Sketches of two more recent—but already fully entrenched—dynasties in other rural districts of Cebu provide examples of alternative paths to capital accumulation and machine building for "political clans" in the province. Taken together, these three case studies exemplify patterns of dynastic bossism while emphasizing the coercive—rather than clientelistic—nature of production and social relations in the coal mines, factories, sugar plantations, and fishing fleets owned by these district-level dynasties.

In the pre-martial-law era, dynastic entrenchment was evident in several congressional districts in Cebu. In the 4th district, for example, various members of the Argao-based Kintanar clan, the dominant political force in the district's most populous town, held the congressional seat from 1938 through 1969. More impressively, the Cuenco family, proprietor of the bus company that linked the small and impoverished towns of the southern coast to Cebu City,[1] represented the 5th district in the national legislature with only two interruptions from 1912 through 1969, while a distant relative and longtime crony, Manuel A. Zosa, the scion of a prominent landowning clan in the town of Barili, stood for the neighboring 6th district in Congress from 1949 through 1965 and again from 1969 to 1972. Yet the most enduring political machine and economic empire constructed in all the rural congressional districts of Cebu was that of Ramon M. Durano Sr., who claimed the 1st district seat from 1949 through 1972, retained significant influence during the post-martial-law Marcos era, and passed on his bailiwick in dynastic form to his son Ramon ("Nito") Durano III, who has represented what now constitutes the 5th district since 1987.

## Congressional District Dynasties: The Duranos of Danao

In Barrio Dungo-an, Danao City, just a 45-minute drive north from Cebu City, lies a monument to the progenitor of Cebu's most famous congressional district dynasty: the burial site of the late Ramon M. Durano Sr. (1905–88). Covered with fresh flowers that are replenished weekly, his tomb lies in a tiny chapel that is almost encircled by busts of all the Popes in the history of Christianity, each facing the late Durano family patriarch. Framing the chapel and this collection of Popes, life-size dioramas of biblical scenes—such as the Last Supper and the Nativity—fill out the grounds of the Ramon M. Durano Sr. Home for the Aged, which is adjacent to the Church and orphanage that also bear his name and just across the road from his publishing house and bakery. Surrounding these monuments to Durano's beneficence and position in the Catholic community, substantial landmarks of his family's remaining worldly empire radiate out in the four cardinal directions: saltbeds stretch east to the coastline;

several hectares of sugarcane plantation line the highway south toward Cebu City; the "industrial welfare estate"—a sugar mill, ice plant, and cement factory—lie on the northbound road; mines and large landholdings extend west to the mountains. In the neighboring towns, mayors and other local notables remain to this day beholden to the late Durano, having benefited handsomely from his long tenure as representative and acknowledged political kingpin of Cebu's former 1st congressional district. Durano's sons have served as the district's representative to Congress and as the mayors of Danao City and the nearby municipality of Sogod. Elsewhere in the province, in Cebu City (and to a lesser extent in the nation's capital, Manila), scores of Durano relatives and protégés still hold positions in Customs, the Port Authority, the Bureau of Internal Revenue, the ranks of the police, and various law firms and construction companies. From its metaphysical, religious, and political center at his gravesite, Durano's empire lives on.

Longtime Cebu congressman Ramon M. Durano Sr., who ruled Danao City and the surrounding towns from 1949 until his death in 1988.

Ramon ("Nito") Durano III, elected Cebu congressman (5th district) in 1987 and heir to much of his father's local empire. Family patriarch Ramon M. Durano Sr. succeeded in passing on the empire he built up over the years to his sons and daughters.

In its style and structure, this memorial to Durano projects an elaborate myth about the late congressman's hold over the former 1st district of Cebu. Situating Ramon Durano Sr. among the larger pantheon of Christianity and emphasizing his public commitment to the Catholic Church,[2] the layout of the burial site locates the source of the Durano family patriarch's power in his putatively privileged access to the spiritual world and identification with the institutions of organized religion, thus obscuring the roots of his political success and economic fortune in the exploitation of state-based resources, privileges, and perks. While highlighting Durano's well-publicized reputation as a great patron and philanthropist, the design of the surrounding testimonies to his beneficence conceals his extraction of monopoly rents, exploitation of labor, and expropriation of scarce resources from the broad mass of the local population.[3] His derivative authority and state resources masked as personal prowess and beneficence, Durano thus appears as the source of all life and death, wealth and power in his bailiwick.

Yet however impressive in scope and remarkable in style, this monument's projection of Durano's authority claims little in the way of an attentive audience. The burial grounds remain almost entirely empty, the church has fallen into disrepair, and the old-age home and orphanage are virtually deserted. Only the caretaker, Durano's longtime personal body-guard, maintains a permanent vigil, standing by the memory of the boss whose life he protected for many years. Less closely affiliated local residents, meanwhile, evince little nostalgia for the late Durano's use of violence, intimidation, and fraud during elections, his implication in several murders, his sponsorship and protection of illegal economic activities, recalling too his penchant for pilfered government funds, fixed concessions and contracts, behest loans, landgrabbing, low-wage labor, and union-busting. Regardless of popular sentiment, Ramon Durano Sr.'s worldly empire lives on, his political machine, business enterprises, and land-holdings passed on to his family in classic dynastic form.

Before the election of Ramon M. Durano Sr. in 1949, the 1st congressional district of Cebu was the bailiwick of the Rodriguez family,[4] a Bogo-based clan with extensive landholdings in the northern sugar-belt towns of the province.[5] Celestino Rodriguez, for example, held the 1st district seat in the Assembly from 1907 to 1912 and again in 1935–38 and 1941–46; he also served in the Senate from 1916 to 1925. Celestino's brother, Pedro Rodriguez, held Cebu's 7th district seat in the Assembly from 1907 to 1909 and succeeded Celestino for two terms in the Senate (1925–28, 1928–31); his son, José V. Rodriguez, represented Cebu's 7th district in the House of Representatives (1941–46, 1946–49) and served as mayor of Cebu City (1952–55). A nephew, Buenaventura Rodriguez, represented both the 1st district (1931–34) and the 7th district (1934–35, 1935–38) of Cebu in the national legislature and was provincial governor of Cebu from 1937 through 1940. Owning large haciendas in the Bogo-Medellin sugar belt, claiming genealogical and cultural ties to Spain, and fraternizing and intermarrying with wealthy Chinese mestizo families from Cebu City, the Rodriguezes were prominent representatives of the provincial oligarchy.[6]

In the late 1930s, however, the Rodriguezes came into conflict with another prominent political clan in Cebu, the Cuencos. Don Mariano Jesus Cuenco, the family patriarch, had represented Cebu's 5th district in the national legislature for five consecutive terms (1912–28) and served two terms as governor of Cebu (1928–31, 1931–34) while his brother, Miguel Cuenco, settled into the 5th district seat (1931–65). Although they did not have large landholdings, the Cuencos enjoyed close ties with prominent commercial interests in Cebu City and owned one of the two major bus companies in the province, the Bisaya Land Transportation Company. In 1936, Mariano Jesus Cuenco was appointed secretary of public works and chairman of the National Power Corporation, positions that allowed him to build up a province-wide patronage machine in Cebu against Vice-President Sergio Osmeña Sr., longtime Cebu provincial king-pin and political rival of both Quezon and Cuenco.[7] In 1937, with Quezon's blessings, the Cuencos and the Rodriguezes forged an alliance against Osmeña and succeeded in electing Buenaventura Rodriguez to the provincial governorship of Cebu. Soon after the elections, however, the Rodriguezes' claims to provincial leadership of the Partido Nacionalista evidently upset the Cuencos and their supporters, who helped a prominent landowner from the town of Borbon, Tereso Dosdos, to unseat the new governor's uncle, Celestino Rodriguez, in the 1st district in the following year's congressional elections.[8]

Yet with the Rodriguezes renewing their alliance with Vice-President Osmeña and Dosdos bowing out in 1941, Secretary of Public Works Mariano Jesus Cuenco needed a new foil against Celestino Rodriguez in the 1st district.[9] Danao, the most populous municipality in the district, was the ideal site for a beachhead against Rodriguez, yet the dominant politician in the town, longtime mayor and wealthy landowner Paulo Almendras, was closely identified with the Osmeñas. Almendras, however, had married Elicia Durano, the daughter of Demetrio Tan Durano, a local merchant of Chinese mestizo extraction who served several terms as municipal councilor in Danao in the first decade of the twentieth century. Moreover, Elicia's brother, Ramon Durano, was the baptismal godson of the wealthy landowner and municipal councilor Salvador Gonzales and had married the daughter of Severo Duterte, another local notable who had won twelve consecutive terms on the municipal council of Danao. In 1934, Ramon Durano won a seat on the Danao municipal council on the Almendras-Osmeña ticket, but his aspirations clearly stretched beyond the small-town political entourage of his brother-in-law. Already the owner of several sailing vessels and proprietor of a modest but successful interisland trading network, Durano entered law school in Cebu City in 1935 and within a few years had passed the bar examination and begun practicing as an attorney.[10] Blessed with political capital from his father and baptismal godfather, affinal ties to the Almendras clan, and considerable ambition, Durano was an ideal candidate for Cuenco's scheme to weaken the local Osmeña machine and build up a counterforce to Rodriguez in the district.

In the late 1930s, moreover, a significant development in the economic life of Danao provided Cuenco with the perfect opportunity to earn the allegiance—and advance the fortunes—of Ramon Durano. In 1924 the National Development Company, a government agency, had founded the Cebu Portland Cement Company (CEPOC) and set up a cement factory in Naga, Cebu. Requiring massive amounts of coal for production, the company established its own mining operations—the Danao Coal Mines—on a 128-hectare plot in a mountainous area of Danao, where geological surveys had indicated coal deposits of more than 1 million metric tons. In 1938, moreover, CEPOC increased its Naga plant's capacity to 2,500 barrels (10,000 bags) of cement per day, necessitating accelerated extraction from its Danao Coal Mines and expanded reliance on private mine operators for its supply of coal.[11] Already installed as secretary of public works and chairman of the National Power Corporation, Mariano Jesus Cuenco won appointment in 1939 as president and general manager of CEPOC. Offering capital and contracts, Cuenco generously set up Durano as one of the company's primary suppliers of coal.[12] Enriched by his coal-mining contracts and backed by Cuenco, Durano ran for Congress against Rodriguez in the 1941 elections but failed to defeat the well-heeled sugar baron.

Wartime and postwar developments, however, improved the position of Durano over his potential rivals in Cebu's 1st district. During the Japanese occupation of the Philippines (1942–45), Durano joined an anti-Japanese guerrilla group operating in the mountains of Cebu, which was led by an American, Aaron Feinstein (aka Harry Fenton), who had worked as a radio announcer in Cebu City before the war. Fenton was feuding with another American, Captain James Cushing, for supreme control over the guerrillas and developed a reputation as a megalomaniac, murderer, and rapist.[13] In a brutal campaign ostensibly aimed at eliminating Japanese collaborators and spies within the guerrilla movement, Fenton and his subordinates, U.S. military intelligence reports dryly noted, "went to extremes and many wanton killings of innocent citizens were reported."[14] Durano, rising in the ranks from lieutenant / judge advocate to captain and intelligence officer (G-2) in Fenton's staff, exploited his discretion over guerrilla "justice" to order the "executions" of his prewar political enemies in the 1st district. In 1942 and 1943, Durano arranged for the murders of more than 40 of Congressman Celestino Rodriguez's *líders*, including the mayors of Tabogon, Sogod, Carmen, and Danao. These killings effectively decimated Rodriguez's political machine.[15]

Early postwar national and provincial political trends also favored Durano's ascendancy to the 1st district seat. Although Quezon's death had left Osmeña as the president of the republic in 1945, and Osmeñistas—including Jovenal Almendras, Durano's nephew—swept the congressional elections in Cebu in April 1946, Manuel Roxas's victory over Osmeña in the presidential election of May 1946 boosted the fortunes of the Cuenco family in the province. In April of that year, Mariano Jesus Cuenco was reelected to the Senate, and in June Roxas appointed

Cuenco's son, Manuel Cuenco, provincial governor of Cebu along with 51 municipal mayors selected by the Cuencos.[16] In 1947, Manuel Cuenco won election to the governorship, along with 48 out of 51 municipal mayoral candidates loyal to his family.[17] In 1949, moreover, Senator Cuenco became president of the Senate, the most powerful member of the bicameral legislature.

Meanwhile, Senator Cuenco continued to promote his Danao-based protégé, Ramon Durano. In 1946 he offered Durano a seat on the provincial board and, when Durano declined, arranged for his appointment as general manager of the Cebu branch of the National Coconut Corporation (NACOCO), a government body created before the war ostensibly to support coconut planters against volatile market conditions and monopolistic middlemen. In 1946, for example, the Cebu branch of NACOCO received hundreds of thousands of pesos from the national government for the purchase of copra from local producers at subsidized prices (for resale to private copra exporters) and for loans to coconut planters.[18] Under Durano's stewardship, which coincided with an unprecedented boom in copra exports from Visayan ports,[19] the Cebu branch of NACOCO doctored copra purchase and sales records to deliver a hefty percentage into the aspiring politician's election-campaign war chest.[20] In the early postwar years, moreover, Durano's coal-mining operations received exceedingly favorable treatment from the government: the Rehabilitation Finance Corporation provided a 30,000-peso loan for a 50-kilowatt generator to supply light and power in Danao to both residents and coal-mining companies,[21] and CEPOC increased both the volume and the price of coal it purchased from private suppliers.[22]

Banking on his ample campaign war chest, expanding role in the economy of the 1st district, and close ties to the patronage-rich Cuencos, Durano rode easily to victory in the 1949 elections on the coattails of the incumbent Quirino administration. In an election still remembered today for the unprecedented vote-buying, violence,[23] intimidation and fraud perpetrated by Liberal provincial governors and other local *líders*,[24] coercive interference in the canvassing of votes at the municipal and provincial level led to spurious victories for Liberal candidates to the Senate and helped Quirino win reelection over José P. Laurel.[25]

In Cebu, the Cuencos played the leading role in the Liberal Party sweep of the province in the November 1949 election. With Manuel Cuenco installed as the governor, Miguel Cuenco seated in the 5th congressional district, and Cuenquistas entrenched in 48 municipal mayorships and countless positions in the Constabulary and Commission on Elections, a well-oiled machine was already in place. In addition, in October 1949, one month before the election, Senate President Mariano Cuenco released more than 700,000 pesos of pork-barrel funds in Cebu Province, including 123,000 pesos for the 1st district.[26] On election day, moreover, a campaign of violence and terror orchestrated by the Cuencos swept Cebu Province.[27] As the House Electoral Tribunal later concluded in a 1952 decision on the 1949 election in the 3rd congressional district of Cebu:

A group of armed men, said to be special policemen of the respective municipalities comprised in the Third District of Cebu, ranging between 30 and 50 in number . . . was organized with official sanction in every municipality to round up the houses of the Nacionalistas, to coerce the Nacionalistas to vote for the Liberals or at least to refrain from voting in the election; to threaten and to manhandle all Nacionalistas who were stubborn or who would resist the pressure made to bear upon them and to shoot them if necessary "so that they could no longer vote."

For this purpose, the most notorious characters in the town were drafted as members of the Special Police Force, which usually was under the command and control of the Chief of Police of the town or under some other important local leader but always with official sanction and with some degree of authority emanating from either the Municipal Mayor or from the Chief of Police of the town, and with the apparent tolerance of the officials in high government circles. . . .

[They] were furnished with deadly weapons such as Thompsons, carbines, pistols and other kinds of firearms. The said firearms were usually supplied by the Chief of Police and were given a license to possess them to show official authority and to give upon each member the impression that they were protected by the government.[28]

These so-called Special Police Forces were highly successful in manufacturing the desired election results for the Liberal Party in the municipalities of the 3rd district.

The names entered in the registry list of voters in many instances were dictated and controlled by the Special Policemen; the voting booths were destroyed in many precincts and the voters had to prepare their ballots on the table of the board of inspectors, within the sight and subject to the inspection of the Special Policemen and the Liberal Party watchers. . . .

On election day, voters who were going to or were entering the polls were threatened and driven away; many of them were mauled and maltreated and forced to return to their homes. Two Nacionalista voters were killed and the killers were a regular policeman and two Special Policemen. . . .

Special Policemen . . . went to the polling places and filled up all unused ballots. Complete stubs were taken and filled up by them and the ballots so voted were all deposited in the ballot boxes. And the Board of Inspectors were just impotent to maintain the majesty of the law.[29]

In the 1st district, where Ramon Durano won election to Congress by using similar tactics,[30] an electoral protest filed by Osmeñista Florencio S.

Urot, his defeated opponent, also detailed extensive fraud and violence but was dismissed on a technicality.[31] Once seated in Congress, Durano began to entrench himself in power, using violence and state office to construct a provincial empire that would last his lifetime and survive him through his children.

For Durano, violence proved a valuable tool in consolidating his hold over the 1st district. During elections, in which Durano defeated a succession of local landowners, he fielded scores of armed goons whose intimidation of voters and election inspectors helped to guarantee winning margins in the district for the congressman as well as his candidates for local, provincial, and national office.[32] In the 1965 election, for example, according to his political opponents:

Thousands of goons were hired by Congressman Durano to prevent the voters from casting their votes for his rival. Fourteen political leaders of Mayor Abel Borromeo of San Francisco, Camotes, were kidnapped the day before the election and brought to Danao City. While six managed to escape, eight of them are still unheard of up to the present. Among those kidnapped was Apolinar Cartegena of San Francisco, Camotes, who was crucified and brutally tortured. He is now living in Davao City where he evacuated with his family.[33]

For the pre-martial-law era, these events were hardly anomalous: Danao and other towns in Cebu's 1st district figured among the "sensitive hot spots" listed by the Commission on Elections in every election from 1951 through 1971. During the Marcos era, moreover, Durano deployed the coercive resources at his disposal to deliver massive victories in his bailiwick for Marcos in the presidential races of 1965, 1969, and 1981 and in the various martial-law referenda and plebiscites in the 1970s.[34] In the 1986 "snap" presidential elections, he likewise arranged for the padding of voters' registration lists, oversaw vote-buying and bribery of election inspectors, and fielded scores of armed goons who harassed and intimidated voters, opposition campaign workers, and election-watch volunteers, attacked polling places, and, in a few cases, stole ballot boxes from voting centers.[35]

Aside from elections, Durano also reacted violently to intrusions into his bailiwick by his opponents in the provincial government. In 1952, for example, Durano and Danao's vice-mayor Manuel Yray were tried for the murder of Danao's acting mayor, Pedra Tecala, whom Governor Sergio Osmeña Jr. had appointed after suspending the congressman's protégé, Pedro Sepulveda, from the municipal mayorship for criminal and administrative violations.[36] In 1966, Durano likewise figured in stories circulating in Cebu about the assassination of Raul Borromeo, the newly named assistant provincial fiscal whose brother served as municipal mayor of San Francisco, Camotes (1963–67), and whose family owned large landholdings on the Camotes Islands, thus infringing upon Durano's bailiwick in the 1st district.[37]

Outside the sphere of electoral competition, Durano also consistently wielded violence to advance his accumulation of proprietary wealth and economic supremacy in the 1st district. With local police and Constabulary forces in his pocket and a bevy of armed retainers at his disposal, Durano always had the upper hand in disputes over rival mining claims in Danao.[38] In the late 1960s and early 1970s, moreover, when demand for sugar on the world market reached a new high, Durano began to acquire large landholdings in towns in the 1st district for conversion into sugar plantations, applying intimidation when necessary to pressure smallholders to vacate their plots.[39] Once, small landowners in a remote barrio of Danao were summarily evicted by Durano, threatened by armed men who accompanied bulldozers to raze the buildings on their lands, and "laughed at by members of the police department" for daring to file a complaint against the congressman.[40] In addition, Durano's monopoly of violence in Danao and the surrounding towns allowed him to enforce harsh labor discipline and maintain appalling working conditions in his enterprises without fear of organized resistance among the workers.[41] Finally, in 1966, Durano established the Insular Police Agency, a company staffed by ex-convicts, thugs, and professional strikebreakers whom he hired out to plantation owners in the Bogo-Medellin sugar belt to drive out the Associated Labor Union locals and to install company unions under the umbrella of the Durano-controlled Free Workers Association.[42]

Durano's monopoly on coercive resources and his control over local law-enforcement agencies also allowed him to sponsor lucrative illegal activities in Danao. After the war and under Durano's aegis and protection, hundreds of small-scale makers of homemade or recycled guns—popularly known as *paltik*—prospered in Danao;[43] their products were used widely throughout the Philippines and exported to markets in Japan and Taiwan. Thanks largely to Durano's intervention and influence, the makers of *paltik* suffered only infrequent and ineffectual police interference in their illegal production and marketing of firearms. Moreover, following the evolution of commercial links between various Durano enterprises and Japan, the construction of a Durano-owned private wharf and drydock facilities in Danao, and the establishment of Danao as an official Philippine port in 1969, Durano was able to smuggle contraband in and out of his hometown.[44]

Along with the benefits of a monopoly on coercive resources in Cebu's 1st district, Durano also enjoyed access to state patronage commensurate with his position in the national legislature. During his long tenure in

Congress, Durano served as a ranking member of committees on mining, public works, franchises, and reparations, his legislative interests in Manila corresponding to his business concerns in Danao. Careful to align himself with the ruling party in every administration, Durano was usually among the more favored congressmen in the disbursement of pork-barrel funds.[45] He evidently used his congressional seat to evade taxes and customs duties, to solicit clients for his law firm, and to win concessions and franchises for his companies.[46] In the early 1960s, for example, he obtained a franchise to operate an electric company and ice plant servicing Danao and neighboring towns. Construction companies owned by the congressman and members of his family likewise prospered through privileged access to government public works projects. Finally, Durano installed numerous relatives and protégés in government posts,[47] especially those that offered rich rent-seeking opportunities (e.g., customs collector, city tax assessor, provincial fiscal).[48] By the late 1960s, Cebu City newspapers began printing annual birthday greetings to Congressman Durano from the public works department, the courts, the tax collector, and other public offices.[49]

For delivering large majorities in Cebu's 1st district to every successful presidential candidate, Durano enjoyed warm relations with Malacañang, especially during the administrations of Carlos P. Garcia (1957–61) and Ferdinand E. Marcos (1966–86), two presidents who rewarded him with special privileges and resources. In 1961, for example, with Garcia's support, Durano succeeded in converting the municipality of Danao into a chartered city, a status that granted the congressman's hometown a significant degree of autonomy from the provincial government of Cebu. Because Durano's relatives and cronies held the Danao mayorship and other elective posts,[50] such offices as city treasurer, engineer, fiscal, judge, and superintendent of schools fell to protégés nominated by the city mayor, appointed by the president, and confirmed by the Congress's Commission on Appointments.[51]

With the blessings of successive presidents and the backing of government financial institutions, moreover, Durano built up an elaborate economic empire in his district. In the 1950s, Durano expanded his control over the coal-mining industry in Danao. In 1954, with President Ramon Magsaysay's assent, two Durano allies won election to the Board of Directors of CEPOC, the government-owned cement firm that purchased coal from Durano's mines in Danao.[52] Through these two well-placed allies, Durano was assured of favorable treatment in his dealings with CEPOC. In 1958, moreover, President Garcia rewarded Durano for his support in the election of the previous year by arranging for the Reparations Commission to finance Durano's construction of a cement plant in

Danao City.[53] Designed as the centerpiece of the Durano-owned Universal Cement Company, the plant was equipped for production of 10,000 bags of cement per day; its construction cost more than 6 million dollars in goods and services provided by the Kobe Steel Works in Japan.[54] Over the next few years, the Universal Cement Company also acquired some 1,600 hectares of property and secured a 900-hectare concession in Danao to expand coal-mining operations for raw materials and fuel.[55]

Durano's empire in Danao further expanded in the late 1960s with generous support from President Ferdinand Marcos. Durano easily obtained loans to pay off his companies' accumulating bills and permission to roll over his mounting debts to the Development Bank of the Philippines (DBP).[56] A multi-million-dollar loan from the DBP also enabled Durano to construct a sugar central in Danao in 1968 with the assistance of the Mitsubishi Corporation.[57] Durano's political clout helped to facilitate crop loans from the Philippine National Bank to planters who pledged their sugar to the Durano Sugar Mills and to ensure favorable treatment from the quasi-government sugar monopsony, the National Sugar Trading Corporation.[58] By the mid-1970s, the Durano central was receiving sugarcane from nearly 5,000 hectares within its milling district and producing more than 300,000 piculs (nearly 20,000 metric tons) of sugar per year.[59]

Though heavily reliant upon privileges and resources derived from the patronage of national politicians, Durano's empire survived intact in the face of adverse economic, political, and personal circumstances. In the early 1980s, falling sugar prices on the world market, slack demand for cement in the Philippines and abroad, and a banking crisis in Manila combined to bankrupt Durano's companies, idling his sugar mill and closing his cement plant.[60] In 1986, moreover, Durano's high-profile support for Marcos in the "snap" election proved a liability once Corazon C. Aquino assumed the presidency. The Ministry of Local Government summarily replaced the Duranos and their protégés in various local government posts with "officials-in-charge" who had supported Aquino in Cebu, while the Presidential Commission on Good Government came under pressure to launch an investigation into the former congressman's "behest loans" and "ill-gotten wealth."[61] Finally, in October 1988, after years of declining health and at the ripe age of 82, Ramon M. Durano Sr. passed away, dying intestate and leaving his empire in considerable disarray.[62] A near-fatal gunfight between two of Durano's sons, Jesus ("Don") and Thaddeus ("Deo"), earlier that year had suggested that a struggle over the patriarch's legacy might divide the family.[63]

Nonetheless, the Durano family weathered this crisis and entrenched itself as a second-generation dynasty in the renamed 5th congressional district of Cebu.[64] Months after Aquino became president, the aging family patriarch had pledged his support to the new administration and, through the intercession of (future House speaker) Ramon V. Mitra Jr., gained ruling party support for the successful candidacy of his favorite son, Ramon ("Nito") Durano III, for the 5th district congressional seat.[65] Less than a year later, Ramon Durano Sr. was elected mayor of Danao City as an official candidate of the Aquino administration.[66] Having skillfully reached a political settlement with the new government, the Duranos salvaged their economic empire, avoided sequestration of their properties by the Presidential Commission on Good Government, and retained ownership of the Durano Sugar Mills.[67] Meanwhile, after the Duranos relinquished control over the heavily indebted Universal Cement Company to government banks in 1986, scions of the prominent Manila-based Araneta and Zobel de Ayala clans teamed up to buy Universal Cement from the Asset Privatization Trust and reopened the cement plant in Danao City in late 1991.[68] Taking note of the Durano family's prominence and ownership of the land on which the cement plant was built, the Aranetas and Ayalas took care to include the Duranos as partners and placed three members of the clan on the new company's seven-member board, including Beatriz Durano, Ramon Sr.'s widow, whom they named chairperson.[69] Moreover, by providing plots of land, assurances of "labor peace," and assistance in securing tax and tariff "incentives," the Duranos coaxed the Mitsumi Electric Company of Japan to set up a factory in Danao City in 1988.[70] Today, the Mitsumi plant employs more than 3,000 residents of Danao City and neighboring towns and, together with the Durano Sugar Mills and the reopened cement plant, has reestablished the Duranos as partners in Danao's "industrial welfare complex."[71]

By 1992, Ramon Durano Sr.'s favorite son, Congressman Nito Durano, had asserted his position as the new family patriarch and consolidated his hold over the 5th congressional district of Cebu. In the absence of a will, the estate of Ramon Durano Sr. went to his widow, but the old man had already transferred control over the sugar mill, titles to numerous properties, and most other valuable assets to Nito before his death in 1988.[72] Though Durano family squabbles may persist,[73] Congressman Nito Durano's supremacy is beyond dispute. In the May 1992 elections, with his feuding brothers Jesus ("Don") and Thaddeus ("Deo") winning reelection to the mayorships of Danao City and Sogod respectively, Congressman Durano recaptured the 5th district congressional seat easily. He received at least 73,000 votes more than his closest rival, including 99 percent of all votes cast in Danao City, and delivered sizable margins to his favored candidates for the provincial governorship and the presidency. In 1995 Congressman Durano was reelected (virtually unchallenged), as were various other family members. In short, although Ramon M. Durano Sr. began his political career as a notoriously predatory and violent aspiring boss, he clearly succeeded in passing on his Danao-based empire to his family.

## The New District Dynasties: *Hacendados* and Fishing Magnates

After the ouster of Marcos in 1986, a gerrymandering of the congressional districts in Cebu created new possibilities for supramunicipal dynasties in the province. The old 1st district monopolized by Ramon Durano Sr. reemerged as the 5th district dominated by his son, but the exclusion of Bogo and its inclusion among the towns of the new 4th district—comprising the nine municipalities of northern Cebu and Bantayan island—helped elevate the Bogo-based Martinez clan to new heights of wealth and power.

The Martinezes, who owned large tracts of land in the Bogo-Medellin sugar belt and on the nearby island province of Leyte, had intermarried with the prominent Espinosa clan of Masbate, and claimed Spanish lineage, resembled at first glance latter-day versions of the well-heeled Rodriguezes, the sugar barons who dominated the old 1st and 7th districts of Cebu for much of the prewar era. But the family patriarch, Congressman Celestino ("Junie") E. Martinez Jr., was far less genteel than his *hacendado* counterparts of yesteryear; he had a wide reputation for ruthlessness and a violent temper. As mayor of Bogo from 1971 to 1986, Martinez asserted his economic domination over the municipality, using the town police to close down his rivals' cockfighting arena and assuming the presidency of the municipal branch of the Coconut Producers' Federation (COCOFED).[74] Once elected to the 4th district congressional seat (in 1987), moreover, Martinez began planning his own coconut oil mill in Bogo.

As owner of only one of many sizable haciendas in the Bogo-Medellin sugar belt, however, Martinez still depends upon the goodwill and support of his fellow *hacendados*, whose economic might dwarfs other concentrations of private wealth in the 4th district. Long the vice-president of the Bogo-Medellin Sugarcane Planters' Association and a shareholder in the Bogo-Medellin sugar central, Martinez earned the praise of other sugar barons for his support of landowners' interests in the national legislature and his resourcefulness in assisting them with other business ventures in Cebu City and Manila.[75] Indeed, his influence may well be responsible for the nonimplementation of agrarian reform in northern

Celestino E. Martinez Jr.,
elected Cebu congressman (4th
district) in 1987. Martinez, a
Spanish mestizo, has enjoyed
the full support of large landowners in the sugar plantation
belt of northern Cebu that
constitutes his district.

Cebu. With generous backing from other sugar planters, ample access to
pork-barrel funds,[76] and a demonstrated willingness to use violence
against his political foes,[77] Martinez has entrenched himself in the 4th
district for the foreseeable future. In the May 1992 elections, he won reelection by a margin of nearly 37,000 over his closest rival, delivering
majorities in the 4th district to his favored candidates for the provincial
governorship and the presidency, and sweeping in his protégés and allies
(including Remedios Escario of Bantayan) in eight out of nine municipalities—results repeated, if not improved upon, in the 1995 elections. With
the congressman's mother, Nilda E. Martinez, elected to the Bogo vice-
mayorship, his 22-year-old son among the winning municipal councilors
in the town, and his kinsman Mariano Martinez seated, along with another protégé, on the provincial board, the Martinez dynasty became virtually unbeatable.

Meanwhile, a new center of political and economic activity has emerged
on the southern tip of the island, where the Abines family has built up a
considerable political machine and economic empire in the new 2nd district. The family patriarch, Apolonio Abines Sr., served two terms as a

municipal councilor (1959–63, 1964–67) and one term as vice-mayor (1968–71) of Oslob, but remained under the shadow of long-term town mayor José Tumulak (1964–80), the owner of large landholdings in the municipality. Although Apolonio Sr. passed away in the 1970s, his son Crisologo ("Sol") captured the mayorship of neighboring Santander town in 1971 and served continuously until 1986. Apolonio Abines Jr., Sol's brother, succeeded the late Tumulak to the mayorship of Oslob in 1980, and various Abines siblings have held the mayorships of the two towns since 1988. In 1987, moreover, Sol Abines won election to Cebu's 2nd district seat in Congress; after being reelected in 1992 and 1995, he helped his brother Apolonio Jr. capture the vice-governorship of the province and swept protégés into local office in several municipalities.

In a district notable for small landholdings, low corn and coconut yields, depleted fishing beds, and massive poverty, the Abines family constructed a supramunicipal empire based on fishing and land transportation enterprises. At the center of the Abines empire is their control over the so-called *muro-ami* fishing industry. *Muro-ami* is a highly effective fishing method introduced to the Philippines by Japanese fishermen in the 1920s: a large cone-shaped bag net is held 40 to 80 feet beneath the surface of the sea; long "scare-lines" of nylon ropes are held by swimmers and attached to stones that are repeatedly dropped on the sea bottom (or often a coral reef) to drive the fish into the net.[78] By one account, Japanese *muro-ami* fishermen who had been fishing since the 1930s on reefs off the coast of nearby southern Cebu lost their nets and other gear during World War II to local "militia," who used the equipment and established methods to revive *muro-ami* fishing in the postwar era.[79] Among the leading recruiters and foremen in these operations was Apolonio Abines Sr.:

He was a tough task master, always exacting the best from his workers in any weather while fishing. But he is also said to have been generous and always on hand to extend assistance to his workers when needed. He had a passion for cockfighting, which he turned to his advantage when he became a manager. When his best fishermen lost money in the cockpit, he lent them money, and so retained them as laborers.[80]

When *muro-ami* fishing began to exhaust the seabeds off the southeastern Cebu coast in the 1960s, Abines started to market his expertise—and his captive labor force—farther afield, supplying *muro-ami* divers to the Cavite- and Manila-based San Diego family, whose fleet took regular expeditions to remote waters off Palawan. When the San Diegos' fishing (and cigarette smuggling) businesses declined in the late 1960s along with the political fortunes of the family's patron, Cavite congressman Justiniano S. Montano Sr.,[81] the Abineses bailed out and formed a successful

Crisologo Abines, elected Cebu congressman (2nd district) in 1987. The Abines family's fishing fleet and bus company constitute the biggest business in the southern part of Cebu.

An Abines family store. The Abines family's district is one of the most infertile and impoverished parts of Cebu Province. Family control over the local economy is monolithic.

partnership with another fishing company based in Navotas, Metro Manila, the Frabal Fishing and Ice Plant Corporation.[82]

With more than 30 large ships, the Abines-Frabal *muro-ami* fleet led regular ten-month expeditions to bring more than 7,000 residents from the southern towns of Cebu (as well as Siquijor and Negros Oriental) to the remote waters of the South China Sea. Based on a small island off the coast of remote Palawan,[83] the fleet made daily fishing trips to nearby reefs, each vessel carrying more than 300 swimmers (*pescadores*) who jiggled the heavily weighted "scare-lines" and worked in tandem with divers who set and retrieved the nets at more than 80 feet below the surface, all under the close supervision of taskmasters (*maestros*) and several overseers (known as *yamada* from the Spanish word for barker or messenger, *llamador*).[84] While these boats commuted every day for ten months between the fleet's home base and the reefs, larger Frabal ships transported the iced fresh fish to the wharves of Dagatdagatan, Navotas, in Metro Manila, for marketing and sale.

With encouragement from the Abines clan's political enemies, these *muro-ami* fishing operations began to attract considerable public controversy in the mid-1980s, and journalistic accounts appeared in a Cebu City–based weekly magazine, Manila daily newspapers, and foreign publications.[85] Prominent marine biologists, for example, released findings that *muro-ami* fishing caused extensive damage to Philippine coral reefs, which led to the imposition of a temporary ban on the fishing method.[86] Scholars and labor rights advocates, moreover, focused on Abines-Frabal's use of child labor, citing confirmed reports that a large number of *muro-ami pescadores* were in fact young boys no more than ten years of age.[87] Subsequent studies exposed the extremely harsh labor conditions on the Abines-Frabal fishing fleet, where the young swimmers, working twelve to fifteen hours a day with only the lightest of meals, suffered from "kidney infection, chest pains, fever, vomiting blood, hepatitis, typhoid fever, stomach cramps, headaches, hunger, and fatigue. Two . . . had been beaten, one on the head with a paddle, leaving a large scar, by their managers for refusing to dive further on a day, in one case because of fatigue, in the other case because of chest pains."[88] One team of researchers compiled a list of 43 *muro-ami* fishermen who died or disappeared from February 1982 through August 1985 alone,[89] while an investigative reporter who visited Talampulan island off Palawan in 1989 discovered "easily over a hundred graves" of *pescadores* who had drowned or otherwise died while at work on the Abines-Frabal fleet. Reportedly, because many of these deaths remain unrecorded the Abineses are able to use the names of their former employees to provide false identities to illegal Taiwanese immigrants whom they have allegedly smuggled into Cebu from rendezvous points in the South China Sea off Palawan. As Ramon Binamira, action officer of the Presidential Committee on Illegal Fishing and Marine Conservation noted: "Even in death, the *muro-ami* operators perpetuate their lies."[90]

In their recruitment and payment of *muro-ami* fishermen, moreover, the Abines family relied upon "credit bondage" to maximize profits from the exploitation of their labor force.[91] Offering a cash advance of 300 pesos to attract recruits, the Abineses also extended credit in kind to fishermens' families—a monthly *bale* (from the Spanish word *vale*, meaning credit receipt or promissory note) of one bag of rice or corn and one sack of pig feed—at their local stores in Oslob and Santander. This arrangement, astute observers have noted, enhanced both labor discipline and surplus extraction:

> Clearly, credit lines and employment are intertwined and by means of this strategy, customers of the Abines stores are not only registered, they are easily prey to overpricing. It was reported that the price of a bag of rice was increased from P50.00 to P80.00 or that 50 kilos of corn grits worth P275 actually weighed only 46 kilos. From the gross incomes, the "vale" still has to be deducted.[92]

While their families accumulated debts at the company store back home in southern Cebu, the *muro-ami* fishermen labored in the remote waters of the South China Sea without benefit of a written contract with Abines-Frabal and in exchange not for wages, but for a small share of the profits—calculated by the companies based on their rendering of accounts in Metro Manila.[93] On a piece-rate basis, the company bosses allowed the *pescadores* to clean and dry rejected fish for sale—at deflated prices—to the *maestros*, who in turn sold the dried fish (*bulad*) to Abines-Frabal for a hefty markup.[94] By paying the fishermen a share of the profits rather than a wage, the Abineses also evaded labor laws that mandated minimum wages and social security benefits. Moreover, the Abines family allegedly made sure that workers' homecomings to southern Cebu from their ten-month expedition coincided with the dates of local barrio fiestas:

> In the cockfights and mah jong games that accompany a fiesta, the fishermen are likely to lose large chunks of their pay in gambling, making it necessary to borrow from their recruiter in exchange for returning to sea on the next voyage. This concatenation of events is probably not accidental. We learned, for example, that the recruiter is a cockfight aficionado and owns a large personal coliseum full of cocks.[95]

Expanding from *muro-ami* fishing operations, the Abines clan's empire in southern Cebu came to encompass key features of the local economy, such as the cockfighting coliseum. In the 1970s, for example, the Abineses responded to growing demand for transport to Cebu City and improved road conditions in the impoverished towns of southern Cebu by starting a bus company. By the late 1980s, the Abines Bus Company coaches virtually monopolized the route from the southern tip of the province to Cebu City—where the Abines-owned ferry also provided the sole link to the neighboring island province of Negros Oriental. The Bacolod City–based Ceres bus company, which had expanded its operations from Negros to include Leyte and large portions of Mindanao, found its moves to obtain a franchise for southern Cebu frustrated and its buses vandalized and thus opted to cede the route to the Abines family. The Librando clan, whose bus company covered the route from Badian on the southwestern coast of the province to Cebu City, likewise yielded to Abines pressures and agreed to settle for an abbreviated schedule and itinerary for its vehicles. As the monopoly franchise holder, moreover, the Abines bus company developed a reputation for pursuing profits ruthlessly. In numerous towns along the southern coast of Cebu province, residents recall incidents in which a speeding Abines bus hit a pedestrian and, in accordance with company policy to avoid costly hospital bills, backed up over the wounded victim to finish the job. Such stories, in which the Abines bus drivers are invariably described as hardened, heavy-set former logging truckers from Mindanao, may in fact be apocryphal, but they capture local sentiment about the Abines clan.

The Abines family thus came to wield nearly monolithic control over the economy of southern Cebu. Where necessary, family members used coercive sanctions to enforce their economic powers: for example, the shop and home of Felix Tan, a Chinese storeowner in Oslob, were burned down (and his father died in the fire) after he stopped borrowing money from the Abineses.[96] On Sumilon, a 23-hectare coral-lined island off the coast of Oslob, the Abineses repeatedly violated an agreement with Silliman University in 1974—and a government order of 1980—designating a 750-meter section of densely populated reef slope on the island's western side a national park and marine sanctuary and fish reserve. Allegedly employing dynamite and *muro-ami* techniques, and using threats of violence to drive out Silliman personnel, the Abines family's fleet fished out the reef by the mid-1980s, destroying much of the coral in the process.[97] Once Sumilon was exhausted of its marine resources and returned to the municipality of Oslob, it became the site of an Abines-sponsored beach and diving resort designed to appeal to upscale Japanese tourists.

In the sphere of electoral competition, moreover, the Abineses have repeatedly used coercion to defeat their rivals in the 2nd district and to deliver solid majorities to their patrons in the national political arena.[98] By attending meetings of local public school teachers' associations,[99] registering scores of *muro-ami* fishermen from Negros Oriental to vote,[100] and offering free passage on Abines buses to local residents and their relatives in Cebu City,[101] Crisologo Abines has taken care to make pre-election preparations against his rivals in the 2nd district.[102] On election day, moreover, the Abines family has saturated the municipalities of the district with armed goons to supervise vote-buying, drive away ward leaders, watchers, and voters identified with his opponents, and, post themselves inside polling places and voting centers, interfere in the casting, counting, and canvassing of votes.[103]

The Abineses' electoral successes, in turn, have protected their business enterprises from government intervention and private competition and enhanced their hold over the 2nd district. Congressman Crisologo Abines, for example, served as chairman of the House Sub-Committee on Fisheries, a position that allowed him to subvert attempts to enforce the ban on *muro-ami* fishing.[104] His brother, Apolonio Abines Jr., elected vice-governor of Cebu in 1992 and again in 1995, headed the Provincial Bantay Dagat Sugbo Council, the interagency body tasked with monitoring and eliminating illegal fishing in the province. With the 2nd district congressional seat, the vice-governorship, and two town mayorships in family hands, the Abineses have also enjoyed considerable discretion over the flow of state patronage into southern Cebu, including funds designated for cooperatives supposedly composed of former fishermen displaced and unemployed because of the nominal ban on *muro-ami*.[105] With a mutually enforcing economic empire and political machine, the Abines family dynasty in the southernmost towns of Cebu will almost certainly live on in the twenty-first century with another generation of the late Apolonio Sr.'s descendants.

## Conclusion

The preceding description of the district-level dynasties of Cebu contrasts with the pattern of provincial-boss entrenchment in Cavite described in Chapter 3. In Cebu, wealthy and powerful families have maintained their economic and political hold over congressional districts for decades at a time, and passed on their bailiwicks, in classic dynastic fashion, to their descendants. These families exercised political power in tandem with command over privately owned empires: coal mines, factories, sugar plantations, bus companies, and fishing fleets. Even longtime congressman Ramon M. Durano Sr., who began his career as a business crony of Senator Cuenco and a rentier capitalist dependent upon government contracts and concessions, established a firm base in proprietary wealth that survived his death and allowed his family to retain its economic preeminence in Danao City and surrounding towns.

To a considerable extent, the diverse political economy of Cebu prefigured the entrenchment of dynasties—rather than individual bosses—in the largely rural congressional districts of the province. In several districts, the concentration of voters in one populous town, command of commercial and transportation chokepoints, or control over sites of intensive production offered district-level dynasties more solid bases for electoral self-perpetuation and capital accumulation than the more heavily state-regulated landscape of Cavite. In each district, dynastic consolidation commenced when the combined processes of capital accumulation and state intervention helped concentrate wealth in the hands of a single family. The introduction and expansion of coal mining in Danao in the 1930s, 1940s, and 1950s, the exhaustion of southern Cebu fishing beds through *muro-ami* fishing by the late 1960s, and the threat of agrarian reform in the Bogo-Medellin sugar belt in the late 1980s thus prefigured the emergence and entrenchment of congressmen Durano, Abines, and Martinez, respectively.

While ruling in dynastic fashion, these families have controlled their respective congressional districts as ruthless bosses. Using state offices, they accumulated wealth from government loans, contracts, concessions, and monopoly franchises. Using the local coercive and law-enforcement agencies of the state, these families have proven willing to employ violence to protect and monopolize illegal economies, defeat political rivals, intimidate potential commercial competitors, and maintain strict labor discipline in their various enterprises. These dynasties have been more diversified than their counterparts at the municipal level in their economic activities and more dependent on state resources and prerogatives than previous analyses have suggested. Contrary to the standard portrait of such families as "patrons" who deliver particularistic goods and services to grateful and loyal clienteles, moreover, these dynasties have combined paternalistic pretensions with violence and intimidation to acquire wealth and property, exploit labor, and mobilize followers during elections. In short, as much as the mafia-style provincial bosses of Cavite, the district-level dynasties of Cebu are examples of the broader phenomenon of bossism in the Philippines.

# A Provincial Dynasty:
# The Osmeñas of Cebu City

The Cuencos, Duranos, Martinezes, and Abineses entrenched themselves as supramunicipal dynasties in the rural districts of Cebu, but these families were less successful in their bids for province-wide power. The Cuencos did succeed—with the help of Manila-based patrons like Manuel Quezon and Manuel Roxas—in achieving provincial hegemony in Cebu for brief periods in the 1930s and 1940s. Ramon M. Durano Sr., moreover, began to approach similar heights of power in the late 1960s,[1] when two sons-in-law, one cousin, and a close crony won election to the legislature, thus granting the longtime 1st district representative effective control over five of Cebu's seven congressional seats.[2] While the abolition of Congress in 1972 cast the extent of Durano's influence in Cebu into doubt, by the mid-1980s his relatives and cronies held two seats in the Batasang Pambansa (National Assembly), the vice-governorship, and a second seat on the provincial board, but Eduardo Gullas, scion of a prominent Cebu City–based family and close associate of First Lady Imelda Marcos, retained the governorship.[3] Only in 1992 did another bid for province-wide power by a rural dynasty succeed, when Congressmen Abines, Durano, and Martinez teamed up to help 6th district representative Vicente ("Tingting") Dela Serna win the governorship.[4] Dela Serna, however, lost his bid for a second term in 1995 when the Cebu City–based Osmeña clan, backed by three other Cebu congressmen and the Ramos administration, successfully fielded a close ally, former 3rd district congressman Pablo Garcia Sr., as their gubernatorial candidate and thus recaptured the provincial capital.

In fact, throughout most of the twentieth century, political power at the provincial level in Cebu remained in the hands of the Osmeña family, whose style of rule, base in Cebu City, and ties to urban commercial interests distinguished them from the Cuencos, Duranos, Martinezes, and Abineses of Cebu's largely rural congressional districts. As one scholar has noted:

> The Osmeñas are an interesting case study of power maintenance not only because their prominence spans a century but because they do not conform to certain stereotypes about political kingpins, or "warlords" in the Philippines. They do not exercise monopolistic economic control in their bailiwick; they do not maintain "private armies" or engage in a rule of systematic, direct repression; and they are not gladhanding, traditional patrons. Their main base of electoral support—Cebu Province, particularly metropolitan Cebu—is a highly urbanized area with a heterogeneous population, a complex occupational structure, a developed media infrastructure, high levels of literacy, and a large concentration of modern, voluntary organizations.[5]

In contrast with the mafia-style bosses of Cavite and the municipal- and district-level dynasties of Cebu, the Osmeñas have practiced a more attenuated—but no less enduring or successful—form of bossism in the Philippines. The pages that follow examine how three successive generations of Osmeñas constructed, defended, and developed a province-wide empire and political machine in Cebu over the course of the twentieth century and how the ingredients of the Osmeñas' success in the province allowed them to emerge time and again as contenders for national power.

## The Founding of the Osmeña Dynasty

As Cebu City evolved from an island entrepôt into a major manufacturing center during the twentieth century, and as the provincial electorate expanded from fewer than 500 voters (in 1906) to more than 500,00 (in 1992), the Osmeña clan remained at the center of politics in both Cebu City and Cebu Province. In the prewar colonial and commonwealth periods, Sergio Osmeña Sr. represented the 2nd district of Cebu (Cebu City and environs) for five terms in the National Assembly and the House of Representatives (1907–22), won a Senate seat for five subsequent terms (1922–35), and served as vice-president (1935–44) and later president (1944–46) of the Philippine Commonwealth. In the postwar, pre-martial-law period, his son, Sergio ("Serging") Osmeña Jr., served variously as

Emilio ("Lito") Osmeña, Cebu governor (1988–92) and vice-presidential candidate of
the Lakas-NUCD Party in 1992, seen here with then presidential candidate Fidel V.
Ramos and then president Corazon C. Aquino. Although he lost his bid for the vice-
presidency, Osmeña's contribution to the Ramos presidency helped to solidify the family's position in the national arena, a strategy deployed by two earlier generations of
Osmeñas. (Nonoy Duran, *Manila Times*)

Cebu provincial governor (1951–55), Cebu city mayor (1956–57,
1960–72),[6] Cebu 2nd district representative (1958–61), and senator
(1966–71); he also ran unsuccessfully for the vice-presidency (1961) and
the presidency (1969) of the Philippine Republic. Finally, in the post-
Marcos era, a revival of Osmeña family fortunes saw a third generation
take power: Serging's son Tomas ("Tommy") won two successive terms
as Cebu City mayor (1988–95), and nephews Emilio ("Lito") Osmeña Jr.
and John ("Sonny") Osmeña served as Cebu provincial governor
(1988–92) and senator (1988–95), respectively. The family's latest representative on the national political scene, Lito Osmeña, lost a 1992 bid for
the vice-presidency of the republic but, as the former running mate of incumbent president Fidel Ramos, gained considerable access to Malacañang and discretion over the flow of national state patronage to Cebu,
even as his cousin, Serge Osmeña, assumed a Senate seat after the 1995
elections.

The backdrop to Sergio Osmeña Sr.'s emergence in 1906 as the preeminent figure in Cebu provincial politics prefigured his family's continuing political success in the province for decades to come. Osmeña was born in 1878 into one of Cebu City's most prominent and wealthy Chinese mestizo families. His grandfather, Severino Osmeña, owned extensive rural and urban properties and was among the leaders of Cebu City's Chinese and Chinese mestizo community. Upon his death (ca. 1860), however, the Osmeña fortune fell to the family of his first wife, leaving Sergio, born out of wedlock to a daughter of Severino's second wife, unable to take full advantage of his family's social and economic resources.[7] Nevertheless, Sergio attended élite educational institutions in Cebu and Manila at the turn of the century and enjoyed close ties with prominent *ilustrado* figures during the short-lived Philippine Republic (1898–1901).[8] Among his closest and most important associates during this period were Juan Climaco, the leading *ilustrado* among the remaining insurgents in the mountains of Cebu province, and Nicasio Chiong Veloso,[9] one of the wealthiest Chinese residents of Cebu City.[10] Chiong Veloso not only sponsored Osmeña's founding of the first daily newspaper in Cebu, *El Nuevo Dia*, but also groomed his young protégé to be a son-in-law.[11] Less than a year after his April 1901 marriage to Estefania Chiong Veloso, Osmeña won another victory when his ally, the surrendered insurgent leader Juan Climaco, with support from Osmeña's newspaper and contacts among both Cebuano urban élites and American colonial officials, won election in February 1902 as provincial governor of Cebu.

Over the next few years, Osmeña passed the bar examination, continued publishing his newspaper, and won two terms on the municipal council of Cebu and appointments as acting provincial governor and provincial fiscal.[12] Thanks to these appointments, the backing of American and Cebuano influentials, and the blessings of his mentor, the ailing (and retiring) governor Juan Climaco, Sergio Osmeña won election by a wide majority to the provincial governorship of Cebu in February 1906.[13] Moreover, after Osmeña emerged as a leading figure in the provincial governors' convention later that year, he joined a Manila-based committee formed ostensibly "to assist the colonial government" in making preparations for the Philippine Assembly.[14] With American support and a close protégé installed as his successor to the Cebu provincial governorship, Osmeña won election as Cebu's 2nd district representative to the Philippine Assembly in 1907 and became majority floor leader soon thereafter. This series of events marked the beginnings of the Osmeña dynasty in Cebu.

In subsequent years, as the Cebu electorate grew, Sergio Osmeña and his descendants used the same ingredients of his ascendance to provin-

cial-level power to maintain their preeminent position—links with national-level political patrons, discretionary powers over the local state apparatus, and ties to the urban commercial élite of Cebu City. Their local
electoral success and national political influence helped the Osmeñas entrench themselves in both Cebu City and Cebu Province and, with mixed
success, they asserted the family's presence in the national political arena.
While Cebu was transformed from a turn-of-the-century agricultural entrepôt into a regional center of export-oriented industry, the Osmeña dynasty's mode of political reproduction remained largely unchanged.

## State Resources and Dynastic Ambitions

Over the years, the Osmeñas used their considerable influence in Manila
to consolidate control over the city and province of Cebu. Like Aguinaldo and Tirona in Cavite, Assembly Majority Leader Sergio Osmeña
enjoyed some measure of discretion over the Bureau of Lands' sale of the
former friar estates in Cebu,[15] which consisted of approximately 10,000
hectares of prime land in the Banilad district of metropolitan Cebu
(roughly 1,900 hectares) and the east coast towns of Talisay and
Minglanilla (roughly 8,100 hectares), just south of the city.[16] Governor-
General Francis Burton Harrison further enhanced Osmeña's control
over these well-situated tracts by issuing an executive order in 1918
handing over more than 6,000 hectares of unsold land to the provincial
government of Cebu for disposal.[17] The implications of these arrangements are apparent in the acquisition by Osmeña relatives and cronies of
large landholdings on the former friar estates, the retention by the provincial government of valuable real properties, and the electoral strength
long enjoyed by successive Osmeñas in the populous towns of Talisay
and Minglanilla.

A 1936 law granting Cebu status as a chartered city, moreover, facilitated the Osmeñas' construction of an urban political machine.[18] The
law, which Vice-President Osmeña had carefully nursed through the legislature and convinced newly elected president Manuel Quezon to sign,
stipulated that the mayor of Cebu City, appointed by the president with
the approval of the Commission on Appointments, would enjoy broad
discretionary powers over the granting of municipal licenses and permits,
the awarding of appointments and salaries to city employees, and the bidding of public works contracts to private companies. While key city
posts—the city fiscal, the judge of the municipal court, the city engineer,
the chief of police, and the city treasurer, assessor, and superintendent of
schools, and all these officials' deputies—were subsequently nominated

by the city mayor, appointed by the president, and confirmed by the Commission on Appointments, the city mayor was authorized by law to appoint, promote, suspend, or remove all other officers and employees of the city government.

Although the Cebu City mayorship became an elective post in 1955,[19] the office—to which Don Sergio's son, Serging, and grandson, Tommy, won repeated election—retained these considerable powers over the local state apparatus. In the pre-martial-law period (1955–72), aside from the personnel prerogatives noted above, the Cebu City mayor also exercised direct control over such diverse bodies as the Osmeña Waterworks System, Cebu Lottery Commission, Board of Assessment Appeals, and Cebu City Planning Board.[20] By 1966, the Cebu City bureaucracy had swollen to almost 4,000 employees (including nearly 1,000 policemen), mostly "nontechnical" workers recommended by the mayor and the elected city councilors, themselves Osmeña protégés. In numerous cases, two or three appointees served in one position, rotating at intervals of ten days each month and splitting the meager pay. Casual laborers appointed by the mayor and the city councilors on a quota basis filled the padded payrolls of public works projects, their numbers reaching well over 14,000 in 1965 alone.[21] In a city whose voting population was at the time less than 80,000, the Osmeña-controlled government bureaucracy clearly constituted a major source of employment. Moreover, in the post-Marcos period, despite the expansion of civil service eligibility to more government employees, the passage in 1991 of a new Local Government Code reaffirmed the Cebu City mayor's control over the significantly expanded local bureaucracy.[22]

In addition, the Osmeñas' hold over the agencies of the local state apparatus through the mayor's office allowed the family to exercise considerable regulatory powers over the economy of Cebu City. Osmeña influence over the Cebu City Police Department and the city fiscal's office also permitted highly selective enforcement of the law in the metropolis.[23] Clearly, political and pecuniary considerations often likewise governed the awarding of licenses for street vendors and stalls in the public market by a division of the bloated Office of the Mayor.[24] Meanwhile, the Osmeñista city council used its manifold prerogatives—in levying taxes, granting business permits, special licenses, public works contracts, and monopoly franchises, and enacting ordinances—to control the local economy.[25] Finally, through the Municipal Board and the Board of Assessment Appeals, as well as the Office of the City Assessor, Osmeña mayors retained the authority to review and revise business and property tax assessments in accordance with local political and economic considerations.[26]

Once entrenched in City Hall, the Osmeñas mobilized an elaborate political machine that mustered majorities for the family and its candidates in local, congressional, and national elections. With thousands of ward *líders*, henchmen, and assorted hangers-on spread throughout populous Cebu City, the Osmeñas have thus been able to carry provincial elections and to deliver large blocs of votes to national-level allies among the candidates for the national Senate and the presidency. Even in 1992, despite Marcos-era revisions of the election code that exclude the Cebu City electorate from voting for candidates to provincial posts, Mayor Tommy Osmeña won reelection by a margin of more than 100,000 votes, garnering a majority in 95 percent of the city's precincts, sweeping in his vice-mayor, the two city congressmen, and fifteen of sixteen Osmeñista city councilors, and delivering an impressive bloc of votes to presidential candidate Fidel V. Ramos.[27] Moreover, throughout Cebu Province the Osmeñas used family alliances and patronage to build up a network of small-town notables loyal to the city-based clan. Enjoying election-day treatment from the Constabulary and the Commission on Elections commensurate with their family's influence in Manila, the Osmeñas and their allies also used "ghost" public works projects with huge padded payrolls to mobilize voters and to bankroll massive vote-buying in Cebu Province.[28]

Over the generations, the Osmeñas enhanced and enlarged their property holdings to become by far the single largest landowner in Cebu.[29] Inherited from Severino Osmeña and Nicasio Chiong Veloso or acquired through purchase (from the Bureau of Lands, the Cebu provincial government, and private individuals), Sergio Osmeña Sr.'s landholdings in Cebu totaled more than 1,700 hectares upon his death in 1961, including haciendas in Carcar (598 hectares), Borbon (398 hectares), Carmen (268 hectares), Aloguinsan (213 hectares), and Medellin (129 hectares), as well as large urban properties in Cebu City.[30]

Over the years, critics repeatedly charged Osmeña family members with using political power to enhance the value of their properties. Opponents of Sergio Osmeña Sr., for example,

pointed to his real-estate speculation in the replanning of the city's burnt downtown district in 1905 (which he helped direct as provincial fiscal), the controversial manner in which he came into the Osmeña inheritance, and his use of public resources in the development of his haciendas in Cebu. . . .

Controversy surrounded the Osmeña-owned Cebu Heights Company. The realty business of the company was built around a big tract of the old Banilad Estate (some 37 hectares), titled to Juana Osmeña, Don Sergio's mother, with a 1919 buying price of P.008 or less than one centavo per square meter. Until 1936, when the construction of the Provincial Capitol began, this area was largely uninhabited (except for the old country house of Don Sergio and four or five other houses). It was only after the Capitol complex was begun that the boom in the real-estate business of Cebu Heights started. Don Sergio was instrumental in the Capitol project and in fact donated the lot for the Capitol building.[31]

Accusations against Serging Osmeña in the 1950s likewise focused on a highly questionable exchange of urban properties between the Osmeña-controlled provincial government and the Osmeña-owned Cebu Heights Company, as well as public works projects allegedly designed to enhance the value of Osmeña lands.[32] Adversaries of Emilio ("Lito") Osmeña Jr. in the 1990s raised similar questions about the properties and profits he acquired in connection with the provincial real-estate and construction projects during his term as Cebu provincial governor (1988–92).[33]

The Osmeñas' political influence in Manila and preeminence in Cebu also facilitated the advancement of the family's various business interests. In the prewar period, the Cebu Autobus Company, managed by a crony of Sergio Osmeña Sr., dominated land transportation in Cebu City and Cebu Province with a fleet of more than 100 buses. In the postwar period, a controlling share of the company's stock was purchased by the De La Rama Steamship Company, whose president was none other than Serging Osmeña himself.[34]

The De La Rama Steamship Company, moreover, received considerable assistance from the national government. The company's founder, Esteban De La Rama, owned substantial sugar lands and shares of a sugar central in Negros Occidental, was on friendly terms with Commonwealth President Manuel Quezon, and won a Senate seat on Quezon's Nacionalista slate in 1941. His steamship company, which had held the franchise for the Negros-Iloilo route since its incorporation in 1931, acquired two interisland vessels and three oceangoing vessels with funding from the government-owned National Development Company (NDC) in the last years before World War II. In 1948, Serging Osmeña, who had married Don Esteban's daughter Lourdes De La Rama in 1942, became president of the De La Rama Steamship Company and, with the help of his *compadre*, President Elpidio Quirino, obtained NDC funds for the purchase from Mitsubishi Heavy Industries of three new oceangoing vessels to replace those commandeered by the U.S. Armed Forces and sunk or worn out during the war.[35] Critics of the 15-million-peso deal noted that the agreement between De La Rama and the NDC was signed in October 1949, less than a month before the elections, and that Serging Osmeña reportedly contributed 100,000 pesos to Quirino's presidential campaign that year and publicly pledged 1 million pesos to his reelection bid in 1953.[36] Following Quirino's defeat in the 1953 elections, the Magsaysay administration began to reconsider the terms of the De La

Rama–NDC partnership (which delivered 15 million pesos in profits to the company and more than 1 million pesos in losses to the government) and eventually terminated the 1949 contract.[37] A similar series of events unfolded in 1962, when an Osmeña-controlled company won an exclusive contract from the Cebu City government to reclaim 160 hectares of foreshore along Cebu City and Mandaue. The Osmeña company repurchased the reclaimed land on favorable terms and with generous financing from the government-owned Development Bank of the Philippines. However, with the election of Osmeña nemesis Ferdinand Marcos to the presidency in 1965, local and national opposition to the reclamation mounted and the project eventually ran aground.[38]

## Brokers for Cebu's Local Oligarchy

Access to state resources and control over state office helped to advance the Osmeñas' real-estate interests and other business ventures, but throughout the twentieth century the family remained at best first among equals in Cebu City's commercial élite. A large entourage of political lieutenants, lawyers, contractors, fixers, ward *líders*, and assorted hangers-on always surrounded the Osmeña's leading members, linking local law firms, construction companies, and a host of small businesses to the family's political machine. Moreover, the predominance of unnaturalized Chinese immigrants, mostly Hokkien-speakers from Fujian Province, as proprietors of commercial establishments in Cebu City strengthened the leverage of those entrenched in City Hall over a local capitalist class self-conscious about its foreign origins.[39] Yet the Osmeñas could never simply parcel out sectors of the thriving Visayan port economy among family members and friends in the manner of the Duranos of Danao or the Abineses of southern Cebu. Instead, a close-knit local oligarchy—comprising a handful of merchant dynasties of Chinese, Spanish, and mestizo lineage—operated a cartel of shipping companies and agricultural processing centers in the city that dominated the copra and corn trade throughout the Visayas and Mindanao and the interisland shipping industry of the entire archipelago for many decades.[40] Over the years, these dynasties—the Gotiaocos, Chiongbians, Lus, Aboitizes, and Escaños—consistently supported, socialized and occasionally intermarried with the Osmeña clan, while refraining from entering Cebu politics themselves.[41] In exchange, the Osmeñas provided these dynasties—along with urban real-estate and merchant families like the Aznars, Gaisanos, and Lhuillers—access to government financing and contracts and guaranteed friendly regulation of their business operations.

Consanguinal and affinal ties, as well as bonds of fictive kinship, have linked the Osmeñas to these Cebu City–based merchant dynasties. Members of the Gotiaoco clan, for example, claimed for many years that Sergio Osmeña Sr. was the illegitimate—but recognized—son of family patriarch Pedro Gotiaoco (1856–1921), a turn-of-the-century Chinese immigrant who established Gotiaoco Hermanos, Inc. (a prominent abaca, rice, and copra-trading firm), the Insular Navigation Company (an interisland shipping fleet), and the Visayan Surety and Insurance Corporation (affiliated with a U.S.-based insurance company) in Cebu in the early years of the twentieth century.[42] In 1918 one of Gotiaoco's sons, Manuel Gotianuy, founded the Cebu Shipyard and Engineering Works, Inc., together with a group of other Chinese businessmen.[43] As of 1999, Gotiaoco's grandson remained on the company's board of directors along with executives from major shipping companies and representatives of majority shareholder (since 1989) Keppel Philippines Shipyard, a Singapore-based corporation with interests in two other marine repair facilities in the archipelago.[44] Meanwhile, in the prewar era, Doña Modesta Singson Gaisano, allegedly Gotiaoco's daughter by another wife, founded the Gaisano family's highly successful restaurant, department store, and real-estate empire, which expanded over the years.[45] Finally, Gotiaoco's grandsons by a third wife included two of the Philippines' most prominent multi-billionaire Filipino Chinese tycoons: banking, food, real-estate, and manufacturing magnate John Gokongwei Jr., and banking and real-estate mogul Andrew Gotianun. In short, successive generations not only maintained but even expanded the fortune passed on to them by family patriarch Pedro Gotiaoco. Although claims to consanguinal ties between various Gotiaocos and Osmeñas may well be apocryphal, reports that Sergio Osmeña Sr. kissed the hand of his supposed father in gratitude for his financial support ring true to those familiar with the intertwined stories of these two dynasties' business and political success.[46]

Over the years, the Osmeñas also maintained close ties to the Aboitizes; a granddaughter of Sergio Osmeña Sr. married a scion of this prominent Spanish mestizo clan. Family patriarch Paulino Aboitiz was a seafarer of Basque extraction who settled in the Visayan island province of Leyte in the late nineteenth century. He married the daughter of a Basque shipowner and became a major figure in the abaca trade between Leyte and Cebu.[47] With generous funding and lenient credit terms from the Cebu branch of the government-owned Philippine National Bank (PNB) in 1917,[48] his descendants expanded their family abaca business but quickly switched to the more lucrative copra trade in the post–World War I boom. By the eve of World War II, the Aboitizes had become the second-largest copra exporters in the Philippines. In 1928, moreover, together with the Escaño clan, the Aboitizes founded La Naviera Filipina, which became the largest interisland shipping company in the Visayas in the interwar era.[49] After World War II, the Aboitiz family established its own shipping lines, diversified into logging (West Basilan Timber Company, Port Banga Timber Company), flour milling (Pillsbury-Mindanao Flour Milling Corporation), banking (Cebu City Savings and Loan Association, First Insular Bank of Cebu, Union Bank of the Philippines), manufacturing (Aboitiz Manufacturing, Pilipinas Kao, Cebu Oxygen & Acetylene), and real estate. With landholdings in Leyte, logging concessions in Mindanao and Basilan (in the 1950s), and four electric companies in their hands, the Aboitizes created an extensive empire linking Cebu to its hinterlands in the Visayas and Mindanao.[50]

Over the years, the Aboitizes depended upon the Osmeñas for a variety of business favors. In purchasing the Cebu Ice and Cold Storage Plant in 1917, founding electric companies in Leyte, Mindanao, and Sulu, and owning shares in Metro Cebu's Visayan Electric Company, the Aboitizes often required—and received—assistance in acquiring and renewing franchises and protection from critics of their local electric power monopolies.[51] Successive Osmeñas handed Aboitiz companies lucrative franchises and contracts, such as the Cebu City jai-alai fronton concession in the 1960s and the controversial provincial road-paving projects of the early 1990s.[52] With Osmeñas as their business partners and political patrons, the Aboitizes also allegedly received preferential treatment for their companies from government regulatory agencies.[53]

Another example of the close personal ties that have bound the Osmeñas and these preeminent merchant dynasties together was the June 1964 marriage of Victor S. Chiongbian and Maria Luisa Cabrera Briones.[54] The bride was the daughter of José Briones, a loyal Osmeña political lieutenant who served as Cebu provincial governor from 1956 through 1961 and held the 2nd district seat in Congress for two terms (1961–65, 1965–69) before stepping down to make way for John Osmeña. The groom was the son of William Chiongbian, a longtime congressman from Misamis Occidental (1953–72, 1987–92)[55] whose family's Cebu-based shipping company—William Lines—had expanded its interisland fleet by purchasing three vessels from Serging Osmeña's De La Rama Steamship Company in 1949.[56] Over the years, William Lines evolved into one of the leading interisland shipping firms, even as the Chiongbians' other business interests expanded to include a fleet of oceangoing vessels (Eastern Shipping Lines), a paper mill, two fishing companies, a food-processing conglomerate (Virginia Food Products, Inc.), and a network of prawn farms, cattle ranches, piggeries, and plantations in Cebu and Mindanao.[57]

Other noteworthy figures in the bridal entourage included principal sponsors Lourdes Osmeña (wife of Sergio Osmeña Jr.), Cayetano Lu Do, Asuncion Escaño, best man Douglas Lu Ym, and bridesmaid Teresita Escaño. Cayetano Lu Do and his nephew Douglas Lu Ym were descendants of family patriarch Lu Do, who immigrated to Cebu in 1889 from Xiamen (Amoy), Fujian. They occupied key managerial positions in the Lu Do & Lu Ym Corporation, a company prominent in the coconut and corn products industry and in the Cebu City real-estate market. The Lu family had operated a coconut oil factory before World War II; in 1945 it used U.S. government contracts to rebuild and in 1951 received U.S. Mutual Security Agency funding to build a large cornstarch manufacturing plant in Cebu.[58] Rebuilt and expanded after World War II, the Lu Do & Lu Ym Corporation's coconut oil refinery, moreover, became the largest in Asia, said to have handled between one-third and one-half of all Philippine coconut exports in the postwar era.[59] The Lus' Philippine Corn Products, founded in the early 1960s, processed corn from all over the Visayas and Mindanao. The family of Asuncion and Teresita Escaño traces its roots back to Spanish merchants who bought up land in Leyte in the late nineteenth century and played a prominent role in the abaca and sugar trade that linked the hinterlands of Leyte to Chinese and Spanish compradors and foreign commercial houses in the Visayan entrepôt of Cebu. Already owners of steamboats by the late 1890s, the Escaños later established their own interisland shipping company, the Escaño Lines, a sizable fleet of passenger and cargo vessels. The centerpiece of the Escaños' business empire, however, has been the Visayan Electric Company (VECO), established in 1905 and managed by family members since they became principal stockholders in 1918.[60] Having won a 50-year franchise from the Philippine legislature (dominated by Sergio Osmeña Sr.'s Nacionalista Party) in 1928,[61] VECO remained the sole distributor of electricity in greater metropolitan Cebu throughout the century, despite recurring attacks on its "exorbitant rates and inefficiency,"[62] persistent power failures and brownouts,[63] and fraudulent billing practices.[64]

In the early 1990s, the Osmeñas' willingness to service the business interests of Cebu City's leading merchant dynasties were apparent in the policies of Mayor Tommy Osmeña and his cousin, former provincial governor Lito Osmeña. While the Cebu City Assessor's Office allegedly undervalued the real-estate holdings of Osmeña allies, the provincial government sold off plots of prime urban land to the Gaisano family and to Michel Lhuiller, one of Lito Osmeña's closest associates.[65] Lhuiller, descendant of a former French consul to Cebu and owner of a nationwide network of pawnshops and jewelry stores, was also reported to have sponsored the import of the illegal narcotic methamphetamine hydrochloride ("shabu") through the Cebu Port and the Mactan-Cebu International Airport, allegedly with the active assistance of Bureau of Customs and Philippine National Police officials installed by the Osmeñas.[66] In 1992, moreover, Lito Osmeña engineered the appointment of Cebu-based attorney Jesus Garcia Jr. as secretary of the Department of Transportation and Communication.[67] Garcia had previously served as legal counsel to the Conference of Interisland Shipowners and Operators, the cartel of mostly Cebu-based shipping lines—including the Aboitiz, Chiongbian, and Escaño companies—whose collusion in setting cargo and passenger rates, oligopolistic practices in sharing and dividing interisland routes, violations of safety and other regulations, and successes in obtaining tax and tariff exemptions had come under mounting criticism in recent years.[68] As transportation secretary, Garcia helped to protect the shipping cartel's interests throughout the archipelago during a period of rapid deregulation, while monitoring the local front as chairman of the newly created, autonomous, and powerful Cebu Port Authority and the Mactan-Cebu International Airport Authority.[69]

Over the years, successive Osmeñas also serviced the interests of Manila-based magnates with investments in Cebu. Sergio Osmeña Sr., for example, assisted and purchased shares in the Madrigal Oil Mill, which was owned by his long-time friend Vicente Madrigal, the Manila-based business tycoon.[70] Serging Osmeña likewise maintained a close alliance with the managers of the Soriano family–owned Atlas Consolidated Mining and Development Corporation, whose operations in Toledo City, Cebu, constituted the largest copper-mining complex in East Asia.[71] He also included prominent Manila businessmen like Francisco Delgado and Carlos Palanca Jr. among the incorporators of his own Cebu-based real-estate company, the Cebu Development Corporation.[72] In his term as provincial governor of Cebu, Lito Osmeña similarly established a close alliance with the Ayala family, whose Makati-based banking, food processing, and real-estate empire teamed up with the Cebu provincial government in a major land development deal and bond issue.[73] In this deal, Cebu Province sold three parcels of land in Cebu City totaling 251 hectares for more than 700 million pesos to the Cebu Property Ventures and Development Corporation, a joint venture between the provincial government of Cebu and the Ayala Land Corporation.[74] A further tie-up has linked the Ayalas' Cebu interests to mining, publishing, and real-estate mogul Alfredo Ramos, the Soriano family, and the Asia-wide empire of Malaysia-born, Hong Kong–based taipan Robert Kuok.[75] Meanwhile, the Osmeñas also reportedly intervened on behalf of major Manila-based companies bidding for two controversial reclamation and construction contracts.[76]

Because the Osmeñas' business and political success always depended on the cooperation of national patrons in Malacañang, the dynasty experienced the greatest difficulties when in conflict with hostile presidents. In the 1930s and 1940s, for example, presidents Quezon and Roxas supported the Cuenco clan in Cebu as a foil against their rival, Sergio Osmeña Sr., whose son subsequently reclaimed supremacy in the province with the support of President Quirino once the Cuencos ran afoul of Malacañang.[77] In the late 1950s, Serging Osmeña likewise found himself under political siege when Boholano president Carlos Garcia attempted to make Cebu part of his Visayan regional bailiwick. Garcia built up Congressman Ramon Durano, filled local government offices and padded public payrolls with his supporters in the province, and supplied the prominent Uytengsu family, long active in the copra trade, with the government licenses and funds to start up a major flour mill in Opon (now Lapu-Lapu City).[78] During Marcos's two elected presidential terms (1966–69, 1970–72), he similarly worked to undermine the Cebu base of Serging Osmeña, who ran against him for the presidency in 1969.[79] During the martial-law era, moreover, while Serging and other Osmeñas were in exile in the United States, Marcos named a close associate of his wife, Eduardo Gullas, Cebu provincial governor and installed a similarly pliable figure as Cebu City mayor.[80]

During this period, Marcos and his cronies also seized key sectors of the Cebu economy. For example, Marcos forged a close alliance with the Associated Labor Unions, based on the Cebu waterfront, promoting its leaders to patronage-rich government posts and high-ranking posts in the Trade Union Congress of the Philippines. Marcos's golf partner, construction magnate Rodolfo Cuenca, obtained the franchise for major stevedoring operations in the Cebu port area, even as Marcos associate Alfonso Yuchengco and frontmen José Yao Campos and Rolando Gapud wrested the contracts for reclamation projects along the foreshore area of Cebu City and Mandaue City from companies controlled by the Osmeñas and their allies.[81] Meanwhile, the coconut industry in Cebu fell under the aegis of an interlocking directorate of government and quasi-government monopolistic/monopsonistic agencies run by Marcos crony Eduardo Cojuangco Jr. and Defense Minister Juan Ponce Enrile.[82] The United Coconut Mills, a Cojuangco-and-Enrile-directed conglomerate of mills and trading companies that monopolized both copra milling and trading, incorporated the Lu Do & Lu Ym Corporation's extensive facilities into its empire and named Douglas Lu Ym executive vice-president for marketing and a member of the Board of Directors.[83] Finally, previously obscure Anos Fonacier, a town-mate of President Marcos from Sarrat, Ilocos Norte, assumed great prominence in Cebu, taking over the

Aboitiz family's jai-alai fronton franchise, publishing his own daily newspaper, and obtaining massive government funding to build a luxury hotel in Cebu City and several tourist resorts on Mactan Island and elsewhere in the province.[84]

This heavy-handed intervention by Marcos in the local economy, however, prompted Cebu's opposition politicians and disaffected élite families to rally around the Osmeña family in the early to mid 1980s. Thus, with the ouster of Marcos and the inauguration of Corazon C. Aquino as president in February 1986, the third generation of the Osmeña dynasty was able to resurrect its urban political machine and its preeminence among the leading Chinese and Spanish mestizo merchant dynasties of Cebu City. Today, with their protégés installed in Cebu City Hall and the provincial capitol, and with a visible presence on the national stage, Don Sergio Osmeña's grandsons—Lito, Sonny, Tommy, and Serge—are well placed to extend the family dynasty well into the twenty-first century.

## Conclusion

At the provincial level, the Osmeña family dynasty dominated the political and economic life of Cebu for most of the twentieth century. It used its urban political machine in Cebu City and its alliances with major mercantile interests in the port metropolis to entrench itself over the generations. Unlike the congressional district–level dynasties in their bailiwicks, however, the Osmeña family never seized monopolistic control over the Cebu economy. While not ashamed to promote family real-estate holdings and other business concerns by means of state resources and powers, the Osmeñas have been careful to identify their interests with those of Cebu City's close-knit local oligarchy, whose cartelized shipping companies, copra and corn-processing facilities, and manufacturing concerns have long benefited from government largesse. Thus Tommy and Lito Osmeña closely associated themselves with the rapid growth of the city and the province, a phenomenon popularly known as "Ceboom." Unlike the dynasties in the rural congressional districts of Cebu, moreover, the Osmeñas have successfully evaded direct implication in electoral violence and illegal economies, though their ward *líders* and business affiliates certainly engaged in coercive and unlawful practices with the family's acquiescence, and even encouragement.

Overall, this two-tiered pattern of dynastic entrenchment at the congressional-district and provincial levels in Cebu reflects both the structure of state institutions and the nature of the local political economy. On the one hand, the division of Cebu Province into seven or more congressional districts laid the groundwork for supramunicipal empires to be constructed with the pork-barrel, patronage, and other privileges afforded all members of the House of Representatives. The broad definition of the Cebu City charter likewise facilitated the emergence and consolidation of an urban political machine in a metropolis whose voting population could—until excluded by a revised electoral code in the 1970s—swing election contests in the entire province. On the other hand, the importance of major production sites outside Cebu City—Danao coal mines, Bogo-Medellin plantations and sugar mill, South China Sea fishing beds—in the provincial economy of Cebu underpinned the empires of supramunicipal dynasties in several rural congressional districts. Similarly, the overwhelming concentration of capital, government resources, and population in Cebu City has guaranteed the long-term hegemony of this preeminent entrepôt and manufacturing center of the Visayas and Mindanao over the hinterlands of Cebu Province. Control over this considerable economic and electoral base has allowed the Osmeñas, unlike their counterparts in Cavite, to assert themselves in national politics, both in the Senate and in recurring bids for the presidency.

Although the dynastic nature and two-tiered structure of boss rule in Cebu contrasts with that observed in Cavite, a similar pattern of variation over time is observable in both provinces. In Cavite and Cebu, bosses have emerged and prospered with the assistance of national-level patrons but foundered upon the intervention of opponents in Malacañang. While the district- and provincial-level dynasties of Cebu have claimed more solid bases in the local economy than their counterparts in Cavite, long-entrenched politicians in both provinces (Justiniano Montano Sr. of Cavite and Serging Osmeña of Cebu) found themselves economically dislodged or (in Montano's case) politically destroyed when their common archenemy, Ferdinand E. Marcos, established himself as the Philippines' first and only national-level boss. The final chapter of this book thus concludes with a reexamination of the small-town, congressional, and provincial bosses of Cavite and Cebu in light of the bossism observed in other parts of the Philippine archipelago and at the national level.

# Bossism in Comparative Perspective

The preceding chapters illustrate the resilience of bossism in the Philippines over the course of the twentieth century. Against the backdrop of an unfolding process of capital accumulation, numerous bosses vied for the spoils of elected office by subordinating—rather than submitting to—the state apparatus in their pursuit of wealth and power. Far less an example of oligarchical and clientelistic politics than it is typically portrayed, bossism as a social formation persisted in the twentieth-century Philippines, due in large part to the imposition of formal electoral democratic institutions upon an underdeveloped state apparatus at an early phase of capitalist development. As E. P. Thompson, commenting on "Old Corruption" England of the eighteenth century, noted:

This is a recognized phase of commercial capitalism when predators fight for the spoils of power and have not yet agreed to submit to rational or bureaucratic rules and forms. Each politician, by nepotism, interest and purchase, gathered around him a following of loyal dependents. The aim was to reward them by giving them some post in which they could milk some part of the public revenue: army finances, the Church, excise. Every post carried its perquisites, percentages, commissions, receipts of bribes, its hidden spoils. The plum jobs of office . . . were worth fortunes. The great commercial interests (whether in merchanting or finance) depended also upon political and military favors, and these could be paid for at a high rate. The great gentry, speculators and politicians were men of huge wealth, whose income towered like the Andes above the rain-forests of the common man's poverty.[1]

As this recognized phase of capitalist development has unfolded in other contexts, however, "Old Corruption" has assumed a variety of new forms. Shaped by the distinctive institutional legacies of U.S. colonial rule, and by its position as a late, late industrializer in the global capitalist economy, the Philippines has seen this social formation crystallize in a system of bossism.

## Local Bosses in the Philippines:
## Beyond Cavite and Cebu

This book has presented case studies of bosses in the Philippine provinces of Cavite and Cebu. Rather than emphasizing the intrinsic "prowess" of these "big men" and family dynasties, the case studies highlight the crucial contextual factors—the structure of state institutions and concentrations of private capital—that facilitated bosses' emergence and entrenchment and that explain the geographic and historical variation in boss longevity.[2] Rather than focusing on the legitimacy these bosses have enjoyed in their respective bailiwicks, the case studies reveal how the projection of charismatic authority and the simulation of patronage obscure the bosses' heavy reliance on derivative, coercive state power and their central role in capital accumulation on a local level.[3]

Defining bosses as power brokers with monopolistic personal control over coercive and economic resources in their territorial jurisdictions or bailiwicks, this study has outlined the structural conditions that explain variations in the emergence, location, and longevity of rule by small-town, congressional district–level, and provincial bosses. In short, bosses have emerged and entrenched themselves when and where the local political economy has lent itself most readily and most fully to monopolistic control, through illegal activities, nodal commercial and transportation chokepoints, public lands, and heavily regulated crops and industries. Insofar as such monopolistic control over the local economy has hinged on state-based derivative and discretionary powers, single-generation mafia-style bosses have depended and heavily on superordinate power brokers for backing; similarly, a backer's hostility has spelled a boss's downfall or death. Insofar as monopolistic control over the local economy has rested upon a solid base in proprietary wealth outside the realm of state intervention, bosses have withstood the hostile machinations of superordinate power brokers and successfully passed on their bailiwicks to successive generations in classic dynastic form. The bulk of the detail laid out in the preceding chapters illustrates these patterns in the provinces of Cavite and Cebu.

Although Cavite and Cebu are not entirely representative of the Philippines as a whole, the patterns observed within their boundaries shed new light upon local politics in other provinces and on the underlying structures and trajectories of bossism throughout the archipelago. At the district and provincial levels, the contrast between Cavite-style state-based bosses and Cebu-style capital-intensive dynasties is readily apparent elsewhere in the Philippines. In Ilocos Sur, for example, the predominance of small landholdings and a heavily state-subsidized and state-regulated tobacco industry have underpinned the long rule of two successive provincial bosses, Floro Crisologo (1946–70) and Luis Singson (1971 to the present).[4] In Negros Occidental, by contrast, the concentration of landholdings in large sugar plantations and the establishment of several sugar centrals in the interwar period prefigured the entrenchment of district-level dynasties such as the Gatuslaos, Gustilos, Lacsons, Ledesmas, Montelibanos, Pueys, and Yulos in the province.[5] Other longtime frontier-zone provincial warlords such as Salipada Pendatun of Cotabato and Ali Dimaporo of Lanao[6] likewise contrast with established landed clans such as the Romualdezes, Tans, and Velosos of Leyte, the Imperials of Albay, the Fortiches of Bukidnon, the Roxases of Capiz, the Teveses and Romeros of Negros Oriental, and the Cojuangcos of Tarlac.

Additional subcategories that fit within the broader scheme outlined in previous chapters include urban bosses who lord over large squatter settlements, Chinese immigrant business communities, and/or lucrative illegal economies;[7] machine politicians operating in condominium with landed clans;[8] small-time political operators who evolve into large landowners and local business magnates;[9] and major logging concessionaires.[10] Nationwide, the diversity of Philippine bossism thus replicates the full spectrum of bosses found in Cavite and Cebu: single-generation, mafia-style bosses without private economic bases (Montano, Remulla); mafia-style bosses who succeed in using state resources to establish private economic empires and political dynasties (Escario, Durano); dynasties whose proprietary wealth provides a solid basis for protracted boss rule (the Abines clan); and dynasties that combine proprietary wealth, state-based resources, and brokerage services to local landed and commercial oligarchies (the Martinez and Osmeña clans).

## A National Boss:
## President Ferdinand E. Marcos, 1966–86

While local bosses flourished in municipalities, congressional districts, and provinces over the course of the twentieth century, the distinctive institutional structures of the Philippine state, the pattern of private capital formation, and the intervention of a superordinate power (the U.S. government) for the most part obstructed the ascension of boss rule to the presidential level. For example, alongside the American-style single-district, single-representative House of Representatives, the bicameral national legislature has a Senate whose 24 members are elected nationally. Because they have no institutionally defined regional jurisdictions and must compete for votes throughout the archipelago, senators depend heavily on party organizations, personal networks of client congressmen, governors, mayors, and ward *líders*, and large sums of money to ensure their reelection.[11]

The Senate has thus been both effectively beyond the reach of most provincial bosses and institutionally unreceptive to the concentration of national power in the hands of a single boss. Unlike the congressional district–level bosses discussed in Chapter 5, the most successful candidates for the Senate have been those able to mobilize votes through region-wide political machines—or populous and wealthy provinces like the Osmeñas' Cebu—or through some claim to popular fame and favor (e.g., television/film/sports stardom).[12] More important, senators have needed to raise large sums of money from private backers and by exploiting state resources.[13] Thus, for example, over the course of the twentieth century, three successive generations of Osmeñas translated their Cebu-wide provincial political machine and close connections to key segments of the national oligarchy into Senate seats.

In any event, Philippine presidents, who in the pre-martial-law period typically emerged from among the ranks of senators, have had to contend with a legislative body whose members claim nationwide interests and electoral strength, and whose support they need to take legislative action, assert administrative control, and win reelection. With its powers enshrined in the Constitution and its 24 members proven in the national electoral arena, the Senate has often served as the Trojan horse and launching pad for anti-administration opposition forces and campaigns against the reelection bids of presidential incumbents, thus preventing the entrenchment of national bosses.

Moreover, a national oligarchy—composed of sugar barons, urban real-estate moguls, shipping magnates, industrial tycoons, and commercial bankers—has further reinforced factional competition for the presidency and thwarted national state-based monopoly by generously funding opposition candidates and preventing the national economy from falling into the hands of a single predatory boss.[14] Finally, the U.S. government, through occasionally heavy-handed intervention and otherwise soft-shoed orchestration, has tended to promote presidential turnover after Manuel Quezon's death and Philippine independence in the mid-1940s.[15]

Longtime president Ferdinand Marcos was the only boss able to overcome these obstacles under conditions strikingly similar to those enjoyed by the small-town, district-level, and provincial bosses examined in the previous chapters. Banking on the increasing availability of foreign loans and assistance programs,[16] exploiting the multiplying opportunities for state intervention in "development,"[17] and manipulating the growing dependence of the oligarchy on government loans and special incentives,[18] Marcos began in his first term (1966–69) to extend the prerogatives of the presidency to include supervisory powers over a National Police Commission and an expanding Armed Forces of the Philippines and regulatory powers over the national economy.[19] Benefiting from the importance of Philippine air and naval bases to the American war effort in Indochina and the support of the Nixon administration in Washington, D.C., Marcos won reelection in 1969 with the U.S. government's blessings and, abolishing Congress, declared martial law in September 1972 with full American backing.[20]

From September 1972 to Marcos's ouster in 1986, the Philippines thus experienced a protracted period of national-level boss rule. Freed from legislative interference, Marcos ruled by decree, centralizing national police forces under the Armed Forces of the Philippines, establishing quasi-government monopolies for major commodity exports, and parceling out regulatory and/or proprietary control over the other strategic sectors of the national economy—banking, construction, energy, food processing, gambling, media, ports, telecommunications, transportation—among a close circle of family members, cronies, and frontmen.[21] As detailed in the chapters on Cavite and Cebu, this centralization of coercive and economic powers in the hands of Marcos and his mafia had dramatic consequences throughout the archipelago. Only in the mid-1980s, when the world recession and the ensuing domestic financial crisis led to government bankruptcy and the U.S. government began to withdraw its support did Marcos's national boss rule come to a close.[22] Like other single-generation, mafia-style bosses, Marcos's inability to establish a solid economic base outside the reach of state intervention prevented him from withstanding the hostile intervention of a superordinate power and passing on his national empire to successive generations.[23]

Yet even as Marcos's long reign demonstrated the possibilities for boss rule at the national level, his downfall in 1986 also highlighted the limitations on bossism in the Philippines imposed by changing domestic and international economic and political circumstances. Just as the flood of private capital into Cavite and Cebu subordinated local bosses to

Manila-based magnates and foreign firms, so has the flow of post-1986 private investment in the Philippines subjugated the national executive and legislative branches to the pressures of international finance and domestic monopoly capital. As the U.S. facilities at Subic Bay and Clark Air Field reverted to the Philippines in the 1990s, presidential control over externally derived "rents" shrank correspondingly. With the restoration of Congress and the subsequent relocalization of control over the coercive, extractive, and regulatory agencies of the state apparatus, moreover, the possibilities for a reassertion of national boss rule in the twenty-first century are severely circumscribed.[24]

## Philippine Bossism in Comparative Perspective

While explaining patterns of bossism found at municipal, district, provincial, and even national levels, this book also portrays the structure of Philippine politics in tones strikingly at odds with the dominant paradigms in the available scholarly literature on the archipelago. Unlike accounts that depict Philippine politics in terms of clientelist networks and portray violence as the symptoms of the breakdown of patron-client ties, this study shows that coercion has persistently and systematically intruded upon electoral competition, economic exploitation, and social relations. An examination of the complex processes through which inequality, indebtedness, landlessness, and poverty are created has highlighted how so-called patrons have expropriated the natural and human resources of the archipelago from the broad mass of the population, thereby generating and sustaining the scarcity, insecurity, and dependency that underpin their rule as bosses. In this context, the myth of small-town and provincial politicians' personal prowess and beneficence obfuscates the derivative and predatory nature of their power while projecting legitimacy claims based on precolonial big-man authority and precapitalist norms regarding the "social use of property."[25]

As a corrective to the many descriptions of the Philippines that emphasize the tenacity and power of the national oligarchy, moreover, this study underscores the extent to which control over the agencies of the state provides the key to capital accumulation, rather than vice versa. From the communal lands of Mayor Casal's Carmona to the government-financed cement factory of Congressman Durano's Danao, myriad forms of state resources have been shown to provide the bases from which small-time political operators ascend to heights of considerable wealth and power. Contesting Migdal and others' caricature of an emasculated "weak" state lacking in autonomy, this study highlights "the abil-

ity of state leaders to use the agencies of the state to get people in the society to do what they want them to do."[26] Successive case studies have detailed the Philippine state's impressive capacity "to *penetrate* society, *regulate* social relationships, *extract* resources, and *appropriate* or use
resources in determined ways"[27] and have underscored the weakness of
constraints imposed upon many state leaders by "any set of organized social interests."[28] In short, while the Philippine state appears relatively
weak in its failings as a "developmental state," it has also been shown to
be somewhat stronger in its capacity as a "predatory state," for "those
who control the state apparatus seem to plunder without any more regard for the welfare of the citizenry than a predator has for the welfare of
its prey."[29]

The Philippine state is neither simply a resource for patron-client relations nor merely an object of oligarchical plunder. It is also a complex set
of predatory mechanisms for the private exploitation and accumulation
of the archipelago's human, natural, and monetary resources. Discrimi-
natory enforcement of laws and regulations, discretionary provision of
monopoly franchises, concessions and contracts, and diversionary collection of public revenues and disbursement of public land, funds, and employment have served as the essential instruments of state-based preda-
tion. Owing to the distinctive institutional legacies of successive stages of
colonial state formation, the main predators have been elected government officials and their allies, who retained control over the state apparatus throughout the twentieth century. With regular elections designed
to provide a measure of competition and turnover, and executive and legislative powers dispersed horizontally and vertically among municipal
mayors, provincial governors, congressmen, senators and presidents, the
Philippine state, even under the authoritarian Marcos regime, remained
essentially a multitiered racket. Though never wholly nor solely a racket,
the Philippine state's racket-like dimensions decisively shaped electoral
competition, capital accumulation, and social relations in the archipelago
over the course of the twentieth century.

Viewed in cross-national historical comparative perspective, Philippine
bossism appears less a unique phenomenon than a particular manifestation of a more generalized social formation found when the trappings of
formal electoral democracy are superimposed upon a state apparatus at
an early stage of capital accumulation. Bossism, in short, reflects a common conjuncture in state formation and capitalist development: the decisive subordination of the state apparatus to elected officials against the
backdrop of what might loosely be termed "primitive accumulation."
Primitive accumulation here refers to a phase of capitalist development in
which a significant section of the population has lost direct control over

the means of production and direct access to means of subsistence, and has been reduced to a state of economic insecurity and dependence on scarce wage labor (before the achievement of "full" employment and modern welfare capitalism). Under conditions of primitive accumulation, moreover, considerable economic resources and prerogatives remain in the "public" domain and secure (private) property rights have not yet been firmly established by the state. Taken together, these features of a society render many voters susceptible to clientelistic, coercive, and monetary pressures and guarantee the centrality of state-based resources and prerogatives for capital accumulation and control over the "commanding heights" of local economies.

Seen in this light, bossism has flourished in various forms around the globe since the days of "Old Corruption" in eighteenth-century England. In southern Europe, for example, the introduction of competitive elections in the last few decades of the nineteenth century prefigured the emergence of Spanish caciques and Italian mafia, local bosses who thrived under the formal auspices of parliamentary democracy.[30] In the nation-states of the postcolonial world, moreover, Filipino bosses had contemporary counterparts in local and state politicians in various parts of India and in the rural and urban caciques of Latin America.[31] Unlike in the Philippines, however, mass struggles for independence, national revolutions, and civil wars and other military conflicts generated major institutional obstacles to national "boss" rule: party machineries with centralized state control over key sectors of the national economy (e.g., Mexico's Partido Revolucionario Institucional, or PRI; India's Congress Party) or military institutions with considerable autonomy from elected officials and potential for decisive and prolonged interventions in national politics.[32] Similarly, in the petty despotisms of Central America and the Caribbean, officers of a centralized National Guard, rather than elected politicians, have succeeded in establishing protracted periods of strongman rule.[33] In short, "bossism" is common in democracies with underdeveloped and weakly insulated state apparatuses and in phases of capitalist "primitive accumulation."

## Bossism in Southeast Asia: The Case of Thailand

This argument linking bossism to democracy and "primitive accumulation" finds considerable support in a comparative analysis of bossism's manifestations throughout Southeast Asia as a whole. Broadly speaking, the only other country in the region where local bosses have achieved power and prominence analogous to what has been illustrated in the

Philippines is, curiously, Thailand. In Thailand and the Philippines, "democratization"—the subordination of the state apparatus to elected officials—was central in facilitating the growth of bossism, but not elsewhere in Southeast Asia. A comparative sociological analysis of the Thai state and institutional structures, moreover, highlights those factors that best explain variations in bossism in the two countries.

The incorporation of the dynastic realm known as Siam into the world economy in the mid-nineteenth century brought with it a centralized bureaucracy virtually unencumbered by concessions to localized forces of sociolinguistic diversity and residual aristocratic privilege.[34] With the fin-de-siècle creation of a Ministry of the Interior and a Ministry of Finance, the famously "modernizing" monarch Chulalongkorn (Rama V) succeeded in subordinating various principalities on the fringes of the realm to the exertions and exactions of policing and revenue-collecting agents dispatched from Bangkok and, with a rapidly achieved regularity, rotated from district to district and province to province.[35] Moreover, after the coup d'état of 1932, control over this apparatus of provincial administration shifted in the postwar era from the hands of absolutizing monarchs to avowedly anticommunist and "development"-oriented military officers, in what came to be known as a well-insulated (if internally factionalized) "bureaucratic polity."[36]

In this context, the institutional constraints upon embryonic local bossism were significant. The steady growth of rice cultivation did provide ample opportunities for capital accumulation through control over the expanding circuitries of production and distribution, and a provincial economic élite accordingly emerged, based in landownership, moneylending, milling, marketing, and transportation as well as such illegal activities as gambling and smuggling. At the local level, moreover, the election of lifetime village headmen (*phuyaiban*) and, for groupings of several villages, commune (*tambon*) headmen (*kamnan*) did allow small-town businessmen to exercise a measure of influence over the flow of central government patronage. A pattern of what James C. Scott has called "market corruption" thrived, with pliable and predatory local agents of various central government ministries open to the "purchase" of their discretionary and regulatory powers over the local economy.[37]

Yet these local government officials were only available, as it were, for temporary rent rather than permanent sale, and at prices to a considerable extent dictated by competitive bidding, because decisions about appointment, promotion, removal, and transfer were made by Bangkok-based bureaucrats rather than up-country bosses. An analogous pattern was observable at the national level: the dominant banking empires were obliged to include ranking army generals on their boards of directors, and the syndicates running the illegal narcotics trade were operated by rival cliques within the military establishment.[38]

By the 1970s, however, three interrelated changes had begun to expand the domain for local bossism in Thailand. First, steady and rapid economic growth, stimulated in no small part by the American-sponsored Vietnam War boom in the country, greatly expanded and multiplied the activities, resources, and external links of the provincial élites in the Thai countryside. Owners of paddy fields and rice mills rechanneled capital into gasoline stations and ice plants, mining claims and logging concessions, construction companies and real-estate firms, and began cultivating Bangkok-based banks for loans and district- and province-level bureaucrats for building permits, land titles, public works contracts, zoning ordinances, and various concessions, franchises, and regulatory breaks. Second, with the growth of armed revolutionary movements in neighboring Laos and Cambodia and the emergence of peasant-based organizations and mobilizational efforts in some areas of the Thai countryside, the government in Bangkok initiated a "counterinsurgency" campaign that entailed both the infusion of considerable state funds for "rural development" and the creation of local paramilitary organizations in rural communities. These intertwined processes broadened the scope and volume of resource flows and state-based prerogatives available to provincial businessmen in rural Thailand.[39]

Third, the social forces generated by the Vietnam War boom began to combine with the internal contradictions of army rule to shift national-level power away from the military establishment and toward previously ceremonial and impotent parliamentary institutions. Although an initial period of unprecedented openness in 1973–76 led to a brutal right-wing backlash against the most vocal proponents of democratization, the intensity of factional rivalries at the highest echelons of the army derailed efforts to reconstruct a military-dominated "bureaucratic polity" and delivered increasing political leverage and legislative authority into the hands of parliament.[40] Thus, although an appointed Senate and threats of a coup d'état left considerable power in military hands, Bangkok's agribusiness, banking, commercial, and industrial magnates began to view parliament as an essential avenue of influence and rechanneled their resources accordingly. Bangkok-based magnates commanded tremendous financial resources, but only province-based businessmen enjoyed links to large blocs of voters in the country's overwhelmingly rural constituencies, and parliamentary seats promised influence over (or inclusion among) Cabinet ministers, central ministries, and local agents of the Thai state.

With the vast majority of parliamentary (multiple-seat) constituencies located in rural areas, it is thus no surprise that by 1990 nearly half of the members of the Cabinet were identified as provincial businessmen.[41]

Against this backdrop, by the mid-1980s, observers of Thai politics had begun to comment on the growing manifestations of local bossism, most prominently with reference to what have come to be known as *chao pho* (or *jao poh*), Thai "godfathers" of a distinctly mafioso variety. These *chao pho* conducted interrelated activities in three realms: the economy, elections, and the state's coercive apparatus. First, the economic activities of *chao pho* are quite visible within loosely defined territorial bailiwicks, where they accumulate proprietary wealth (agricultural land, real estate, mills, processing centers, factories; shares in banks and industrial firms), acquire state-derived concessions, contracts, and franchises (e.g., logging, mining, public works, transport), and operate illegal rackets (e.g., in the drug trade, gambling, smuggling). Second, *chao pho* have achieved great prominence and power through their successful service as—or provision of—vote brokers (*hua khanaen*) in elections, delivering parliamentary constituencies, or regional clusters of constituencies, to Bangkok-based patrons, local clients, or themselves on election day, through a combination of coercion, vote-buying, and electoral fraud. Third, *chao pho* are notorious for their control over the local tentacles of the state, most notably its coercive apparatuses, and their ability to achieve effective local monopolies over the organization of (statal and extrastatal) violence within their bailiwicks, for use in capital accumulation, electoral manipulation, and enforcement of illegal rackets.[42]

Contemporary Thai bossism differs from that in the Philippines in two key respects. First, the transfer of effective control over the state apparatus to elected officials came relatively late in the process of capitalist development, when enormous Bangkok-based financial, agribusiness, and industrial conglomerates and up-country magnates with province- or region-wide empires were already entrenched and equipped with ample resources for electoral competition. Thus prominent Bangkok bankers and industrialists have themselves assumed political party leadership posts or otherwise engineered alliances with regional clusters of *chao pho*, and provincial businessmen have in some cases exercised *chao pho*-like influence over multiple constituencies or even provinces.[43]

Second, the subordination of the state apparatus to a parliament drawn from multiple-seat constituencies and without proportional representation has encouraged a highly fluid system of political parties held together largely by patronage networks (regional and national) and personal ties and coalition governments stitched together through multiparty Cabinets.[44] Thus *chao pho* exercising control over several constituencies have found it relatively easy to install themselves or their stooges in the Cabinet and thereby to wield considerable influence over the internal affairs of key central ministries and their local agencies. This configuration in contemporary Thailand is quite different from the highly decentralized state and presidential system in the Philippines.

In short, in Southeast Asia in the 1990s, bossism began to take root beyond the Philippines. In Thailand, bosses—known as "godfathers" or *chao pho*—have emerged with the entrenchment of electoral democracy since the 1980s, yet in the context of a more industrialized economy, a more centralized bureaucracy, and a European-style parliamentary system. Local executive powers remain in civilian bureaucrats' hands and military generals retain a measure of national influence through an appointed Senate and other forms of political and economic intervention. In short, the case of Thailand supports the argument that the subordination of the state to elected officials, rather than the strength of "traditional élites" and clientelistic demands in society constitutes the crucial precondition for the emergence and entrenchment of local bossism.

Postwar examples of both democratic and authoritarian rule in other Southeast Asian countries provide additional evidence in support of this argument. Local bossism flourished in Burma during the early postindependence period of parliamentary rule, but faded (at least in Burma proper) with the imposition of centralized military rule in 1962.[45] Similarly, in early postindependence Indonesia, local gangs, Outer Island aristocracies, and in some regions the army's territorial commanders (*panglima*), acted as major local power brokers under conditions of lively multiparty electoral competition and weak central army command.[46] However, with the demise of parliamentary rule and the onset of martial law in 1957,[47] and the inception of military rule in 1965, a centralized bureaucratic state emerged to subordinate local aristocracies, magnates, and gangsters alike under provincial governors and territorial army commanders rotated regularly by the ministries in Jakarta.[48] Meanwhile, under conditions of highly restricted parliamentary competition and effective one-party rule in Malaysia, local politicians have very limited realms of influence and power,[49] squeezed between the perennial dominance of the ruling Barisan Nasional (and the United Nationalist Malays Organisation, or UMNO, within it) and the centralization of the state's coercive apparatuses in Kuala Lumpur.[50]

Restricted forms of "local mafia" such as those in Malaysia have evolved under authoritarian (military or one-party) rule in Southeast Asia in the course of capitalist development, but such mafias seem to emerge *from* the (party-)state rather than from among "traditional élites" or other forces in society. In federal Malaysia, for example, the constitutional allocation of land to the sole jurisdiction of state governments[51] has created countless new opportunities for local UMNO politicians to use real-estate development schemes to entrench themselves in their bailiwicks. As one author concluded:

The dominance of UMNO within the district bureaucracy made it imperative for any business ventures to have connections with top district UMNO politicians. . . . The entire district development machinery has become an integral party of the total ruling party organization [in the locality]. . . . The machinery has also become the most effective instrument within the district, not only for the suppression of opposition from other political parties, such as the Parti Islam SeMalaysia (PAS), but also for dealing with opposition from within the ruling party ranks. The large pool of material rewards that this machinery can offer through the implementation of the NEP [New Economic Policy] programs, and the potential power that one can gain by association with the organizations or their officials, have created highly significant political and economic configurations in the district and in its various *mukim* and villages.[52]

In a slightly different vein, numerous local Communist Party cadres in rural areas of Vietnam have reportedly used their discretionary powers over land-use rights, taxation, and policing to seize the lion's share of evolving opportunities in the market transformation of the countryside, leading to charges that economic reform in the country has led to a revival of "local mandarins."[53] Meanwhile, in Indonesia, some observers have traced the emergence of "local mafias" from lower- and middle-ranking military personnel serving in provinces of the archipelago:

They have the opportunity to build powerful long-term local bases in the regions, first as representatives of the Center, later as real-estate speculators, fixers, commission-agents, local monopolists, and racketeers. These long-term prospects, meaning retirement in the regions, are helped by local alliances, including marriage connections (themselves or their children), business partnerships with local elites, and personnel manipulations through former subordinates within the active military. As "old hands," such military men are in a strong position to inveigle or obstruct "new broom" officers sent in from the Center. Essentially, we are speaking of the formation of local mafias, which often have their eye on such "civilian" political positions as bupati, provincial secretary, and even governor.[54]

In short, state-based "mafias," rather than local aristocracies or "traditional élites," have begun to exercise a degree of power and influence within local bailiwicks under (both one-party and military) authoritarian regimes in Southeast Asia. But the subordination of these "mafias" to centralized national (party-)state apparatuses has limited their capacity to achieve sustained, local monopolies over coercive and economic resources within their bailiwicks. It is only with the subjugation of the national state apparatus to (competitively) elected officials that opportunities for local "bossism" can be fully realized.

## Philippine Bossism:
## Distinctive Lineages, Patterned Trajectories

Viewed in contrast with these other forms of bossism and against the backdrop of urban political machines and rural county courthouse cliques in the United States, Philippine bossism clearly reveals its American colonial lineage.[55] This American institutional heritage has included a presidential system, a bicameral legislature, a multitiered hierarchy of elected local executives, and a notoriously porous bureaucracy that lacks autonomy from elected officials. American colonial policy left additional legacies in the Philippines: the devolution of executive and legislative powers to elected officials before the creation of a bureaucratic state apparatus and at an early stage of capitalist development; the phasing in of "colonial democracy" and "Filipinization," with local elections preceding those for the national legislature and a highly restricted suffrage gradually expanded over the decades; and the transfer of national-level executive powers to Filipino hands via the commonwealth presidency in 1935 and the granting of formal independence in 1946. Because of these American policies, neither the vestiges of a "bureaucratic polity" nor the remnants of a mass-based independence-movement-cum-political party impeded the ascendance of bosses to the national level in the Philippines. Thus the Philippines' long authoritarian interlude under Ferdinand E. Marcos transpired under the rule of an elected president and machine politician rather than a putschist general or populist independence leader, its peculiar institutional foundations amply evident in the patterns of "crony capitalism" and "constitutional authoritarianism" that distinguished Marcos's dictatorial regime from its counterparts elsewhere in the region.

In comparison with the United States, however, today's Philippines is a very late industrializer, its economy is more heavily dominated by state intervention, its government is more firmly supported by international forces (e.g., Citibank, the International Monetary Fund, the Japan International Cooperation Agency), and its "state-building" trajectory is unlikely to be catalyzed by foreign conflicts. In the aftermath of the "absolutizing" interlude of the Marcos regime, in the context of a reversion to national legislative and local executive supervision of the bureaucracy, and in the absence of strong pressures for civil-service and electoral reforms, it is difficult to identify the nature or direction of change in the structure of boss rule in the contemporary Philippines. At most, the processes of capital accumulation and the occasional rumblings of class conflict may provide the basis for the gradual erosion or transmutation of bossism in the Philippines, as the more parasitic features of this social formation give way to the pressures of global capitalism. Yet, as the examination of Cavite and Cebu has illustrated, even the most "advanced" regions of the archipelago are likely to remain susceptible to boss domination well into the twenty-first century.

In projecting trends in the Philippines, it is tempting to draw on examples of bossism elsewhere. Certainly today's labor activists, nongovernmental organizations (NGOs), and reformist movements in the Philippines are reminiscent of analogous forces arrayed against manifestations of bossism in other eras and in other places, and the structural logic of global capitalism does tend to shift casinos and construction contracts from gangster to corporate hands. Yet the resilience of English "Old Corruption," American county court cliques and urban machines, Italian (and no doubt Russian) mafia, and Latin American caciques is also worthy of note. Filipino bosses will undoubtedly retain control over countless rackets, real-estate deals, and elected offices for many years to come, as will their counterparts in India, Thailand, and some countries in Latin America.

In this context, scholars and other observers who claim an interest in the problems of "democratization" in the developing world should strive to examine and encourage challenges to the various forms of local despotism that thrive when there is electoral competition for control over the state. In the Philippines, for example, NGO activists, investigative journalists, and organizers of laborers, peasants, and the urban poor have worked hard in recent years to expose and oppose the predations of local bosses. In countless towns and villages in other "democratic" countries, opposition to local bossism is also under way. Such efforts are amply deserving of both attention and support. Although this study emphasizes the resourcefulness of local bosses and the resilience of bossism in the face of socioeconomic change and popular challenges, it also underscores the urgency of identifying potential paths for resistance and reform, a task that demands further scholarly attention.

# Notes

1. Migdal, *Strong Societies and Weak States*, p. 33.
2. Ibid., p. 256.
3. Hagopian, *Traditional Politics and Regime Change*, p. 281.
4. See Fox, "The Challenge of Rural Democratization," "The Difficult Transition," and "Latin America's Emerging Local Politics."
5. Migdal, *Strong Societies*, p. 65.
6. Ibid., p. 27.
7. Hagopian, *Traditional Politics and Regime Change*, p. 48.
8. In this regard, it is noteworthy—and astonishing—that authors such as Migdal, Hagopian, and Fox ignore the role of the police and other coercive apparatuses of the state, and of violence and intimidation, in the establishment and perpetuation of local strongman rule.
9. Shefter, "The Emergence of the Political Machine," p. 41. Emphasis added.
10. Erie, *Rainbow's End*, p. 9.
11. Ibid., p. 205.
12. Chubb, *Patronage, Power, and Poverty in Southern Italy*, p. 215.
13. Ibid.
14. See Soriano, *Political Clans and Electoral Politics*; Gutierrez, *The Ties That Bind*; and Gutierrez, Torrente, and Narca, *All in the Family*.
15. Kerkvliet and Mojares, *From Marcos to Aquino*, p. 5.
16. For moralizing American colonial attacks on the supposedly Spanish legacies of "caciquism," see, for example, Mayo, *The Isles of Fear*; and Hayden, *The Philippines*, p. 278. For a more recent and scholarly formulation of this "caciquism" thesis, see Miyagi, "Neo-Caciquismo."

17. Gutierrez, *The Ties That Bind*, p. 9.

18. See, for example, the attention paid to patron-client relations in Wurfel, *Filipino Politics*. A tentative critique of the clientelist "factional model" is provided in Kerkvliet and Mojares, *From Marcos to Aquino*, pp. 8–11.

19. Scott and Kerkvliet, "How Traditional Rural Patrons Lose Legitimacy," p. 502.

20. See, for example, Grossholtz, *Politics in the Philippines*, pp. 78–100; and Lynch and de Guzman, *Four Readings on Filipino Values*.

21. Scott and Kerkvliet, "How Traditional Rural Patrons Lose Legitimacy," p. 511.

22. See, for example, Hollnsteiner, *The Dynamics of Power in a Philippine Municipality*.

23. See Landé, *Leaders, Factions, and Parties*.

24. Agpalo, *Pandanggo sa Ilaw*, p. 23.

25. Landé, *Leaders, Factions, and Parties*, p. 18.

26. Ibid., pp. 115, 101–2.

27. Machado, "From Traditional Faction to Machine."

28. Nowak and Snyder, "Clientelist Politics in the Philippines."

29. Paredes, *Philippine Colonial Democracy*; McCoy, *An Anarchy of Families*.

30. On vote-buying, see Baterina, "A Study of Money in Elections in the Philippines." On violence, media reports contradict unsubstantiated claims of "escalating electoral violence" during this era. Compare the November 1949, 1959, and 1969 issues of the *Philippines Free Press* on this point. "In the provinces," one commentator claimed, "election frauds were the rule rather than the exception" (Hayden, "The Philippines," p. 409). By the 1920s, according to another source, "various practices of electoral fraud (vote-buying, fake ballots, flying voters, and others) were already quite common" (Mojares, *Vicente Sotto*, p. 94). Allegations of vote-buying and fraud in the highly restricted 1902 provincial elections underline that these practices in fact preceded the expansion of the suffrage.

31. See, for example, Hawes, *The Philippine State and the Marcos Regime*, esp. pp. 20–54; and Rivera, "Class, the State and Foreign Capital." For a much earlier formulation of this thesis, see Simbulan, "A Study of the Socio-Economic Elite."

32. See, for example, Soriano, "The Return of the Oligarchs"; McCoy, "The Restoration of Planter Power in La Carlota City"; Gutierrez, Torrente, and Narca, *All in the Family*; and Gutierrez, *The Ties That Bind*.

33. Crouch, *Economic Change, Social Structure and the Political System in Southeast Asia*, p. 10.

34. See, for example, A. Guerrero, *Philippine Society and Revolution*.

35. See, for example, the discussion of the Philippines' "soft state" in Wurfel, *Filipino Politics*, p. 327.

36. By 1898 an estimated 2 million hectares, comprising a mere 7 percent of the colony's total land mass, were privately owned, nearly 10 percent of which were in the hands of the religious orders. On this point, see O. J. Lynch, "Land Rights, Land Laws," p. 84. For a comparison of large landholdings in 1897 and

1953, for example, see Rivera, "Class, the State and Foreign Capital," p. 87; see also Ansay-Miranda, "Early American Imperialism."

37. See Dañguilan-Vitug, *Power from the Forest*; and Lopez, *Isles of Gold*.

38. See Mejia, *Philippine Virginia Tobacco*; Tiglao, *Looking into Coconuts*; Billig, "Syrup in the Wheels of Progress."

39. See, for example, Porter with Ganapin, *Resources, Population, and the Philippines' Future*; Gamalinda, *Saving the Earth*; Kummer, *Deforestation in the Postwar Philippines*; and Broad and Cavanagh, *Plundering Paradise*.

40. See Yoshihara, *Philippine Industrialization*; Rivera and Koike, *Chinese-Filipino Business Families*; and Gutierrez, *The Ties That Bind*.

41. Putzel, *A Captive Land*, pp. 93–95; Simbulan, "A Study of the Socio-Economic Elite," p. 410; Yoshihara, *Philippine Industrialization*, p. 137; and Edgerton, "Americans, Cowboys, and Cattlemen."

42. Prominent urban bosses and "dynasties" include Pablo Cuneta, mayor of Pasay City since the 1950s, Rodolfo Ganzon, longtime "kingpin" of Iloilo City, and the long-entrenched Asistio clan of Caloocan City, none of whom began their careers as owners of urban real estate. On the causal link between small landholdings and the endurance of political dynasties and bosses in the provinces of the Ilocos region, for example, see Lewis, *Ilocano Rice Farmers*, pp. 138–43.

43. For the most compelling and influential articulation of the revisionist view of Siam's supposed "escape" from colonial rule, see B. Anderson, "Studies of the Thai State."

44. See Ockey, "Business Leaders, Gangsters, and the Middle Class," "Chaopho," and Ockey, "Political Parties, Factions, and Corruption in Thailand."

45. See, for example, the enlightening and influential articles written by B. Anderson, "Cacique Democracy in the Philippines"; and Hutchcroft, "Oligarchs and Cronies."

46. On "prowess" and "inner-soul stuff," see O. W. Wolters, *History, Culture, and Region*, pp. 4–10, 101–4.

47. See W. H. Scott, *Barangay*.

48. See Lieberman, "Local Integration and Eurasian Analogies."

49. On these points, see J. Francisco, *The Philippines and India*, and *Indian Culture in the Philippines*.

50. Corpuz, *The Roots of the Filipino Nation*, pp. 40–51.

51. The *encomiendas* were temporary Crown grants to private individuals of jurisdiction over territories and the populations within them. See Elliott, *Imperial Spain*, p. 69.

52. On the the broad powers of the parish priest in municipal affairs, see Bankoff, "Big Fish in Small Ponds."

53. On this process, see Larkin, *The Pampangans*, pp. 63–102.

54. May, "Civic Ritual and Political Reality," p. 13.

55. See, for example, May, "Civic Ritual," pp. 24–25.

56. Bankoff, "Redefining Criminality."

57. With rapid population growth and the expansion of the franchise, the electorate grew from a mere 100,000 (1 percent of the total estimated population) in

1907 to 1.6 million (10 percent) in 1935 and almost 3 million (15 percent) in 1946.

58. On mayoral and gubernatorial control over the police and constabulary, see Baja, *Philippine Police System*, pp. 203–21, 280–86; and C. Campos, "The Role of the Police in the Philippines," pp. 159–65. On the power of legislators, see Cullinane, "Playing the Game," p. 75. On bureaucratization and Filipinization, see Corpuz, *The Bureaucracy in the Philippines*, pp. 166–86.

59. W. Wolters, "Rise and Fall of Provincial Elites," pp. 54–74.

60. A 1940 constitutional amendment provided for the creation of a Commission on Appointments, consisting of twelve senators and twelve members of the House of Representatives, elected by each house and presided over by the Senate president, with veto power over presidential nominations for various government positions. See Hayden, *The Philippines*, pp. 229–30.

61. Stanley, *A Nation in the Making*, pp. 238–48.

62. On the formal powers vested in this "extraordinarily strong presidency" and their similarity to the prerogatives of American state governors, see Hayden, *The Philippines*, pp. 60–86. On the distinctive institutional structures of the American state during this period, see Skowronek, *Building a New American State*, esp. pp. 3–120, 165–247, 285–92.

63. As Benedict Anderson concludes, "unlike all the other modern colonial regimes in twentieth-century Southeast Asia, which operated through huge, autocratic, white-run bureaucracies, the American authorities in Manila . . . created only a minimal civil service, and quickly turned over most of its component positions to the natives." B. Anderson, "Cacique Democracy," p. 11.

64. Hayden, *The Philippines*, p. 291.

65. Tinio served as provincial governor of Nueva Ecija (1907–9), director of the Bureau of Labor (1909–13), and director of the Bureau of Lands (1913–16), while close relatives and protégés held numerous municipal, congressional, and provincial positions in Nueva Ecija with Tinio's blessings. See Crisostomo, *Governor Eduardo L. Joson*, pp. 110–38. According to Kerkvliet, "At the turn of the century, much of his land was still virgin forests and meadows. But between 1900 and the 1920s Tinio took on more and more peasants, who staked out small parcels and laboriously turned the land into neatly diked rice fields." Kerkvliet, *The Huk Rebellion*, p. 6.

66. Rivera, "Class, the State and Foreign Capital," p. 87; Quirino, *History of the Philippine Sugar Industry*, p. 56; McCoy, "Sugar Barons," pp. 125–26.

67. McCoy, "Quezon's Commonwealth," p. 118.

68. See Friend, *Between Two Empires*, pp. 117–18, 154–55; and Caoili, "Quezon and His Business Friends."

69. On this key counterfactual point, see B. Anderson, "Cacique Democracy," pp. 9–10.

70. J. C. Scott, "Patron-Client Politics," p. 96.

71. Owing to the sensitive nature of the material treated in the book, interviews conducted by the author are rarely cited in the text and endnotes. Although discussions with residents of Cavite and Cebu between 1990 and 1994 informed the analysis herein, prudence and concern for the welfare of those individuals dictated

a heavy reliance upon (and reference to) documentary and newspaper sources to substantiate controversial *but previously published* assertions in the text.

72. See the censuses of 1903, 1918, 1939, 1948, 1960, 1970, and 1971, as well as the following materials: *Handbook on Philippine Land Resources*, pp. 70–73; Japan International Cooperation Agency, *The Master Plan Study on the Project Calabarzon*; *Cavite Provincial Profile 1990*; and McAndrew, *Urban Usurpation.*

73. Vandermeer, "Corn on the Island of Cebu," pp. 35–85.

74. See the censuses of 1903, 1918, 1939, 1948, 1960, 1970, 1971, and 1990, as well as *Handbook on Philippine Land Resources*, pp. 74–78; *Province of Cebu: Socio-Economic Profile CY 1990*; 1990 Census of Population and Housing: Cebu; Juario, Avila, and Lastimosa, "Vanishing Swamps and Ruined Reefs"; Hallare-Lara, "A Profile of the Philippine Corn Industry"; and Dones, *Visayas Agriculture.*

CHAPTER 2

1. See, for example, Hollnsteiner, *The Dynamics of Power in a Philippine Municipality.*

2. See, for example, the classic study of this period, Landé, *Leaders, Factions, and Parties.*

3. Landé, *Southern Tagalog Voting*, p. 24.

4. See Machado, "From Traditional Faction to Machine."

5. Letter of September 13, 1935, from Juan Rabellana of Dolores, Tayabas, to Senate President Manuel L. Quezon, "Elections—1935—September 13—R" folder, Box 123, Series 7, Manuel L. Quezon Papers (hereafter Quezon Papers). Translation by the author.

6. Ibid.

7. In 1992–93, for example, representative news items included: "Mayor, Cafgus Face Illegal Logging Raps," *Philippine Daily Inquirer*, February 2, 1992; "Negros Mayor Charged with Robbery, Graft," *Philippine Daily Globe*, March 19, 1992; "Leyte Mayor in Murder Rap," *Manila Standard*, July 5, 1992; "Kin Seek Suspension of Mayor over Slay," *Philippine Daily Inquirer*, July 28, 1992; "Mayors, Cops Charged with Illegal Logging," *Manila Chronicle*, July 22, 1993; and "Mayor with Gun-for-Hire Gang," *Manila Chronicle*, August 6, 1993.

8. See, for example, the July 11, 20, 22, and 26, issues of the *Manila Chronicle* for related stories on the Sanchez case.

9. McBeth, "A Life for a Life," pp. 16–17.

10. Ibid., p. 16; *Manila Chronicle*, August 5, 1993.

11. See Baja, *Philippine Police System*, pp. 202–21.

12. C. Campos, "The Role of the Police in the Philippines," pp. 218–26.

13. On this point, see, for example, Romani and Thomas, *A Survey of Local Government in the Philippines*, pp. 27–28; and Villanueva et al., *Government and Administration of a Municipality*, pp. 20, 108–9.

14. On the structure of municipal finances in the postwar Philippines, see Vergara, "The Fiscal Position of Philippine Local Governments."

15. Caoili, "Real Property Tax Administration in the Province of Leyte," pp. 319–20; and Ocampo and Panganiban, *The Philippine Local Government System*, p. 19.

16. Villanueva et al., *Government and Administration of a Municipality*, pp. 91–92; Castillo, *Property Tax Administration in the Philippines*, p. 107.

17. See, for example, M. Szanton, *A Right to Survive*, p. 16.

18. See, for example, the conclusions of a study of election results in nine provinces: Landé, *Southern Tagalog Voting*, pp. 96–97.

19. Curry, "The Determinants of Philippine Political Competition," p. 68.

20. In the seven pre-martial-law local elections, an average of 70 percent of the municipal executives elected belonged to the party of the incumbent administration, as did an average of 68 percent of the provincial governors elected. Ibid., pp. 77, 224–25.

21. Blok, *The Mafia of a Sicilian Village*, p. 6.

22. In Cavite, the number of votes cast shot up from roughly 25,000 in 1934 to more than 50,000 in 1941. Throughout the Philippines, population growth and the removal of suffrage restrictions led to a rapid rise in electoral participation during this period. On election fraud, see, for example, the September 17, 1935, October 3, 1935, and September 6, 1939, issues of *The Tribune*; and "Cavite Officials Convicted," *Philippines Free Press*, January 20, 1940. On the resistance movement, see Tria, "The Resistance Movement in Cavite."

23. On the 1953 election, for example, see *Daily Mirror*, November 11, November 18, and November 27, 1953; and *Manila Times*, November 17, 1953.

24. "Election Protest," filed March 21, 1988, by Sixto S. Brillantes Jr. and Juanito G. Arcilla, in *Election Protest Case No. NC-1*.

25. "Petition" filed May 22, 1992, by Teodorico C. Ramirez, in *Election Protest Case No. NC-2*.

26. Republic of the Philippines, Commission on Elections, *Report of the Commission on Elections to the President of the Philippines and the Congress on the Manner the Election Was Held on November 10, 1959* (Manila: Bureau of Printing, 1960), p. 36.

27. *Electoral Case No. 137*, "Memorandum for the Protestant," p. 145.

28. See, for example, *Ang Pahayagang Malaya*, April 27, 1985; and *Manila Chronicle*, March 11, 1992. For a complete list of these casualties, see *Philippine Daily Inquirer*, March 3, 1995.

29. Medina, "Cavite Before the Revolution," pp. 120–210.

30. Letter of October 27, 1922, from Claro Cuevas, "Bacoor, Cavite: 1921–1923" folder, Box 41, Series 7, Quezon Papers; Forbes, *The Philippine Islands*, p. 167; "The Jueteng Business," *Philippines Free Press*, November 4, 1933; Baja, *Philippine Police System*, p. 356.

31. For the 1909 report of Cavite provincial fiscal Francisco Santamaria, see Villamor, *Criminality in the Philippine Islands*, pp. 59–60. On the connivance of local officials and police with cattle rustlers in later years, see *Philippines Free Press*, January 13, 1940, pp. 20–21.

32. *Manila Daily Bulletin*, April 15, 1922; *The Tribune*, December 19, 1928, October 10 and October 14, 1939.

33. On prostitution and illegal gambling in Cavite City, for example, see *Manila Times*, July 26, 1954, and *Daily Mirror*, February 18, 1955. On marijuana cultivation and carnapping in Imus, see *Manila Daily Bulletin*, March 22, 1962, and *Manila Times*, May 27, 1963.

34. See, for example, the *Manila Times* for June 9, 1956, March 30, 1957, August 27, 1959, and September 4, 1966.

35. These estimates appeared in documents submitted by Acting Executive Secretary Calixto O. Zaldivar to Secretary of Justice Salvador Marino in March 1964 and were later published in the Manila press. See "Documents Expose Extent of Smuggling Operations," *Manila Chronicle*, March 19, 1964.

36. On illegal gambling, see, for example, *Manila Standard*, August 26, 1992; *Philippine Star*, September 7, 1992; *Manila Standard*, November 13, 1992; *Philippine Daily Inquirer*, August 21, 1993. On narcotics smuggling, see, for example, *Diyaryo Pilipino*, July 22, 1991; *Philippine Daily Globe*, November 15, 1991; *Philippine Daily Inquirer*, January 27, 1992. On illegal trawling, see Hingco and Rivera, *The History of Trawling Operations in Manila Bay*; *Bulletin Today*, December 22, 1984, and November 1, 1985; *Ang Pahayagang Malaya*, January 10, 1986; *Manila Bulletin*, September 6, 1988; *Philippine Daily Inquirer*, December 5, 1992. On the illegal labor market, see *Philippine Daily Globe*, October 18, 1990. See also Kaplan and Dubro, *Yakuza*, pp. 139–41, 209–11.

37. *Fifth Annual Report of the Philippine Commission, 1904*, Part I, "Report of the Governor of Cavite," p. 450.

38. For classic descriptions of the emergence of the largely Chinese mestizo landowning élite in the provinces during the nineteenth century, see Larkin, *The Pampangans*, esp. pp. 63–102; and Wickberg, *The Chinese in Philippine Life*, esp. chaps. 2 and 3.

39. Borromeo, "El Cadiz Filipino," p. 68.

40. Alvarez, *The Katipunan and the Revolution*, p. 72 (English), pp. 307–8 (Tagalog).

41. Medina, "Cavite Before the Revolution," p. 216.

42. See, for example, Manuel, "Biography of Tomas Tirona," p. 290.

43. Medina, "Cavite Before the Revolution," p. 222; Manuel, "Biography of Tomas Tirona," p. 303.

44. *Fifth Annual Report of the Philippine Commission*, "Report of the Governor of Cavite," pp. 454–58. By 1933, nearly 95 percent of the 47,111 hectares of friar estate land in Cavite had been redistributed. See Endriga, "The Friar Lands Settlement," pp. 397–413.

45. See, for example, "Documentos Tomados . . . Expediente Incoado por el Comite de Defensa de los Derechos de los Proprietarios de Terrenos en Imus, Cavite . . . I.F., Despues de su Organizacion, Marzo 1911," in the 1908–11 folder, Box 238, Series 7, Quezon Papers.

46. See, for example, the letter of March 1, 1926, from Tomas Mascardo to Quezon in the "Imus, Cavite—1926" folder, Box 42, Series 7, Quezon Papers. Similar correspondence is found in the "Naic, Cavite—1928," folder, Box 44, and the "April 1–June 30, 1934" folder, Box 250, Series 7, Quezon Papers.

47. *Philippines Free Press*, February 1934, pp. 8, 37.

48. First National Assembly, First Session, Bill No. 1101, Commonwealth Act No. 32, "An Act Providing for the Subdivision and Sale of All the Portion of the Friar Lands Estates Remaining Undisposed Of," Approved, September 15, 1936.

49. *Philippines Free Press*, January 7, 1950; *Manila Chronicle*, July 20, 1955.

50. Interview conducted by the author with Benjamin P. Resus, former municipal secretary of Naic, Cavite, at his home in Barangay Humbac, Naic, Cavite, on November 5, 1992. See also "Republic Act 1199: An Act To Govern the Relations Between Landholders and Tenants of Agricultural Lands (Leasehold and Share Tenancy)," in Starner, *Magsaysay and the Peasantry*, pp. 211–24.

51. *Manila Times*, March 6, 1955.

52. The number of approved building permits increased, on average, 27 percent annually for the period 1980–90. In the peak year of 1989, private construction activities in the province were valued at nearly 1 billion pesos. *Business Star*, October 29, 1991. On the use of government land, see, for example, *Bulletin Today*, December 25, 1979. On public works, see *Manila Bulletin*, July 23, 1991. On the ambitious plans for reclamation along the Cavite coast, see, for example, the 16,000-hectare proposal outlined in *Regal Bay Philippines* (Manila: Regalado Development Corporation, 1992).

53. *Midweek*, April 11, 1990; *Business World*, June 10 and July 31, 1991; Canlas, "Industrializing the Countryside or Undermining Agriculture?" In various Municipal Agrarian Reform offices in Cavite visited by the author in 1991–92, log books and files bulged with records of local elected officials' visits and letters of recommendation in support of land conversion. In the town of Dasmariñas, the Municipal Agrarian Reform Office processed applications for the conversion of more than 2,300 hectares of land in a period of less than five years. Municipal Agrarian Reform Office, Dasmariñas, Cavite, "Dasmariñas Land Use Conversion Status, March 1988 to July 1992."

54. On market stalls, see *Philippine Daily Inquirer*, June 3, 1992. On the system of local monopoly franchises for ice plants, see Hinkle and Aquino, *A Report on Factors Affecting the Cost of Ice*. An appendix to this study lists seven ice plants in various Cavite municipalities. See also "Municipal Tax Ordinance No. 02-S-92: An Ordinance Imposing Tax on Winnings of Cockfighting Fronton," in *Excerpts from the Minutes of the Regular Session Held by the Sangguniang Bayan of Dasmariñas, Cavite on October 9, 1992* (Dasmariñas, Cavite: Office of the Sangguniang Bayan, 1992); *Civil Case No. 537-91* (1991).

55. In Cavite City, for example, Mayor Dones forced the Rojas family to cough up 88,000 pesos in "amusement taxes" on its two cinema houses after the passage of a city ordinance imposing a tax on amusement establishments.

56. See, for example, *Manila Times*, March 14, 1962: "According to the complaint, Dones demanded P15,000 from Prospero Sarapdon, contractor of the Cavite City public market, in consideration for the awarding of the bid which Sarapdon won. Dones was also charged with having received an additional P1,500 from Sarapdon before authorizing the release of the amount for the construction of the market."

57. The late Captain Victor Miranda, until his death the mayor of Bacoor, for example, owned shares in a savings bank as well as a recruitment agency that

placed Filipino merchant marines on international vessels. On the heavily regulated, abuse-ridden, and profitable business of recruiting seamen in the Philippines, see Chapman, *Trouble on Board*, pp. 23–32.

58. *Ang Pahayagang Malaya*, November 4, 1986. Customs and EIIB officials estimated in the 1980s that various forms of "technical" smuggling amounted to billions of dollars a year and involved over one-fourth of all Philippine imports. See Alano, "Import Smuggling in the Philippines"; Economic Intelligence and Investigation Bureau, "Economic Subversion in the Philippines"; and Parayno.

59. Umehara, "Green Revolution for Whom?"; Fegan, "Accumulation"; McAndrew, "Urbanization and Social Differentiation."

60. These landholdings are listed in land tax records ("Farm Land Holdings of 50 Hectares or More," Department of Finance, December 31, 1953), which were used as the basis for Sorongon's study. The author also double-checked the location and size of these landholdings with the provincial and municipal offices of the Department of Agrarian Reform in Cavite.

61. Land tax records from the early 1950s indicate that the Triases owned several hundred hectares of prime land in the towns of General Trias and Silang, Cavite.

62. From 1949 to 1953: Mayor Gulapa of Maragondon (1949); Mayor Beratio of Magallanes (1949); Mayor Rillo of Maragondon (1952); Mayor de la Torre of Silang (1953); from 1969 to 1972: Mayor Reyes of Magallanes (1972); Mayor Rojas of Cavite City (1972); and Mayor Dalusag of General Aguinaldo (1972).

63. In 1980 and 1988, Remulla's candidates won 17 of the 22 elective mayorships in the province. In 1992, 19 of 23 elected mayors, 16 of 23 vice-mayors, and 129 of 182 municipal councilors were on Remulla's slate.

64. Gervasio Pangilinan y Enriquez, *La Historica Cavite* (Manila, 1926), pp. 226–29.

65. *Manila Times*, January 7, May 23, and September 16, 1954; *Manila Chronicle*, January 10, 1954; *Daily Mirror*, January 25 and September 16, 1954.

66. "Complaint," filed May 12, 1955, by Bernardo B. Hebron, in Bernardo Hebron, Plaintiff, versus Eulalio D. Reyes, Defendant (Manila: Supreme Court).

67. *Manila Times*, May 4, 1955.

68. Republic of the Philippines, Commission on Elections, *Report of the Commission on Elections to the President and the Congress on the Manner the Elections Were Held on November 8, 1955* (Manila: Bureau of Printing, 1956), pp. 19, 139, 141–42.

69. Land tax records from 1953 indicate, however, that the Ermitaños owned less than 50 hectares of land in Carmona.

70. On the key role of Senator Montano in the passage of this legislation, see Starner, *Magsaysay and the Peasantry*, pp. 168–69, 176, 181–84.

71. See "The Land Reform Bill of 1955: A Summary and an Evaluation," and "Republic Act 1400: An Act Defining a Land Tenure Policy, Providing for an Instrumentality to Carry Out the Policy, and Appropriating Funds for Its Implementation," in Starner, *Magsaysay and the Peasantry*, pp. 184–87, 231–36.

72. Wurfel, "The Bell Report and After," p. 763.

73. José P. Mojica, a Caviteño protégé of Senator Montano and a former head of the landed estates division of the Bureau of Lands, served as the chief of the survey division of the Land Tenure Administration, the agency created for and tasked with the expropriation and redistribution of landed estates under R.A. 1400.

74. The Cavite Court of First Instance fixed the price for the Yaptinchay estate at 2,000 pesos per hectare of sugar land and 4,000 pesos per hectare of irrigated rice land, rates that Land Tenure Administration chairman Manuel Castañeda deemed inordinately high and "contrary to the spirit envisioned in the land reform law." *Manila Times*, August 14, 1956.

75. A copy of this decree is found in Marciano P. Mapanoo, *Tenants Association of Carmona, Cavite* (Manila: Commonwealth of the Philippines, Department of Public Instruction, 1940?). Translation by the author.

76. On the complex political economy of the Philippine sugar industry, see Billig, "Syrup in the Wheels of Progress."

77. Simbulan, "A Study of the Socio-Economic Elite in Philippine Politics and Government," p. 412; Yoshihara, *Philippine Industrialization*, pp. 137, 141.

78. "The Oppositors' possession has been disturbed when the Applicants, by brute force, ejected them from the premises. This force has been maintained, monitored and continuously employed up to the present, the principal applicant Cesar Casal having, since 1955, been the Mayor of Carmona, Cavite. Evidence of such use and employment of physical force is the death of one of the heirs (Severino Medina) which up to now has remained unsolved and a mystery" ("Opposition," filed May 18, 1990, by Arnold A. Savella, Counsel for the Oppositors, in *RTC LRC b-90-6*, "Application for Registration of Title," Cesar Casal et al., Applicants [Bacoor: Regional Trial Court, Fourth Judicial Region, Branch 19]).

79. Although Manila newspapers fail to mention any incidents of election-related violence in Carmona, the Commission On Elections reports on the 1959, 1963, 1967, and 1971 local elections note that Comelec declared Carmona a "critical" area and placed the town's police force under Comelec and Constabulary control in every single election after Casal became mayor. Carmona shares a history of banditry, cattle rustling, carnapping, and marijuana cultivation with other lowland Cavite towns. See, for example, *Manila Times*, March 29, 1962; *Taliba*, July 9, 1972; and *NBI Annual Report 1976* (Manila: National Bureau of Investigation, 1977), p. 38.

80. University of the Philippines students hired by the author to observe and report on the election in Carmona on May 11, 1992, described election-eve visits by armed men, vote-buying for 500 pesos a head, ballot-switching, and "selective disenfranchisement" by Casal's camp during the election.

81. Saulo and de Ocampo, *History of Cavite*, pp. 163–64.

82. See *Manila Times*, April 15, 1970; Poethig, "An Assessment of the Carmona Resettlement Project," pp. 12, 17; and "Carmona Relocation," pp. 62–67.

83. *Daily Mirror*, December 11, 1970; *Manila Times*, June 9, 1972; *Daily Mirror*, July 5, 1972.

84. Senior Specialist Angelita R. Legaspi, "Memorandum for the Director, Examiners and Appraisers Department Re: Southern Heights Land Development Corporation," submitted August 15, 1982, found among documents filed by the

Southern Heights Land Development Corporation with the Securities and Exchange Commission.

85. On Campos, see Manapat, *Some Are Smarter Than Others*, pp. 353–67.

86. Tracy Posis, "The Birth of a New Horizon," *Metro Manila Real Estate Magazine*, September–October 1992, pp. 10–12.

87. Knowledgeable sources in Carmona recall that a lawsuit against Casal for landgrabbing (subsequently dismissed) formed the backdrop to this deal.

88. This *engkargado*, a notoriously unsavory character, has been named as a prime suspect in the killings of two real-estate brokers in a nearby town in January 1992. *Manila Chronicle*, March 11, 1992.

89. See "Complaints," filed October 20, 1988, by Elpidio F. Barzaga Jr., Counsel for the Plaintiffs, in *RTC-BCV-88049.*

90. On the dumpsite controversy, see Guillermo Guerrero Jr., "Garbage or Land Reform: The Case of Carmona, Cavite," *Center for Advanced Philippine Studies Monitor Series No. 90-1* (March 1990), pp. 1–19; *Manila Standard*, December 19, 1990; *Philippine Daily Inquirer*, March 16, 1992; *Business World*, April 7, 1992; *Manila Chronicle*, April 30, 1993; *Philippines Free Press*, July 3, 1993.

### CHAPTER 3

1. The author's description of the Velasco murder is based on eyewitness accounts contained in *Criminal Case No. NC-579*, "Information," filed March 13, 1992, by acting Cavite provincial prosecutor Ferdinand R. Abesamis. Attached affidavits and "sinumpaang salaysay" (a sworn statement) supplement Abesamis's summary of the events of March 3, 1992.

2. Juan B. Zaldarriaga Jr., M.D., "Postmortem Findings," *Autopsy Report No. 92-20* (Manila: Republic of the Philippines, Department of Justice, National Bureau of Investigation, Medico-Legal Division, 1992).

3. *Manila Chronicle*, March 5 and March 11, 1992; *Philippine Daily Inquirer*, March 5 and March 11, 1992; *Newsday*, March 11, 1992.

4. Velasco ran against Nuñez's protégé in the 1988 local elections, lost, and filed a protest case that dragged on until late in 1991, when he was officially proclaimed the winner and assumed the Ternate mayorship. During registration in February 1992, Nuñez, armed and accompanied by his brother and several bodyguards, confronted Velasco over the detention of alleged illegal registrants in the Ternate police station. Velasco subsequently filed a case before the Commission on Elections charging Nuñez with violation of the gun ban.

5. According to sources sympathetic to Bonifacio and hostile to Aguinaldo, the revolutionary officers guarding the Bonifacio brothers received written orders to carry out the execution. See Alvarez, *The Katipunan and the Revolution*, pp. 118, 353–54.

6. Walsh, "Perceptions of Gubernatorial Authority," pp. 72–75; and Williams, "Center, Bureaucracy, and Locality," pp. 29–30.

7. Vergara, "The Fiscal Position of Philippine Local Governments," pp. 55–56.

8. On this point, see C. Campos, "The Role of the Police in the Philippines,"

p. 205; and "Republic Act No. 6875, An Act Establishing the Philippine National Police Under a Reorganized Department of the Interior and Local Government, and for Other Purposes," approved December 13, 1990, in Gutang, *Pulisya*, pp. 145–76.

9. Walsh, "Perceptions of Gubernatorial Authority," p. 91.

10. See Francisco and De Guzman, "The '50–50 Agreement"; Roxas, "The Pork Barrel System"; and Vidallon-Cariño, *The Politics and Administration of the Pork Barrel*.

11. On governors and congressmen in the pre-martial-law era, see, for example, Curry, "The Determinants of Philippine Political Competition," p. 64; and *Roster of Philippine Legislators: 1907 to 1987*, pp. 95–201. On governors and congressmen in the post-Marcos era, see Gutierrez, *The Ties That Bind*; Gutierrez, Torrente, and Narca, *All in the Family*; and Soriano, *Political Clans and Electoral Politics*.

12. *Fifth Annual Report of the Philippine Commission*, "Report of the Governor of Cavite," p. 450.

13. Borromeo, "El Cadiz Filipino," p. 68.

14. Medina, "Cavite Before the Revolution."

15. Aguinaldo, *Mga Gunita Ng Himagsikan*, pp. 5–6, 25.

16. Ibid., pp. 45–68.

17. The names of these revolutionary figures also appear in the list of Chinese mestizo *principales* in Cavite towns provided in Borromeo, "El Cadiz Filipino," p. 75. This pattern of revolutionary recruitment of the provincial élite in Cavite is similar to that described by Glenn May in his revisionist article "Filipino Revolutionaries in the Making," and more recently in his book *Battle for Batangas*.

18. Aguinaldo, *Mga Gunita Ng Himagsikan*, p. 49. May's article and book elaborate on this argument with reference to the pattern of mobilization in Batangas (see note 17 above).

19. On the Magdalo-Magdiwang conflict, see the conflicting accounts in Aguinaldo, *Mga Gunita Ng Himagsikan*, pp. 139, 142–43; and Alvarez, *The Katipunan and the Revolution*, esp. pp. 94–119, 331–54. On the overall pattern of "revolutionary" mobilization in Luzon, see the important revisionist accounts of M. Guerrero, "Luzon at War," and May, *Battle for Batangas*.

20. See the various fine essays in Paredes, *Philippine Colonial Democracy*.

21. *Fifth Annual Report of the Philippine Commission, 1904*, Part I, "Report of the Governor of Cavite," pp. 454–58.

22. *Manila Times*, February 5, 1902.

23. *Fifth Annual Report of the Philippine Commission, 1904*, Part I, "Executive Order No. 8, The Government of the Philippine Islands, Executive Bureau, Manila, January 27, 1904," pp. 692–93.

24. See Cullinane, "*Ilustrado* Politics," pp. 437–516.

25. For references to election-related skulduggery in Cavite, see, for example, the February 11 and April 23, 1907, issues of the *Manila Times*, as well as Caballero and Concepcion, *Quezon*, p. 440, and *The Tribune*, October 3, 1935.

26. "Confidencial" letter of September 11, 1935, from Juan Nolasco (president, Comité Nacional de Campaña) to General Basilio Valdes (brigadier general,

Philippine Constabulary), "Elections—1935—September—V" folder, Box 121, Series 7, Quezon Papers. In the original Spanish, this passage reads as follows: "Tenemos informes confidenciales que los Aguinaldistas forzaran a los electores en dichos municipios a votar por el General Aguinaldo, y que durante el escrutinio los mismos Aguinaldistas obligaran a los inspectores de eleccion para que leyeran las balotas a favor del General Aguinaldo." Translation by the author.

27. Quirino, *Quezon*, p. 149.

28. Successful *revolucionario-politicos* included longtime Laguna governor Juan Cailles, Bulacan kingpin Teodoro Sandiko, and Nueva Ecija *hacendado* Manuel Tinio.

29. Clariño, *General Aguinaldo and Philippine Politics*, p. 37.

30. *The Tribune*, August 13, 1935; *Philippines Free Press*, June 11, 1949.

31. See Jorgé B. Vargas, "General Aguinaldo and the Bureau of Lands" (dated September 30, 1927) in the "January 20–December 31, 1927" folder, Box 250, Series 7, Quezon Papers.

32. Ibid.

33. See the July 27, 1929, letter of Director of Lands Serafin P. Hilado to Quezon in the "1922–1927" folder, Emilio Aguinaldo file, in the Major Correspondents' Series, Quezon Papers. See in particular the attached "Statement of the Accounts of General Emilio Aguinaldo with the Bureau of Lands (Friar Lands Division)."

34. See Caballero and Concepcion, *Quezon*, pp. 213, 315.

35. See the letter of September 14, 1938, from Antero Ganuja et al., of Naic, Cavite, in the "Bureau of Lands—1918" folder, Box 248, Series 7, Quezon Papers.

36. *The Tribune*, July 22, 1929.

37. See *The Tribune*, November 29, 1934 (two articles); and Quirino, *Amang*, pp. 49–50.

38. See the September 17, September 19, and October 3, 1935, issues of *The Tribune*, as well as the "Confidencial" letter of September 11, 1935, from Juan Nolasco to General Basilio Valdes, in "Elections—1935—September 11—V" folder, Box 122, Series 7, Quezon Papers.

39. First National Assembly, First Session, Bill No. 1101, Commonwealth Act No. 32, "An Act Providing for the Subdivision and Sale of All the Portion of the Friar Lands Estates Remaining Undisposed Of," Approved, September 15, 1936.

40. Doronila, *The State*, pp. 89–113, 123–33.

41. Manufacturing grew at the fantastic rate of 12 percent per year on average in the 1950s and increased its share of net domestic product from 10.7 percent in 1948 to 17.9 percent in 1960. See Villegas, "The Story (So Far)," p. 4.

42. According to census figures, the population of Metro Manila swelled from roughly 1.5 million in 1948 to just under 4 million in 1970.

43. 1970 Census of Population and Housing, *Cavite*, p. xxi.

44. On these developments, see the more thorough account in John P. McAndrew's fine study, *Urban Usurpation*, pp. 34–57.

45. Justiniano S. Montano Sr., interviews with the author, October 18, 1990, and August 15, 1991, Greenhills, San Juan, Metro Manila.

46. "Upon the fiscal's energy, legal ability, and sense of public responsibility largely depends the enforcement of the law within his jurisdiction. If he is lazy or incompetent, uses his offices for personal or political advantage or is dominated by the gambling interests, the political boss, or the important landowners of the province, the cause of justice and the interests of the state will suffer. Because of its political significance, the office has always been more or less in politics. . . . Politically minded fiscals have gone on to be provincial governors, representatives, senators, or assemblymen. In fact, the position has been one of the best stepping-stones to a career in provincial and national politics" (Hayden, *The Philippines*, pp. 257–58).

47. *Philippines Free Press*, November 4, 1933, pp. 2–3, 40–41.

48. *Philippines Free Press*, September 9, 1935.

49. Montano interviews, October 18, 1990, and August 15, 1991.

50. See the September 17, 1935, November 11, 1938, and October 17, 1939, issues of *The Tribune*, as well as the December 3, 1938, and October 21, 1939, issues of the *Philippines Free Press*.

51. See, for example, *Manila Daily Bulletin*, December 3, 1946; and *Manila Chronicle*, November 11, 1953.

52. *Manila Chronicle*, February 26, 1949; *Philippines Free Press*, May 8, 1954.

53. See the September 2, September 21, and September 23, 1961, issues of the *Manila Times*, as well as the November 4, 1961, issue of the *Philippines Free Press*.

54. *Electoral Case No. 137*, "Memorandum for the Protestant," pp. 3–4, 10.

55. Camerino's "armed goons and special agents roamed around the barrios," a later court decision noted, and "in some instances went from house to house, [and] threatened the leaders and adherents of the opposition against voting on election day," warning them to stay home "if they wish[ed] to remain alive." May 18, 1957, "Resolution" of the Electoral Tribunal of the House of Representatives, in *Electoral Case Number 102*, p. 452.

56. *Manila Times*, January 7 and September 16, 1954; *Sunday Chronicle*, January 10, 1954; *Daily Mirror*, January 25 and September 16, 1954.

57. *Manila Times*, July 26 and August 7, 1954; *Daily Mirror*, August 9, 1954, and February 18, 1955.

58. *Manila Times*, May 4, 1955.

59. The relocation of the capitol building and other provincial offices to this unlikely site allegedly doubled the value of the Montanos' land. *Asia-Philippines Leader* 1, no. 4 (April 30, 1971), p. 47.

60. See the July 19, 1969, April 21, 1970, and May 14, 1972, issues of the *Manila Times*. See also Administrative Order No. 339, "Removing Mr. Justiniano N. Montano Jr. from Office as Chairman of the Games and Amusements Board," signed September 26, 1972, by President Ferdinand E. Marcos, *Official Gazette* 68, no. 40, pp. 7776 D–H.

61. See also the discussion of the Cavite Department of Public Safety, a special police unit consisting of 38 agents created in 1964 by the provincial board of Cavite and placed under the supervision of the governor of Cavite, in "Decision,"

ordered February 27, 1967, by Judge Alberto V. Averia, in *Civil Case No. TM-178*, Rodolfo Salgado, Plaintiff, versus Delfin N. Montano et al. (Trece Martires City: Court of the First Instance of Cavite, 7th Judicial District, Branch 1).

62. See *Manila Chronicle*, March 24, 1964. By 1958, Sandakan, British North Borneo, had become the world's largest importer of American cigarettes, the overwhelming majority of which were bound for Philippine shores. See "Import Control, High Taxes, and Smuggling," *American Chamber of Commerce Journal* 24, no. 5 (May 1959), p. 197.

63. These estimates appeared in documents submitted by Acting Executive Secretary Calixto O. Zaldivar to Secretary of Justice Salvador Marino in March 1964 and were later published in the Manila press. See *Manila Chronicle*, March 19, 1964.

64. Mejia, *Philippine Virginia Tobacco*.

65. *Asia-Philippines Leader* 1, no. 11 (June 18, 1971), pp. 44–45.

66. See the records of Senate hearings on smuggling held on March 9, March 16, and April 13, 1964, in *Congressional Record*, Senate, Fifth Congress, Third Session, Volume 3, nos. 30, 35, and 49, pp. 562–67, 667–77, and 1049–59.

67. Documents detailing the syndicate's operations cited the following monthly payoffs: major AFP command chief: P20,000; CIS chief: P10,000; area CIS chief: P5,000; major, unit commander: P10,000; captain, unit commander: P5,000. See *Manila Chronicle*, March 20, 1964. In 1966, revelations identified the secretary of defense, the chief of the Philippine Constabulary, and Constabulary officers in Cavite as recipients of hush money. See *Saturday Chronicle*, September 3, 1966; *Philippines Free Press*, September 10, 1966.

68. Numerous articles in the *Manila Times*, 1963–70, as well as Securities and Exchange Commission documents offer insight into the machinations of such Montano companies as Cirmont Industries, Monta-Monte Realty, C. N. Montano and Associates, Trece Martires Development Corporation, Cavite Farms Corporations, Naic Farms Corporation, and Tanza Farms Corporation.

69. See, for example, *Daily Mirror*, January 9, 1964.

70. See, for example, the January 13, 1964, June 4, 1964, and March 6, 1965, issues of the *Daily Mirror*.

71. See the May 29, 1964, August 6, 1964, and September 14, 1965, issues of the *Daily Mirror*, as well as the December 17, 1970, January 16, 1972, and January 22, 1972, issues of the *Manila Times*.

72. See, for example, *Manila Chronicle*, September 5 and September 9, 1966.

73. *Daily Mirror*, July 9, 1968; *Manila Times*, July 10, 1968.

74. Commission on Elections, *Report of the Commission on Elections to the President and the Congress of the Philippines on the Manner the Elections Were Held on November 14, 1967* (Manila: Bureau of Printing, 1969), pp. 98–100, 118–19, 133–39, 140–42; Commission on Elections, *Report of the Commission on Elections to the President and the Congress of the Philippines on the Manner the Elections Were Held on November 11, 1969* (Manila: Bureau of Printing, 1971), pp. 187–89, 197–99, 264–80.

75. *Daily Mirror*, February 11, 1967; *Manila Chronicle*, November 1, 1967.

76. Jovito R. Salonga, Abraham F. Sarmiento, and Antonio José Cortes, "Mo-

tion for Reconsideration and Rehearing," filed January 1, 1968, in Fernando C. Campos et al., Petitioners, versus Commission on Elections et al. (Respondent G.R. No. L-28439, Supreme Court, Republic of the Philippines, Manila).

77. *Daily Mirror*, March 19, 1971; *Manila Times*, March 23, 1971; Primitivo Mijares, *The Conjugal Dictatorship of Ferdinand and Imelda Marcos I* (San Francisco: Union Square Publications, 1976), p. 159.

78. The Commission on Elections placed eight towns with pro-Montano mayors under Constabulary control, allowing Bocalan's own *compadre*, Second Constabulary Zone Chief Brigadier General Zosimo Paredes, considerable discretion in monitoring electoral fraud and violence in Cavite. Moreover, the commission decided to hold the final canvassing of Cavite election returns in its central offices in Manila, thus further "sanitizing" the election in Bocalan's favor.

79. These developments are well documented and discussed in McAndrew, *Urban Usurpation*, pp. 187–93.

80. *Provincial Profile: Cavite*, pp. 14–17.

81. *Manila Chronicle*, June 8, 1992.

82. *Provincial Profile: Cavite*, pp. 76–81.

83. Oscar F. Reyes, "Petition," filed January 11, 1986, Annex "B," in Special Action Case No. 73646. See also *Ang Pahayagang Malaya*, April 12 and May 21, 1984.

84. Fernando C. Campos, "Petition," in Special Civil Action Case No. 73646; *Ang Pahayagang Malaya*, February 21, 1986.

85. *The NAMFREL Report*, p. 88.

86. Although it claims less than 5 percent of the population as members, the Iglesia Ni Cristo (INC) is an independent church whose strict internal discipline holds certain attractions for politicians like Remulla. Forbidden to join labor unions, INC members received favorable treatment from Governor Remulla in his recommendations to factory owners in search of employees, as has the INC hierarchy in its efforts to build new churches in Cavite. In exchange for these favors, INC clergymen reportedly urged their congregations to support Governor Remulla in his successive bids for reelection.

87. According to Dragon's opponents, he milked the Royal Savings Bank before the 1984 National Assembly elections and then allowed his close friend and fellow-elected assemblyman from Cavite, Finance Minister Cesar Virata, to arrange a government bailout for the bank through its sale to the Government Service Insurance System (GSIS). See *Ang Pahayagang Malaya*, July 23, 1984. Rumors in early 1994, moreover, suggested that Dragon, by then chairman of the House Committee on Banking, was working to buy back the bank from the GSIS.

A sheaf of documents provided to the author by veteran investigative journalist Marites Dañguilan-Vitug chronicles Dragon's persistent lobbying of the Department of Environment and Natural Resources (DENR) on behalf of Woodland Domain, Inc. (of which he is a major stockholder), which is accused of violating various forest laws. According to Dañguilan-Vitug, the DENR suspended Woodland's license in 1986 for nonpayment of forest dues, illegal subcontracting agreements, and logging operations outside Woodland Domain's 72,680-hectare concession in Agusan del Norte. In 1988, however, thanks to Dragon's intercession and influence, the DENR lifted Woodland Domain's suspension. On these developments, see Dañguilan-Vitug, *Power from the Forest*, pp. 97–98.

88. As noted in the previous chapter, Remulla's opponent in the 1992 election estimated that the governor spent over P200 million (US$8 million) to guarantee his reelection and that of his protégés in Cavite.

89. As noted in the previous chapter, Remulla's candidates won 17 of the 22 mayorships in the province in the elections of 1980 and 1988. In 1992, 19 of 23 elected mayors, 16 of 23 vice-mayors, and 129 of 182 municipal councilors were on Remulla's slate.

90. *Manila Times*, March 23, 1950.

91. *Manila Chronicle*, May 31, 1967.

92. Caoili, "Quezon and His Business Friends," pp. 81, 105.

93. *Ang Pahayagang Malaya*, June 3, 1987.

94. "Extrajudicial Foreclosure of Real Estate Mortgage," Manila Banking Corporation, Applicant-Mortgagee, versus Capitol City Farms, Inc., Mortgagor (Tagaytay City: Republic of the Philippines, Regional Trial Court, 4th Judicial Region, Branch 13, 1991).

95. Manapat, *Some Are Smarter Than Others*, pp. 274–92.

96. Ibid., pp. 267–73, 353–67.

97. "Information," filed August 8, 1989, by M. A. T. Caparas, PCGG Chairman, in *Criminal Case No. 143784*.

98. *Bukang Liwayway: Official Newsletter of the First Cavite Electric Cooperative, Inc.* (Dasmarinas: FCECI, 1983); Paulo C. Campos, *Odyssey of a Cooperative: History of the First Cavite Electric Cooperative, Inc.* (undated and unpublished manuscript).

99. See "Complaint," filed July 30, 1987 by PCGG Chairman Ramon A. Diaz and Solicitor General Francisco I. Chavez, in *Civil Case No. 0035*.

100. See, for example, "Urgent Motion for Temporary Restraining Order and Urgent Fair Decision of the Case," filed September 15, 1982, by Desales A. Loren, in *G.R. No. 57625*.

101. Ibid. Translation from the Tagalog by the author.

102. On land conversion cases in Cavite, see McAndrew, *Urban Usurpation*, pp. 115–36, 160–79.

103. Municipal Agrarian Reform Office, Dasmariñas, Cavite, "Dasmariñas Land Use Conversion Status, March 1988 to July 1992."

104. *Business World*, June 10 and July 31, 1991.

105. Commentary in Manila newspapers on the state of industrial relations in Cavite under Remulla is instructive. See, for example, the March 8, March 14, and April 19, 1992, issues of the *Philippine Daily Globe*; *Manila Chronicle*, February 24, 1995; and *Philippines Daily Inquirer*, May 1, 1995.

106. *Business World*, October 18, 1990; *Manila Bulletin*, July 29, 1991.

107. Interview by the author with a former Cavite provincial treasurer, July 24, 1991; interview by the author with a former president of the Cavite Contractors' Association, October 20, 1992.

108. "Complaint," filed January 26, 1989, by PCGG Chairman M. A. T. Caparas, in *Civil Case No. 0062*.

109. *Annual Audit Report of the Province of Cavite for the Calendar Year 1985; TBP Case Nos. 87-01808 through 87-02029.*

110. No less than Remulla's personal driver confirmed the veracity of this widely circulated anecdote.

111. As the acting secretary of the Department of Interior and Local Government, Sarino played a key role in budgetary allocations for local government units. The Aquino administration was regularly accused of selectively delaying and expediting the release of these funds to local officials throughout the country in order to secure promises of support for Ramos's presidential candidacy. Sarino also handpicked a heavily armed 81–man PNP task force that operated in Cavite in the week preceding the election of May 11, 1992.

112. *Philippine Daily Inquirer,* May 12, 1995.

113. Remulla allegedly provided protection to Manila-based drug-trafficking syndicates and Yakuza "sex-trade" recruiters operating in Cavite. See, for example, *Philippine Daily Globe,* October 18, 1990.

CHAPTER 4

1. See, for example, Gutierrez, *The Ties That Bind;* Gutierrez, Torrente, and Narca, *All in the Family;* and Soriano, *Political Clans and Electoral Politics.*

2. In this regard, this chapter follows the analytical direction suggested in McCoy, *An Anarchy of Families,* pp. 1–32.

3. Resil B. Mojares, "Political Change in a Rural District in Cebu Province," in Kerkvliet and Mojares, *From Marcos to Aquino,* p. 67.

4. On violent incidents in the 1924 elections, for example, see the February 8, May 9, and June 27, 1924, issues of the Cebu City–based weekly, *Bag-ong Kusog.*

5. *Pioneer Press,* December 5, 1947.

6. "Petition," filed May 22, 1992, by Bienvenido R. Sanid Jr. and Vitto A. Kintanar, Counsel for the Petitioners, in *S.P. Case No. EC-11,* pp. 1–2.

7. On Cebu municipal mayors implicated in election-related violence, see *Republic Daily,* May 4 and May 9, 1954; *Daily News,* February 7, 1958; *Daily News,* August 1959; *Daily News,* September 19, 1959; *The Freeman,* October 24, 1971.

8. The three town mayors killed in the province were Pedro Tecala of Danao (1952), Samson Cerna of Pinamungahan (1970), and Oswaldo de Dios of Carmen (1989). On one of the few cases of murder filed against a town mayor in Cebu, see the July 14 and 15, 1972, issues of *The Freeman.*

9. *Manila Times,* November 5, 1951; *The Freeman,* February 22, 1970; *Sun-Star Daily,* August 4, September 2, and September 24, 1992.

10. "Special Report re Illicit Activities of Mayor Daniel Sesaldo of Argao, Cebu," filed August 20, 1990, by PC Major Pedro V. Nicolas, District Commander, Headquarters, 344th Philippine Constabulary Company/INP District II, Sibonga, Cebu, to PC Brig. Gen. Triunfo P. Agustin, Regional Commander/Regional Director, Regional Command 7, Camp Sergio Osmeña, Sr., Cebu City; letter of September 5, 1990, from PC Brig. Gen. Triunfo P. Agustin, Regional

Commander/Director, INP, Headquarters, Philippine Constabulary Integrated National Police Regional Command 7, Camp Sergio Osmeña Sr., Cebu City to Director Juliano Z. Barcinas, Regional Director, Department of Local Government, Region 7, Cebu City.

11. See, e.g., PC Lt. Col. Hiram C. Benatiro, "An Evaluation of the Government's Campaign Against Illegal Fishing in the Province of Cebu" (M.A. thesis, National Defense College of the Philippines, 1990); *Sun-Star Daily*, April 3 and July 13, 1984, July 9, 1991, and July 3, 1992.

12. See Provincial Bantay Dagat Sugbo Council, 1989 Annual Report; and *Sun-Star Daily*, July 20, 1992.

13. See Bacani and Cailao, *Raiders of the Philippine Treasury*.

14. A 1992 "Report on Existing Tenements in Cebu" submitted by the Mines and Geosciences and Development Service of the Department of Environment and Natural Resources, notes that there were 111 mining concessions in 35 of Cebu Province's 52 municipalities.

15. The Argao quarry case is described in great detail in the following documents: Resolution No. 20, Series of 1990, Argao Irrigators' Service Association, Argao, Cebu; Resolution No. 4, Series of 1991, Argao Irrigators' Service Association, Argao, Cebu; and Letter of April 25, 1991, from Rodolfo C. Orais, Regional Director, Regional Office No. VII, Department of Agriculture to Jeremias Dolino, Regional Executive Director, DENR Region 7, Cebu City. See also the related articles in the April 13, 16, and 19, 1991, issues of the Cebu City–based *Sun-Star Daily*.

16. As one cockfighting aficionado noted after the passage of the 1991 Local Government Code, "the local government has acquired almost absolute licensing power over cockpits in their respective area of responsibility. The local officials are now in possession of authority to grant licenses or deny the same to operators for cause." *Sun-Star Daily*, February 8, 1992.

17. On this point, see, for example, the documents relating to *Civil Case No. CEB-4412*. See also *Sun-Star Daily*, February 8, 1992, on mayoral interests in cockpits in the towns of Barili and Balamban.

18. These landholdings are listed among the "Farm Land Holdings of 50 Hectares or More" culled from the Department of Finance's 1953 land tax records. The size and location of these landholdings was double-checked with the Department of Agrarian Reform's "Master List of Landowners and Their Properties: Cebu: Landholdings Over 50 Hectares," which was compiled in 1992 and provided to the author by the Department of Agrarian Reform's provincial office in Cebu City.

19. As the local heads of COCOFED, these Cebu mayors could corner "cocofund" receipts supposedly earmarked for the coconut farmers in their municipalities who had paid the coconut levy. On the political economy of COCOFED, see Virgilio M. David, "The Barriers in the Development of the Philippine Coconut Industry" (M.B.A. thesis, Ateneo de Manila University, 1977), pp. 142–55. On complaints about price manipulation and nonissuance of Cocofund receipts in Cebu, see A. M. Valiente Jr., *Coconut Socio-Economic And Marketing Study Part VIII: Central Visayas* (Quezon City: Department of Agriculture, Planning Service,

Special Studies Division, 1977), p. 57.

20. The Abines clan, whose bus company dominates the southern Cebu route and whose descendants have long occupied the mayorships of Oslob and Santander and today include the vice-governor of Cebu Province and a congressman, is discussed in Chapter 5.

21. See Ragas, *Handumanan mga Punoan Lungsodnon*, pp. 20, 39, 56. The case of the Allers of Alegria is typical: Miguel Aller, who served as town *presidente* from 1919 to 1937, is listed as "one of the hard-working landowners in his municipality" (usa sa makugihang magyayuta sa iyang lungsod). His son, Benito Aller, served as municipal mayor of Alegria from 1951 through 1986.

22. Endriga, "The Friar Lands Settlement," p. 403; *Handbook on Philippine Land Resources*, pp. 74–78.

23. Cullinane, "The Changing Nature of the Cebu Urban Elite," p. 268.

24. Wickberg, "The Chinese Mestizo in Philippine History."

25. Fenner, "Colonial Cebu," pp. 119–27, 128.

26. Ibid., p. 164.

27. Only towns south of Argao on the east coast and Dumanjug on the west coast, where the soil was "too broken and rocky to support extensive sugar cultivation," remained free of haciendas and large-scale tenancy. Ibid., p. 176.

28. Ibid., pp. 184–85.

29. Cullinane, "The Changing Nature of the Cebu Urban Elite," p. 273.

30. Cebu-based Chinese businessmen from Fujian Province describe themselves as speakers of "Amoy," a dialect spoken around the port city of Xiamen (Amoy) and similar to "Taiwanese," which is widely spoken by the population of Taiwan. On Amoy and other dialects used in Fujian, see Norman, *Chinese*, pp. 228–36; and Ramsey, *The Languages of China*, pp. 107–10.

The preeminence of Spanish mestizo and Chinese families in the regional economy of the Central Visayas and Mindanao centered in Cebu City is discussed extensively in Chapter 6.

31. See, for example, the account of political change in Carcar provided by Mojares, *Theater in Society*, pp. 20–54.

32. *Pioneer Press*, June 2 and June 21, 1946, and November 15, 1947; *La Prensa*, November 18, 1951; *Morning Times*, November 18, 1951.

33. The breakdown of the two-party system in the post-Marcos period rendered this form of analysis inapplicable for the 1988 and 1992 local elections. On those two elections, see below.

34. Towns and mayors of the 5th district: Alcantara: Demetrio Romero (1967–86); Alegria: Benito Aller (1951–86); Boljoon: Elias Gumera (1946–67); Ginatilan: Cresenciano Aranas (1955–63, 1967–80); Malabuyoc: Roque Vilbar (1946–80); Moalboal: Pedro Cabaron (1955–63, 1967–86). Towns and mayors of the 6th district: Aloguinsan: Aracile Gantuangco (1947–59) and Recaredo Echavez (1959–71); Barili: Librada Pace (1959–80); Dumanjug: José Macoy (1947–63); Pinamungahan: Samson Cerna (1963–71); Ronda: Lucio Ortiz (1955–71); Toledo: Marcelo Barba (1955–71).

35. Vicente C. Arcenas, "Kasaysayan Sa Pila Ka Banay Sa Lungsod Sa Bantayan, Lalawigan Sa Sugbu" [History of Several Families in the Municipality of

Bantayan, Cebu Province], an unpublished and undated manuscript kindly provided to the author by Mr. Arcenas. Translation by the author.

36. Ragas, *Handumanan mga Punoan Lungsodnon*, p. 79.

37. Available sources do not make clear Escario's factional affiliation in 1937, but he is listed among municipal mayors loyal to Osmeña in 1941. *Bag-ong Kusog*, January 17, 1941.

38. Remedios Escario was reelected mayor of Bantayan in 1992 and served with her daughter, Geralyn Escario Cañares, as vice-mayor.

39. Salvador Abello, brother of Remedios Escario, served as the chief of police in Bantayan for most of the pre-martial-law period.

40. As of 1983, Bantayan was home to 2,630 officially listed municipal fishing operators and nineteen commercial fishing operators. "Number Of Municipal Fishing, Commercial Fishing And Aquafarm Operators and Area of Aquafarm by Location: 1980 Central Visayas Region," *National Census and Statistics Office Special Release*, Number 444 (March 4, 1983), Table 1.

41. On this point, see, for example, "Information," filed August 13, 1991, by Atty. Anecita G. Pasaylo, Provincial Coordinator, Provincial Bantay Dagat Sugbo Council, in *Criminal Case No. CBU-22920*.

42. "Information," filed July 15, 1991, by Adolfo S. Alcoseba, 4th Asst. Provincial Prosecutor, in *Criminal Case No. CBU-22860*; "Resolution," filed July 15, 1991, by Florencio Villarin, Regional Director VII, National Bureau of Investigation, Complainant, versus Rogelio Japitana et al., Respondents, IS No. 91–7290. See also Michelle P. So's stories entitled "Illegal Gambling in Bantayan," in the April 6, 8, and 10, 1991, issues of the *Sun-Star Daily*.

43. Isidro Escario's brother Rafael, who served for many years as the barrio captain of Botiguis, owned a preponderance of the land on the islet and played a dominant role in supplying its fishermen with credit and, allegedly, dynamite.

44. See Judge Alfonso B. Baguio, "Decision," promulgated March 21, 1970, in *Criminal Case No. CCC-XII-27 Negros Occidental*.

45. On Rex Escario's involvement in the October 5, 1990, robbery of the Mandaue City branch of the Far East Bank and Trust Company, during which nearly 3 million pesos were stolen and the bank's chief security guard was killed, see the documents relating to *Criminal Case No. DU-1891*.

46. Violeta B. Lopez-Gonzaga, "The Sugarcane Workers in Transition: The Nature and Context of Labor Circulation in Negros Occidental," A Final Report Submitted to the Visayas Research Consortium and the Philippine Social Science Council, February 1985 (Quezon City: PSSC, 1985), p. 49.

47. Ibid., pp. 50, 59, 72.

48. Thanks to Bantayan's extremely hot and dry climate, residents of the three municipalities on the island are said to consume more San Miguel beer than the entire province of Bohol, a point of local pride that San Miguel salesmen are only too happy to confirm.

49. These arrangements are described in considerable detail in a letter of July 1, 1991, from Bantayan vice-mayor Diosdado Dosdos and municipal councilors Vidal Escanuela, Jupiter Pacio, and Arthur Despi to Philippine Ports Authority team manager Romeo S. Alviso, Cebu City.

50. The Escarios have owned several large fishing boats known locally as *kubkub* and supplied credit to numerous small-time Bantayan fishermen. Isidro Escario long served as president of the municipal COCOFED and, together with Bantayan vice-mayor Diosdado Dosdos, was accused of abusing his position in a manner typical of local COCOFED officials (see note 19 above). Bantayan residents, moreover, recall efforts by Geralyn Escario and Jesus Escario's estranged wife to monopolize copra trading in the town in the 1970s and 1980s.

51. For newspaper accounts of the 1973 fire, see the April 17 and 18, 1973, issues of *The Freeman*.

52. On Nicolas Escario, see Santiago U. Tan, "A Study of the Life of Dr. Nicolas G. Escario and His Contribution to Education" (M.A. thesis, University of the Visayas, 1969).

53. *OMB-VIS-90-006171* and *OMB-VIS-90-0074*, Diosdado Dosdos et al., Complainants, versus Rex A. Escario et al., Respondents (Cebu City: Office of the Ombudsman [Visayas], Provincial Capitol, 1990).

54. See the painfully trite account by Isidro Escario's vice-mayor, Sebastian M. Escalona, *Life-Laughter: Funny Sketches of My Hometown* (Bryn Mawr, Penn.: Dorrance and Company, 1982), pp. 123–27.

55. Commonwealth Act 725, enacted in 1946 and reinforced by Republic Act 599 (known as the Electoral Code), stipulated that boards of election inspectors consist of one member of the party polling the largest number of votes in the last national elections, one member of the party polling the second largest number of votes, and a third inspector to be chosen from among the public schoolteachers by the Commission on Elections.

In this regard, Isidro Escario benefited not only from his father-in-law's longstanding influence in the school system, but also from his own discretion over the hiring of new teachers once he assumed the mayorship. Knowledgeable sources in Bantayan estimate that at the end of the twentieth century 90 percent of the schoolteachers in the municipality were Escario supporters.

56. Cebu City–based newspaper reports on the acts of violence committed by Escario henchmen include: *Daily News*, January 26, 1960; *The Freeman*, February 1, 1968, April 30, 1970, and November 5, 1971.

57. This incident is well documented in "Information," filed January 10, 1991, by Nancy H. Madarang, Director, Law Department, Commission on Elections, in *Criminal Case No. CBU-20741*. See also the attached Annex "A": Affidavit of Wilson V. Fernandez of Bantayan, February 24, 1988. This incident is also discussed in the "Decision," issued October 25, 1991, by Judge Renato C. Dacudao in *Criminal Case No. CBU-15864*.

58. The original Cebuano text is cited in a Resolution filed October 4, 1989, in the above-mentioned case by Manuel N. Oyson Jr., Provincial Election Supervisor and Investigating Officer, Commission on Elections, Cebu City, p. 9. Translation by the author.

59. The 40 "goons" from Negros Occidental were allegedly provided by Tito Escario (son of Isidro and Remedios), who married into a wealthy family with large landholdings and a major interest in a sugar mill in the province. The remainder are said to have been supplied by Congressman Celestino E. Martinez

Jr., whose mother's family, the Espinosa clan, has long dominated the political and economic life of Masbate.

On the May 1992 elections in Bantayan, see, for example, the May 12 and 14, 1992, issues of the *Sun-Star Daily*.

60. The head of a local poultry cooperative told the author in 1992 that more than 500,000 eggs were hatched in Bantayan every day.

61. Nonong Laysan, for example, told the author in 1991 that he might eventually sell off the general store and the gasoline station to raise more capital for his family's already extensive poultry farm operations, which were funded in part with small-business loans from the Development Bank of the Philippines and the China Banking Corporation.

62. Several clans of less established lineage in the town (e.g., the Batayolas, Despis, and Montemars) have come to play prominent roles in the local fishing trade.

63. In 1992, the company supposedly paid out more than 500,000 pesos a week in wages and in purchases of fresh crabs. *Sun-Star Daily*, September 5, 1992.

CHAPTER 5

1. On the Cuenco-owned Bisaya Land Transportation Company, see *Bag-ong Kusog*, September 10 and September 17, 1937; and *Kagawasan*, November 7, 1951.

2. On Durano's use of generous donations to win influence in the Catholic Church hierarchy, see Cullinane, pp. 195–202, esp. pp. 195, 202. This thoughtful and carefully researched essay provides many sources of information as well as insights that I have borrowed in the following pages.

3. On Durano's self-promotion as patron and philanthropist, see ibid., esp. pp. 212–13; and Ramon M. Durano, *Ramon M. Durano: An Autobiography* (Danao: Ramon Durano Foundation, 1987), esp. pp. 156–239, which include extensive accountings of Durano's donations to civic and religious organizations.

4. The 1st district of Cebu comprised the towns of Bogo, Borbon, Carmen, Catmon, Danao, Pilar, Poro, San Francisco, Sogod, Tabogon, and Tudela on the northeastern coast of Cebu and the three municipalities of the Camotes Islands. Since 1987 these towns have formed the new 5th district, with the exception of Bogo and Tabogon, which belong to the 4th district.

5. Gerry Yaun Desabelle, *Sugar Basin Of Cebu: The Municipality of Medellin (September 1881–January 1988)* (Cebu City: Our Press, 1988).

6. See the brief biographical sketches of the Rodriguezes in Luna, *Ang Bogohanong Kasaysayan*, pp. 24–25, 145–47.

7. On Cuenco's use of his control over public works projects to build up a political machine in Cebu, see, for example, *Bag-ong Kusog*, February 16, 1940. Cuenco's father, Mariano A. Cuenco, who enjoyed close ties with the wealthy Spanish mestizo Escaño family, lost a bid for the provincial governorship of Cebu to an Osmeña protégé in 1907. On this point, see Cullinane, "Playing the Game," pp. 92–93, 110–11.

8. Land tax records from the early 1950s indicate that Dosdos's children inherited more than 400 hectares of coconut land in Borbon. See also Cayetano M. Villamor, *Senator Cuenco As I Know Him* (Cebu City: Villamor Publishing House, 1947), p. 95.

9. Congressman Dosdos apparently dropped out of the race after the Cuencos agreed to support a provincial Nacionalista slate with a mixture of Cuenquista and Osmeñista candidates that included Celestino Rodriguez, rather than Dosdos, for the 1st district seat.

10. T. D. Avila, "Poblacion: History and Cultural Life of the Town of Danao," in *Historical Data Papers: Cebu Province* (Manila: National Library, 1953); Durano, *Ramon M. Durano*, pp. 52–72; and Cullinane, "Patron as Client," pp. 166–69, 222–24.

11. Cebu Portland Cement Company, *Annual Report*, pp. 7–11.

12. For a list of all holders of permits to mine coal in Cebu, see *The Tribune*, November 15, 1941.

13. *Bisaya*, April 9, 1947; Celerino V. Uy, *Karon Mosulti Na Ako: Basahon Sa Gubat* (Cebu: Mercer Book Company, 1947); Manuel F. Segura, *Tabunan: The Untold Exploits of the Famed Cebu Guerrillas in World War II* (Cebu City: MF Segura Publications, 1975), p. 194.

14. Maj. Gen. Charles A. Willoughby, U.S.A. (Ret.), *The Guerrilla Resistance Movement in the Philippines 1941–1945* (New York: Vantage Press, 1972), p. 476. Willoughby's account is based on reports prepared by the Philippine Subsection, G-2 General Headquarters, Southwest Pacific Area.

15. See Rodriguez's embittered account of Durano's wartime atrocities: Celestino L. Rodriguez, *Episodios Nacionales: Horas Tragicas De Mi Pueblo* (undated, unpublished manuscript available at the Cebuano Studies Center, University of San Carlos, Cebu City), pp. 66–67, 126–28, 235–36.

16. *Pioneer Press*, June 2 and 21, 1946; *Morning Times*, June 8, 1946.

17. *Pioneer Press*, November 14 and 15, 1947.

18. On these developments in Cebu, see *Pioneer Press*, September 15, November 27, and December 11, 1946, and February 9, 1947; and *Morning Times*, September 28, 1926.

19. Copra exports from Cebu amounted to nearly 13 million pesos in 1947 alone. *Manila Times*, December 7, 1947.

20. *Morning Times*, July 16, 1947; *Pioneer Press*, December 17, 1947; *Manila Times*, February 27 and February 28, 1948; and *Philippines Free Press*, September 25, 1948.

21. *Pioneer Press*, August 6, 1947.

22. Lolita Gil Gozum, "A Historical Survey of the Postwar Operation of the Cebu Portland Cement Company, with Particular Attention to the Province Of Cebu" (M.A. thesis, University of San Carlos, 1955), pp. 33–35.

23. *Manila Times*, November 9, 1949.

24. See, for example, *Philippines Free Press*, February 3, 1951.

25. In Cebu Province alone, Liberal Party candidates were given 65,000 votes in excess of those tabulated in a subsequent recount. See "Decision," promul-

gated April 3, 1952, by the Senate Electoral Tribunal, in Claro M. Recto, Alejo Mabanag et al., Protestants, versus Quintin Paredes, Esteban R. Abada, et al., Protestees (Manila: Senate Electoral Tribunal).

26. *Ang Republika*, October 1, 1949.

27. *Philippines Free Press*, November 26, 1949.

28. "Decision," promulgated November 22, 1952, by Enrique Medina, in *Electoral Case No. 42*, Maximino Noel, Protestant, versus Primitivo Sato, Protestee (Manila: Electoral Tribunal of the House of Representatives), pp. 424–25.

29. Ibid., pp. 433–35.

30. For a vivid, if exaggerated, account of the violence and intimidation perpetrated by Durano in the 1949 election, see "Message to President Marcos," privileged speech of Senator Sergio Osmeña Jr., delivered on the floor of the Senate on June 14, 1966, p. 4.

31. The House Electoral Tribunal dismissed Urot's protest because he allegedly submitted his filing fee late, although he had a registered mail receipt proving he had submitted it on time. See "Resolution," promulgated November 21, 1950, by Congressman Manuel Concordia, in *Electoral Case No. 52*, Florencio S. Urot, Protestant, versus Ramon M. Durano, Protestee (Manila: Electoral Tribunal of the House of Representatives).

32. On the local elections of 1959, for example, see the October 1, October 7, and November 10, 1959, issues of the Cebu City–based *Daily News*. On Durano's use of violence in other elections, see, for example, *Daily News*, November 1, 1953; and *Morning Times*, November 21, 1967.

33. Osmeña, "Message to President Marcos," p. 3.

34. On this point, see University of San Carlos Political Science Majors Class, 1977–78, *A Study of People Participation in the Conduct of Local Government, Administration and Politics of Danao* (Cebu City: University of San Carlos, 1977), pp. 48–51; as well as the Commission on Elections, *Report of the Commission on Elections on the Manner the Election of the President of the Philippines Was Held on June 16, 1981* (Manila: Commission on Elections, 1984), p. 174.

35. *The NAMFREL Report*, pp. 33, 46, 61, 92.

36. On the celebrated Tecala murder case, see, for example, the May 27, 1952, January 10, 1953, and February 28, 1954, issues of the Cebu City–based *Republic Daily*.

37. *The Freeman*, June 16, 1966.

38. See, for example, *Sun-Star Daily*, May 11, 1983.

39. See, for example, the January 27, 28, and 30, 1972, issues of *The Freeman*.

40. On labor conditions, see "Answer," filed February 20, 1974, by José W. Diokno and Francisc E. Garchitorena, Counsel for the Defendants, in *Civil Case No. DC-56*. A 1959 Cebu newspaper account claimed that thousands of employees in various Durano-owned establishments in Danao received only half of the measly salaries they had originally been promised. See *Daily News*, September 25, 1959.

41. In 1983, for example, a series of fatal accidents, which resulted in the deaths of more than twenty Durano workers, drew attention to the lax safety standards in the Durano coal mines in Danao. See the Cebu City–based *Sun-Star Daily* for February 3, 4, and 5, April 3, and November 23, 1983.

42. *The Freeman*, April 9 and May 1–3, 1970.

43. Proponents of legislation that would have legalized *paltik* production estimated in the mid-1980s that at least 5,000 residents of Danao were directly involved in the illegal trade. See *Sun-Star Daily*, March 3 and April 12, 1985.

44. On November 26, 1968, then commissioner of customs Juan Ponce Enrile issued a Customs Administrative Order opening Danao as an official port of entry for international vessels and naming a Durano protégé, attorney Jesus Pepito, the customs collector at the new port. See *Cebu Bulletin*, March 5, 1969.

45. See, for example, *Republic Daily*, April 2 and May 22, 1955.

46. On tax evasion, see *Daily Mirror*, March 19, 1952; *Philippines Free Press*, March 22 and September 6, 1952. On his evasion of customs duties, see *Republic News*, June 9, 1962. On soliciting clients, see *Manila Daily Bulletin*, June 2, 1954. In 1962 the House Committee on Franchises passed a bill granting a franchise to Cebu Heavy Industries, a Durano company, to operate taxicabs in Manila at a preferred rate; see *Daily Mirror*, April 23, 1962.

47. See, for example, *Republic News*, February 10, 1963, for a list of appointments—including the Cebu City police chief and a number of assistant fiscals and municipal judges—recommended by Durano.

48. In 1964, for example, Paulo M. Durano, acting surveyor of the Port of Cebu, fell under a cloud of suspicion for his handling of a case involving a large shipment of confiscated contraband. See *Star Monthly*, June 1964.

49. See, for example, the December 24, 1968, edition of the Cebu City–based *Morning Times*.

50. Beatriz D. Durano (the congressman's wife) served as mayor of Danao from 1956 through 1971; she was succeeded by their son, Ramon D. Durano Jr. (1971–86).

51. Cullinane, "Patron as Client," pp. 209–10.

52. One of the new directors of CEPOC was Durano's partner in the Universal Cement Company; the other was a Cuenco protégé.

53. Durano and his close ally, Cebu 6th district congressman Manuel Zosa, had backed Garcia in the Nacionalista convention and delivered solid majorities in their districts on election day. On the role of political considerations in the awarding of Reparations Commission funds, see the articles by Napoleon G. Rama in *Philippines Free Press* for September 12, 19, and 26, 1959, and October 3 and 10, 1959.

54. *Report of the Reparations Commission for the Period from July 23, 1956 to December 31, 1958* (Manila: Reparations Commission, 1959), pp. 483–85; A.V. H. Hartendorp, *History of Industry and Trade of the Philippines* (Manila: Philippine Education Company, 1961), pp. 323–34.

55. *Cebu Trade Directory: 25th Anniversary: Cebu City 1937–1962* (Cebu City: Antonio A. Altonaga, 1962), p. 229.

56. Durano protégé Gaudencio Beduya, for example, held high posts at the

Development Bank of the Philippines (DBP) and the Central Bank of the Philippines; on Beduya, see *The Freeman*, June 30, 1966. See also "Subject: Ramon Durano Enterprises" of March 11, 1971, from Leonides S. Virata, Chairman, Bangko Sa Pagpapaunlad Ng Pilipinas, for President Ferdinand E. Marcos, Malacañang, Manila. A letter of April 23, 1974, from Emerito S. Calderon, President, Durano & Co., Inc., to the Development Bank of the Philippines (DBP) refers to a 5-million-dollar loan obtained by Durano & Co. and requests that the proceeds of the loan be applied to the outstanding debts of various Durano companies with the DBP. A note handwritten and signed by President Ferdinand E. Marcos reads as follows: "Chairman Virata, What happened to this request? Let us act on this."

57. Durano company debts to the DBP allegedly totaled more than 10 million dollars in 1971. See *Philippines Free Press*, July 31, 1971.

58. A letter dated December 5, 1979, from Ramon M. Durano to José A. Unson, vice-president and executive officer of the National Sugar Trading Corporation, Intramuros, Manila, accompanied by a handwritten note by President Marcos, requests special treatment of some 341,244 piculs of sugar from the Durano Sugar Mills designated as substandard and deteriorated according to analysis by the Philippine Sugar Commission (C7, LC Box 1, Folder 6, Document 07–001–0228, p. 278).

59. See *Data Series on Sugarcane Statistics in the Philippines* (Los Baños: Philippine Council for Agriculture and Resources Research, 1980), p. 23; and *Philippine Sugar Handbook, 1976 Edition* (Manila: Sugar News Press, 1976), pp. 49, 67.

60. For example, the Durano-owned electric company and ice plant, losing money and embattled in a dispute with the National Power Corporation, eventually waived its franchise in favor of a Cebu City–based electric cooperative. See *Sun-Star Daily*, August 9, 1984, and January 10, 1985; *Ang Pahayagang Malaya*, June 3, 1985, and November 4, 1986.

61. *Sun-Star Daily*, June 5, 1986 (two articles).

62. *Sun-Star Daily*, October 12, 1988.

63. Deo Durano had waged an unsuccessful campaign against his father for the mayorship of Danao City, while Don had won the vice-mayorship as his father's running mate. See the related stories in the January 22, 26, 27, and 28, 1988, issues of the *Sun-Star Daily*.

64. The newly formed 5th district closely resembles the pre-martial-law 1st district but includes the former 2nd district municipalities of Liloan and Compostela and excludes the former 1st district municipalities of Bogo and Tabogon.

65. Durano won by 20,000 votes in the district (and 19,000 votes in Danao City). *Sun-Star Daily*, May 18, 1987.

66. Senator Ernesto Herrera proclaimed Durano an official LABAN coalition candidate at a rally in Danao City reportedly attended by 20,000 supporters. See *Sun-Star Daily*, January 12, 1988.

67. *Ang Pahayagang Malaya*, October 23, 1986.

68. *Sun-Star Daily*, June 1, 1991.

69. *Sun-Star Daily*, September 2, 1991; *Philippine Daily Globe*, September 11,

1991.

70. *Manila Chronicle*, February 28, 1989; *Philippine Daily Globe*, September 10 and 19, 1991.

71. *Sun-Star Daily*, January 14, 1992; *Philippine Daily Globe*, April 27, 1992.

72. See "Petition," filed December 28, 1988, by Beatriz D. Durano, in *S.P. Proceeding No. 76-SF*. Documents provided by the provincial office of the Department of Agrarian Reform list more than 300 hectares of sugar land owned by the RMD Agricultural Development Corporation, a company now controlled by Congressman Durano. See *Department of Agrarian Reform 1992 Provincial Master List: Cebu: Landholdings Over 50 Hectares* (Cebu City: Department of Agrarian Reform, 1992); see also "Supplemental Inventory for Purposes of Collation," filed April 29, 1991, by Gonzalo D. David, Counsel for Paulino Durano, Virignia A. Durano-Aguiling, and Jesusa A. Durano-Macrama, Intervenors, in *S.P. Proceeding No. 76-SF*.

73. *Philippine Daily Globe*, March 30, 1992.

74. See *Civil Case No. CEB-4412*; *Sun-Star Daily*, November 7 and 10, 1985. On the discretion of municipal presidents of COCOFED over the copra trade, see the sources cited in Chapter 4, note 19.

75. *Sun-Star Daily*, July 28 and August 15, 1987. Engineer Horacio "Dodong" Franco, known as the owner of perhaps the largest sugar plantation in northern Cebu and one of the biggest construction companies in Cebu City, described Martinez to the author as extremely responsive to his requests for "assistance" and "favors."

76. *Sun-Star Daily*, January 12 and September 2, 1991.

77. For newspaper reports of Martinez's use of armed goons, especially those imported from his mother's family's home turf in Masbate, during election campaigns, see *Sun-Star Daily*, April 19 and April 29, 1984, and May 16, 1987; *The Freeman*, May 18 and 19, 1984.

78. On the Japanese introduction of *muro-ami* fishing to the Philippines in the prewar period, see M. Guerrero, "A Survey Of Japanese Trade and Investments," pp. 110–11; and Heraclio R. Montalban and Claro Martinez, "Two Japanese Fishing Methods Used by Japanese Fishermen in Philippine Waters," *Philippine Journal of Science* 42, no. 4 (August 1930), pp. 465–78.

79. See "Appendix I: Notes on the History of Muro-ami Fishing in Southern Cebu," in Bernie Cañizares, Farah de José, and Harold Olofson, "A People in Travail: Veteran Muro-Ami Fishermen in Southern Cebu and Adjacent Negros Oriental" (Cebu City: Development Management Group, Area Research and Training Center, University of San Carlos, September 26, 1991), pp. 47–50.

80. Ibid., p. 49.

81. *Manila Chronicle*, March 25 and 26, 1964.

82. Owned by the Dee family, the Frabal Fishing and Ice Plant Corporation was registered with the Securities and Exchange Commission in 1973.

83. Charges that the Abines-Frabal fleet has forcefully and illegally occupied private land on Talampulan Island, Busuanga, Palawan, are detailed in letters written by attorney Ofelia P. Miguel of Puerto Princesa City, Palawan, to the

deputy minister for local governments and Palawan governor Salvador Socrates on July 9, 1982, and to attorney Emerito Calderon, Samboan, Cebu, on August 20, 1986.

84. For a sense of the coercive resources available for the enforcement of labor discipline on the Abines-Frabal fleet, see the description of one *maestro*'s personal arsenal, featuring M-16 Armalite rifles and a Thompson submachine gun, in "Resolution," filed November 18, 1986, by Eric F. Menchavez, Assistant Provincial Fiscal, in *I.S. No. 86-5463*, 7th CIS District, Complainant, versus Quinciano Labiste, Respondent (Cebu City: Office of the Provincial Fiscal), p. 4.

85. See stories by Godofredo M. Roperos in the December 10, 17, and 24, 1986, issues of the Cebuano-language magazine *Bisaya*. See also *Ang Pahayagang Malaya*, October 4, 1986; *Philippine Panorama*, December 21, 1986; *Manila Chronicle*, March 16, October 10, 11, 12, 13, 1989, and September 5–11, 1992; Howard Hall, "Swimming into Danger?" *International Wildlife*, September–October 1985, pp. 4–13; "Sea Urchins," *Asia Magazine*, June 1, 1986, pp. 22–26.

86. See, "Marine Lab Helps City Council on Muro-Ami Issue," *Marine Laboratory Newsletter* (Silliman University, Dumaguete City) 1, no. 2 (April–June 1985), pp. 1, 3, 9; Fisheries Administrative Order No. 163, "Prohibiting the Operation of Muro-Ami and Kayakas in All Philippine Waters," signed November 20, 1986, by Minister of Agriculture and Food Ramon V. Mitra Jr.

87. Henk van Oosterhout, "The Muro-Ami: Some Observations on Child Labor in the Fishing Industry," *Philippine Journal of Industrial Relations* 8, no. 1 (1986), pp. 75–93; and Ruby L. Dimaano, "Muruami Fishing and the Youth," *Philippine Labor Review* 10, no. 1 (January–June 1986), pp. 53–62.

88. Cañizares, de José, and Olofson, "A People in Travail," p. 3.

89. A "Partial List Of Fishermen Dead/Missing" was kindly provided to the author by attorney Emerito S. Calderon, a leading political rival of the Abines family and a prominent opponent of *muro-ami* fishing in the Philippines.

90. *Manila Chronicle*, November 1, 1989.

91. Harold Olofson and Araceli Tiukinhoy, "'Plain Soldiers': Muro-Ami Fishing in Cebu," *Philippine Studies* 40 (First Quarter 1992), pp. 35–52.

92. Van Oosterhout, "The Muro-Ami," p. 78.

93. "Class Suit of Fishermen Against Operators/Recruiters of Muro-Ami," letter of August 11, 1986, from Emerito S. Calderon to Vice-President Salvador H. Laurel, for example, estimates that individual *pescadores* earn a few thousand pesos per expedition, while total gross profits for the fleet's operations amount to 450 million pesos, figures that jibe with other calculations of *muro-ami* earnings.

94. Olofson and Tiukinhoy, "Plain Soldiers," pp. 38–39.

95. Cañizares, de José, and Olofson, "A People in Travail," pp. 8–9.

96. See the sworn statements and NBI reports included among the documents filed in *Criminal Case No. AR-898*, The People of the Philippines, Plaintiff, versus Edgardo Almozar and Benjamin Rodrique, Accused (Argao: Regional Trial Court, 7th Judicial Region, Branch 26).

97. The Abines family also used the threat of violence to drive out a parish priest in Santander who did not agree with their tastes. On this incident, see *Sun-*

*Star Daily*, February 20, 21, and March 8, 1989.

98. See "SU Marine Laboratory to Re-Survey Sumilon," *Marine Laboratory Newsletter* (Silliman University, Dumaguete City) 1, no. 3 (July–November 1985), pp. 1, 4; and Alan T. White, "Philippine Marine Park Pilot Site," *Solidarity*, no. 115 (November–December 1987), pp. 73–78.

99. A letter of October 16, 1986, from an anonymous resident of Samboan, Cebu, to the editor of the *Sun-Star Daily* noted that "during the Teachers Night, September 28, 1986, Fiesta of Samboan, ex-Mayor Crisologo Abines attended the affair with three car loads and one *panel* [truck] of bodyguards. As the purpose is to impress on the people of Samboan, and their guests, that the Abineses are that powerful, naturally everybody . . . noticed the long and side arms with silence and practically submission." The public schoolteachers, of course, constitute the Board of Election that oversees the casting and counting of ballots on election day.

100. *Sun-Star Daily*, February 4 and 5, 1992.

101. See, for example, the charges against Abines in the *Sun-Star Daily*, May 8, 1987. The article also notes accusations that Abines bodyguards were suspects in the murders of a town vice-mayor and a barangay captain.

102. The Abines family's political foes have included former congressman and assemblyman Emerito S. Calderon (son-in-law of Durano and heir to large properties in Samboan) and landowners and politicians based in populous towns (e.g., Argao, Badian, and Dalaguete) closer to Cebu City, richer in natural resources, and more independent from the *muro-ami* economy than Santander and Oslob. On the political landscape of Cebu's 2nd district, see "Candidates in the 2nd District, Cebu," *Sun-Star Daily*, April 9, 1987.

103. See "Protest," filed November 3, 1987, by Edgar F. Gica and Elias L. Espinoza, Counsels for the Protestant, in Emerito S. Calderon, Protestant, versus Crisologo Abines, Protestee (Manila: House of Representatives Electoral Tribunal), pp. 7–9. See also pages 5–7 for a reiteration of the other charges against Abines listed above.

104. On discussions in the national legislature on *muro-ami* fishing, see the *Manila Chronicle* for October 7 and 14, 1989, and November 4 and 8, 1989.

105. See, for example, *Sun-Star Daily*, September 18, 1990.

CHAPTER 6

1. Durano had earlier made failed bids for the provincial governorship (in 1959) and the mayorship of Cebu City (in 1963).

2. In 1969 the winners of congressional seats from Cebu included Durano sons-in-law Emerito Calderon (5th district) and Celestino Sybico Jr. (7th district), cousin Manuel A. Zosa (6th district), and protégé Gaudencio Beduya (4th district).

3. *Sun-Star Daily*, March 13 and June 2, 1985.

4. The post-1987 6th district consists of the northern Metro Cebu towns of Cordova, Consolacion, Lapu-Lapu City, and Mandaue City. Dela Serna also received considerable support from two Cebu-based senators: ALU secretary gen-

eral Senator Ernesto "Boy" Herrera, and longtime mentor Senator John ("Sonny") Osmeña, whose strained relations with the rest of the Osmeña clan led him to oppose the gubernatorial bid of his sister-in-law, Annete Osmeña.

5. Resil B. Mojares, "The Dream Goes On and On: Three Generations of the Osmeñas, 1906–1990," in McCoy, ed., *An Anarchy of Families*, p. 312.

6. Although Serging Osmeña won every election to the Cebu City mayorship in the pre-martial-law period, his other responsibilities—as 2nd district representative and senator—necessitated that an Osmeñista vice-mayor (e.g., Carlos Cuizon or Eulogio Borres) be allowed to fill his shoes.

7. Cullinane, "Playing the Game," pp. 76–77.

8. Ibid., pp. 77–79.

9. On Nicasio Chiong Veloso and other Chinese and Chinese mestizo merchants in late-nineteenth-century Cebu, see Bruce L. Fenner, "Business Partnerships In Nineteenth-Century Cebu City," *Filipinas* 2 (1981), pp. 43–56; as well as Concepcion G. Briones, *Life in Old Parian* (Cebu City: Cebuano Studies Center, 1983), esp. pp. 20–21.

10. Cullinane, "*Ilustrado* Politics," pp. 314–15. This chapter forms the basis for much of the essay cited in note 7 above.

11. The name of Nicasio Chiong Veloso is among those mentioned as holding the exclusive franchise for the sale of opium in Cebu in "Anfion," Cebu Y Bohol, N.A. 75 Book 1, 1873–1898, in the Philippine National Archives, Philippine National Library, Manila. Osmeña's bride, Chiong Veloso's daughter Constancia, fell ill and died shortly before the announced wedding day, but her sister, Estefania, married him in a "grand ceremony" in Cebu less than one year later. See Cullinane, "Playing the Game," p. 79, and "*Ilustrado* Politics," p. 315.

12. On Provincial Fiscal Osmeña's success in negotiating the surrender of recalcitrant rebels (*pulahanes*) in the mountains above Cebu City, see Resil B. Mojares, "The Pulahanes Of Cebu: Case Study in Human Geography," *Philippine Quarterly of Culture & Society* 4 (1976), pp. 233–42; and *Bag-ong Kusog*, October 14, 1932.

13. Cullinane, "Playing the Game," pp. 84–98, and "*Ilustrado* Politics," pp. 325–62.

14. Cullinane, "Playing the Game," p. 101.

15. On the notoriously corrupt Bureau of Lands during the American colonial period, see Kelly, *His Majesty King Torrens*.

16. Endriga, "The Friar Lands Settlement," p. 76.

17. See Francis Burton Harrison, Governor-General of the Philippine Islands, "Executive Order No. 20," issued June 2, 1918, by the Office of the Governor-General of the Philippine Islands, in *Official Gazette* 16, no. 28 (July 10, 1918), pp. 1049–50.

18. "Commonwealth Act No. 58—An Act Creating the City of Cebu," Approved October 20, 1936.

19. Revision of the charter's provisions in Republic Act No. 3857 of 1964 still left the Cebu City Charter, in the words of one knowledgeable source, "the most autonomous city charter in the Philippines today." *The Freeman*, February 24, 1966.

20. Belinda A. Aquino, *Report on the Cebu City Government* (Quezon City: Local Government Center, College of Public Administration, University of the Philippines, 1967), p. 9.

21. Ibid., pp. 11, 15.

22. See Nolledo, esp. pp. 532–33.

23. For relatively recent accounts of Cebu City Police Department activities, see, for example, stories in the November 24, April 2, and April 3, 1991, issues of the *Sun-Star Daily*.

24. On this point, see Aquino, *Report*, p. 30; and *Sun-Star Daily*, October 19, 1991.

25. A 1967 newspaper article, for example, notes that, in 1996, of 7,000 business establishments that applied to renew their permits, 500 were denied for violating fire and safety regulations and various city ordinances. See *Morning Times*, January 29, 1967. See also Emma Montecillo-Acosta, "A Subject Guide to the Ordinances Enacted by the City Council of Cebu, 1945–1975" (M.S. thesis, University of San Carlos, 1977).

26. The 1966 report on the Cebu City government mentions chronic property tax underassessment as well as "insufficient" enforcement of city ordinances. Aquino, *Report*, pp. 22–23. For accounts of property tax assessment disputes and scandals in 1967 and 1991, see *Morning Times*, January 8, 1967; *Sun-Star Daily*, April 5, September 2, and September 24, 1991; *Philippine Daily Globe*, December 24–25, 1991.

27. *Manila Chronicle*, June 5, 1992.

28. On the Osmeñas' uses of public works projects in the pre-martial-law period, see, for example, *Manila Chronicle*, April 17, 1946; *Manila Times*, February 10, 1954; and *Manila Times*, March 28, 1954. On recent charges of a similar nature against 3rd district congressman Pablo Garcia, a close Osmeña ally, see "Petition of Protest," filed November 13, 1987, by Regalado E. Maambong, Counsel for the Protestant, in Celestino N. Sybico Jr., Protestant, versus Pablo P. Garcia, Protestee (Manila: House of Representatives Electoral Tribunal), pp. 8–9.

29. Land tax records from 1953 list Sergio Osmeña as the owner of 2,015 hectares of land in Cebu Province and show Osmeña family properties as amounting to 3,258 hectares, thus dwarfing the listed holdings of all other individuals and families in Cebu. See "Farm Land Holdings of 50 Hectares or More: Cebu," Department of Finance, December 31, 1953, records used in Sorongon, *A Special Study of Landed Estates in the Philippines*.

30. Mojares, *The Man Who Would Be President*, p. 100. This chapter draws heavily on the insights and information provided by Mojares in this fine study, as well as his excellent essay cited in note 5 above.

31. Mojares, *The Man Who Would Be President*, p. 67.

32. Ibid., pp. 68–69; *Manila Chronicle*, August 22, 1951; and *Republic Daily*, December 27, 1956.

33. *Philippine Daily Inquirer*, June 15, 1991, and August 30, 1992.

34. *Cebu Trade Directory*, p. 217.

35. Mojares, *The Man Who Would Be President*, pp. 36–38; *Manila Times*, November 21, 1948; Hartendorp, *History of Industry and Trade*, pp. 288–89.

36. *Manila Times*, March 29, 1953.

37. Ibid., March 10, 1954; Mojares, *The Man Who Would Be President*, pp. 37–38.

38. On the reclamation controversy, see Mojares, *The Man Who Would Be President*, pp. 111–12; *Philippines Free Press*, October 2 and 16, 1965; *Manila Chronicle*, November 6, 1965; and "Complaint," filed July 12, 1966, by Candido Vasquez et al., Attorneys for the Plaintiffs, in *Civil Case No. R-9455*, Manuel O. Ponce, Manuel S. Ponce Jr., Rosario Ponce Soriaga, and M. S. Soriaga, Plaintiffs, versus Sergio Osmeña Jr. et al., Defendants (Cebu City: Court of the First Instance of Cebu, 14th Judicial District).

39. In the latter part of the nineteenth century, more than 100,000 people a year emigrated to Southeast Asia from Amoy on British and Chinese vessels; 200,000 passengers traveled to Manila from 1875 to 1898. See Cartier, "Mercantile Cities," pp. 137, 196–97, 217–24. A 1962 list of 142 small commercial establishments in Cebu City—bakeries, corn mills, furniture stores, soap and candle factories—included only 29 names that were not obviously unlocalized Chinese. *Cebu Trade Directory*, pp. 317–21.

40. Compare the lists of prominent copra dealers in the early postwar era, ranking Cebuano taxpayers in the mid-1960s, and the richest families in the 1990s in *Morning Times*, May 10, 1947; *Star Monthly*, March 1965; and *Say*. On the Uytengsu family, see below.

41. A 1953 newspaper report, for example, cites alleged illegal campaign contributions by members of Cebu's Chinese Chamber of Commerce to Serging Osmeña; see *Daily Mirror*, September 5, 1953. A 1938 report of a major gathering at the exclusive Club Filipino in Cebu City noted the presence of assorted Aboitizes, Escaños, Gaisanos, Gotianuys, and Osmeñas; see *Bag-ong Kusog*, December 28, 1938.

42. Michael Cullinane, in published writings and personal communications with the author, expressed doubt about the veracity of these claims, noting evidence that suggests that the real father of Sergio Osmeña Sr. was another Chinese merchant, and that the putative kinship ties between the Osmeñas and Gotiaocos were convenient bases for a long-lasting business-cum-political alliance between the families. See Cullinane, "Playing the Game," pp. 106–7, and "*Ilustrado* Politics," p. 364.

43. Manuel Gotianuy also served as president of the Chinese Chamber of Commerce of Cebu and as honorary consul of the Chinese government in the prewar period. George F. Nellist, ed., *Men of the Philippines* (Manila: Sugar News, 1931), p. 121.

44. Tiglao, "Stacked Decks," p. 60. The article notes 1992 revenues for Cebu Shipyard and Engineering Works of P267.6 million in 1992 alone.

45. While family matriarch Doña Modesta Singson Gaisano enjoyed warm personal relations with Sergio Osmeña Sr., her grandsons apparently received preferential property tax assessments from Cebu City mayor Tomas Osmeña, grandson of the former president. See *Sun-Star Daily*, December 21, 1991; and *Philippine Daily Globe*, August 21, 1992.

46. This account of the Gotiaoco family's relations with the Osmeñas draws

heavily on "She-wu Hua-shang Ching-ying" [Cebu's Outstanding Chinese Businessmen], *Forbes Zibenjia*, March 1992, pp. 64–65. Carol Hau kindly translated this article into English for the author; Elizabeth Remick provided help with the title and family tree.

47. *The Story of Aboitiz & Company, Inc. and the Men Behind It* (Cebu City: Aboitiz, 1973), pp. 6–7.

48. Ibid., pp. 17–18. José Martinez, who as Cebu manager of the PNB provided "liberal credit" (P800,000) to the Aboitizes and extended the repayment period of their loans, resigned from the PNB in 1924 to become the auditor of Aboitiz y Cia.

49. Ibid., p. 19.

50. The four electric companies were Cotabato Light & Power Company, Davao Light & Power Company, Jolo Power Company, and Ormoc Electric Company. The Aboitizes also own substantial shares in the Visayan Electric Company of metropolitan Cebu, according to Securities and Exchange Commission documents, while their relative, Fr. Francisco Silva, managed three electric cooperatives elsewhere in the province. See *The Story of Aboitiz & Company*, pp. 39–61. See also *Mindanao Incorporated: A Primer and Directory of Major Corporations Operating in Mindanao* (Davao City: Alternative Forum for Research in Mindanao, 1990), esp. p. 150.

51. On charges that Aboitiz electric companies charged excessively high rates, see, for example, *Philippine Daily Globe*, August 30, 1991; *Philippine Daily Inquirer*, January 20, June 21, and November 9, 1992.

52. See *The Freeman*, December 29, 1966, and April 6, 1967; and the 1964 Articles of Incorporation of the Cebu Jai-Alai Corporation filed with the Securities and Exchange Commission. An Aboitiz-controlled company was subcontracted to pave more than 40 kilometers of Cebu provincial roads. A controversy subsequently arose over the bidding procedure for the contracts and the company's dubious fulfillment of contract requirements. See *Philippine Daily Globe*, April 30, 1992; *The Freeman*, August 10, 1992; and *Sun-Star Daily*, August 27, 1992.

53. See, for example, *Manila Chronicle*, January 12 and March 14, 1990; *Business World*, January 12, 1990; *Philippine Daily Globe*, January 18 and March 2, 1990;

54. *Daily Mirror*, June 18, 1964.

55. William's brother, James Chiongbian, also served as congressman from South Cotabato (1967–72, 1987–92) and from Saranggani (1992– ). A half-brother, Benito P. Chiongbian, won election as governor of Misamis Occidental in 1992.

56. *Manila Times*, May 3, 1949. A later account of the Chiongbians' postwar shipping expansion also notes the acquisition by William Lines of salvaged Japanese vessels for interisland passenger and cargo traffic in 1945, when Sergio Osmeña Sr. was president of the Philippine Commonwealth. See *The Freeman*, September 23, 1972.

57. In 1987, 1988, and 1989, William Lines was the top shipping company in

the Philippines in gross revenues and ranked 114 among the top 1,000 corporations in the country. See *Manila Chronicle*, June 14, 1989. See also Gutierrez, *The Ties That Bind*, p. 110.

58. *Daily News*, February 25, 1953, and April 10, 1958.

59. *Daily News*, April 10, 1958; and "The Lu Family," in *Shih-chieh Hua-jen Fu-hao Lieh-chuan* [Biographies of Wealthy Chinese of the World] (Hong Kong: San Si Chuanbo Company, 1992), pp. 155–63. Elizabeth Remick kindly translated the latter article from Chinese to English for the author. Statistics on the Philippine coconut industry in 1965 indicate that the Lu Do & Lu Ym Corporation was responsible for 44 percent of the total volume of coconut oil exported and 34 percent of the copra meal and cake exported. See George L. Hicks, *The Philippine Coconut Industry: Growth and Change, 1900–1965* (Washington, D.C.: National Planning Association, 1967), pp. 27a, 30a.

60. Mojares, *Escaño*.

61. *Cebu Trade Directory*, pp. 234–36.

62. Mojares, *Vicente Sotto*, p. 156.

63. Political Science 130 Class and Carolinian Political Science Society, 1975–76, *An Inquiry into the Visayan Electric Company, Inc. Power Failures* (Cebu City: University of San Carlos, 1976), pp. 3–4.

64. *Sun-Star Daily*, July 2, 1991.

65. *Sun-Star Daily*, September 14, 1988 and December 22, 1991.

66. On these allegations against Lhuiller, see the related articles published in the March 4, 6, and 11, 1992, issues of *Newsday*. See also *Sun-Star Daily*, December 20, 1991, March 11, 1992; *The Freeman*, June 12, July 14, and August 19, 1992; *Newsday*, March 5, 1992.

67. Garcia's uncle, two-term 3rd district congressman (1987–92) and current Cebu governor Pablo Garcia, was a close ally of Lito Osmeña.

68. On the setting of cargo and passenger rates, see Senator Teofisto T. Guingona Jr., "The Price Is Wrong," speech delivered on May 4, 1990, in *Speeches of the Senators* (Manila: Senate, 1990), pp. 130–34; on interisland routes, see *Business World*, December 20, 1991, and August 12, 1992; on violations of shipping regulations, see Stella Tirol-Cadiz's series, "The Perils of Shipping," published in the September 30, October 1, and October 2, 1993, issues of the *Philippine Daily Inquirer*; on tax exemptions, see *Business World*, November 3, 1988, and *Philippine Star*, September 26, 1992; see also *Asian Wall Street Journal Weekly*, July 4, 1994.

69. For a sense of the considerable autonomy and generous charter of the Cebu Port Authority, see the text of Republic Act No. 7621, "An Act Creating the Cebu Port Authority, Defining Its Powers and Functions, Providing Appropriation Therefor, and for Other Purposes," approved June 26, 1992, by President Corazon C. Aquino. The author of Republic Act No. 7621, and of Republic Act No. 6958, "An Act Creating The Mactan-Cebu International Airport Authority," was Cebu City (1st district) representative Raul V. Del Mar, a close ally and distant relative of Tommy and Lito Osmeña.

70. Resil B. Mojares, "Worcester in Cebu: Filipino Response to American

Business 1915–1924," *Philippine Quarterly of Culture & Society* 13 (1985), pp. 1–13. On Madrigal, see Quirino, *Philippine Tycoon*, esp. pp. 1, 9, 15–16 on his relationship with Osmeña; and Amada Tipace-Valino, "Family Portraits: The Madrigals," *Mr. & Ms.*, June 26, 1984, pp. 16–20, 22–23.

71. On Osmeña's backing of the Atlas manager for the 6th district congressional seat in 1965, for example, see *Daily Mirror*, December 24, 1965. On Atlas, see *The Impact of Corporate Mining on Local Philippine Communities*, pp. 21–92; and Lopez, *Isles of Gold*, pp. 216–18, 374, 380.

72. See the Articles of Incorporation dated August 28, 1962, among documents in the corporation's file at the Securities and Exchange Commission.

73. *Prospectus: Cebu Equity-Bond Issues* (Cebu City: Province of Cebu, 1991).

74. "Deed of Exchange," executed July 15, 1990, by and between the Province of Cebu and Cebu Property Ventures and Development Corporation. The CPVDC's articles of incorporation (dated June 15, 1990) are found among documents in the corporation's file at the Securities and Exchange Commission.

75. See the articles of incorporation of Cebu Holdings, Inc. (dated November 21, 1988) and Kuok Philippine Properties Inc. (dated October 18, 1989) on file at the Securities and Exchange Commission. On Ramos's wide-ranging business interests, see Jonathan Friedland, "Scatter-Gun Strategist," *Far Eastern Economic Review*, November 1, 1990, pp. 63–65. On Kuok's sprawling empire (including sugar refineries, flour mills, rubber plantations, tin mines, shipping lines, banks, insurance companies, a major international hotel chain, a Hong Kong newspaper, and properties in several Asian countries), see Sally Cheong, *Corporate Groupings in the KLSE* (Kuala Lumpur: Modern Law Publishers and Distributors, 1990), pp. 121–26; Robert Cottrell, "The Silent Empire of the Kuok Family," *Far Eastern Economic Review*, October 30, 1986, pp. 59–66; Rigoberto Tiglao, "More to Offer: Kuok Group Emerges as a Major Manila Developer," *Far Eastern Economic Review*, February 1, 1990, p. 49.

76. *The Freeman*, August 17, 1992; "Decision," promulgated September 4, 1992, by Associate Justice Carolina C. Grino-Aquino in *G.R. No. 101469*, Malayan Integrated Industries Corporation, Petitioner, versus the Hon. Court of Appeals, City of Mandaue, Mayor Alfredo M. Ouano et al., Respondents (Manila: Supreme Court); *Manila Chronicle*, May 22, 1992; *Business World*, November 18, 1992.

77. Mojares, *The Man Who Would Be President*, pp. 1–6, 27–52.

78. Mojares notes that Garcia reportedly extended more than a thousand appointments to his political *líders* in Cebu and spent from 7 to 14 million pesos in the 1959 elections in the province; see Mojares, *The Man Who Would Be President*, pp. 90–93. Uytengsu family patriarch Tirso Uytengsu (b. 1899) immigrated to Cebu City from Amoy, became president of the Cebu Chinese Chamber of Commerce, and headed Uy Matiao and Company, Inc., one of the biggest copra exporters in the Philippines. The flour mill built with Garcia's assistance became the centerpiece of the General Milling Corporation, the Uytengsus' food processing conglomerate. See also "Observations in Cagayan de Oro, Cebu, Bacolod, and Iloilo," Foreign Service Despatch #136 of August 22, 1958, from U.S. Em-

bassy Manila to the Department of State, in *Confidential U.S. State Department Central Files: Philippine Republic 1955–1959* (Frederick, Md.: University Publications of America, 1987); Yoshihara, *Philippine Industrialization*, p. 113.

79. Mojares, *The Man Who Would Be President*, pp. 115–52.

80. Marcos's revision of the electoral code also stipulated that residents of "highly urbanized" cities such as Cebu and Mandaue could not vote in provincial elections, thus minimizing the chances of an Osmeña comeback in Cebu Province through a revival of the family's urban political machine. See *The Freeman*, December 28, 1979.

81. On the rise and fall of Cuenca's business empire, see Manapat, *Some Are Smarter Than Others*, pp. 274–92; and Tiglao, *The CDCP Sting on Campos and Gapud*, see *Sun-Star Daily*, May 20, 1986, and Manapat, *Some Are Smarter Than Others*, pp. 353–67. See also *Civil Case No. CEB-9658*.

82. See Hawes, *The Philippine State*, pp. 55–82; Manapat, *Some Are Smarter Than Others*, pp. 174–98, 221–29; and Virgilio M. David, "20 Million Coconut People Are Victims of Levy Racket," in *The Coco-Dile File* (Manila, 1992), pp. 85–114.

83. Manapat, *Some Are Smarter Than Others*, pp. 190, 192.

84. "Complaint," filed July 22, 1987, by PCGG Chairman Ramon A. Diaz and Solicitor General Francisco J. Chavez, in *Civil Case No. 0012*. The "expanded" version of this "Complaint," dated December 8, 1987, notes that Fonacier won loans from the Development Bank of the Philippines "upon the express and personal approval of Defendant Ferdinand E. Marcos."

CHAPTER 7

1. E. P. Thompson, *Whigs and Hunters*, pp. 197–98.

2. Van Velzen, "Robinson Crusoe and Friday."

3. See John T. Sidel, "The Philippines: The Languages of Legitimation," in Muthiah Alagappa, ed., *Political Legitimacy in Southeast Asia: The Quest for Moral Authority* (Stanford, Calif.: Stanford University Press, 1995), pp. 136–69.

4. Lewis, *Ilocano Rice Farmers*; Mejia, *Philippine Virginia Tobacco*.

5. McCoy, "Sugar Barons."

6. G. Carter Bentley, "Mohamad Ali Dimaporo: A Modern Maranao Datu," and Jeremy Beckett, "Political Families and Family Politics Among the Muslim Maguindanaon of Cotabato," in McCoy, ed., *An Anarchy of Families*, pp. 243–310.

7. Leichter, *Political Regime and Public Policy*; Magno, "Politics, Elites"; and Glenda M. Gloria, "Makati: One City, Two Worlds," in José F. Lacaba, ed., *Boss: 5 Case Studies of Local Politics in the Philippines* (Manila: PCIJ/IPD, 1995), pp. 65–101.

8. On longtime Batangas governor Feliciano Leviste, perennial Capiz congressman and governor Cornelio Villareal, and eight-term Laguna governor Felicisimo San Luis, for example, see Machado, "Leadership and Organization in Philippine Local Politics"; and Sagalongos-San Luis, *Gobernador Felicisimo T. San Luis*.

9. On longtime Nueva Ecija governor Eduardo Joson (1960–86, 1988–92), for example, see Crisostomo, *Governor Eduardo L. Joson.*

10. Dañguilan-Vitug, *Power from the Forest.*

11. Before the electoral changes of the Marcos era, only the administration party and the dominant opposition party had the right to appoint members of precinct-level boards of election inspectors. This key provision of the electoral system, reflected in the persistence of two-party competition and coherent national party organizations before 1972, effectively confined races for the Senate to the Liberal and Nacionalista Party slates. Only one pre-1972 senator, Lorenzo Tañada (1947–71), won reelection as a third-party candidate, and only as an incumbent initially elected on the Liberal slate in 1947 and included as a guest candidate of one of the other two leading parties in the succeeding elections.

Massive electoral fraud has always played a major role in determining the outcomes of senatorial elections. For evidence of continuity in the role of fraudulent provincial canvassing of votes in the postwar era, see "Decision," promulgated April 3, 1952, in Claro M. Recto et al., Protestants, versus Quintin Paredes et al., Protestees (Manila: Senate Electoral Tribunal); and Tancangco, *The Anatomy of Electoral Fraud.*

12. The importance of regional voting patterns was reflected in the consistently large number of senators from vote-rich provinces (e.g., Pangasinan and Cebu) and the pattern of regional diversity in senatorial slates in the pre-martial-law period. Since 1987, however, no such pattern has been discernible.

13. In the prewar period, Batangas and Negros Occidental were overrepresented in the Senate because landed magnates from these two extremely rich agricultural provinces banded together to support their province-mates who ran for the Senate. Representatives of the "sugar bloc," prominent corporate lawyers and a few leading industrial magnates themselves, also served in the upper chamber of the national legislature.

Membership in the powerful Commission on Appointments, discretion over pork-barrel funds and legislation, and access to information and media for strategic "exposés" guaranteed a plethora of "rent-seeking opportunities" for incumbent senators.

14. For a systematic and structuralist analysis of the oligarchy's interest in preventing the emergence and entrenchment of a predatory and monopolistic national-level boss, see Hedman, "In the Name of Civil Society," chap. 2.

15. On the U.S. government's efforts to prevent Elpidio Quirino from winning reelection in 1953, for example, see Shalom, *The United States and the Philippines*, pp. 86–93.

16. See, for example, Boyce, *The Philippines*, p. 268. On the role of Japanese assistance in lining the pockets of President Marcos in the late 1960s, see Francisco Chavez, *Aide Memoire on Japanese Kickbacks* (Makati: Office of the Solicitor General, 1991).

17. Doronila, *The State*, pp. 123–52.

18. In the 1960s, as landed magnates began to shift into manufacturing and to buy out American companies, they began relying more heavily on government loans and tax/tariff breaks.

19. On the president's control of the armed forces, see Berlin, "Prelude to Martial Law"; C. Campos, "The Role of the Police in the Philippines"; Hernandez, "The Extent of Civilian Control." On his regulatory powers, see Baldwin, *Foreign Trade Regimes*, pp. 65–75.

20. On the importance of Clark Air Field and Subic Naval Base to the U.S. war effort in Indochina, see, for example, "United States Security Agreements and Commitments Abroad: The Republic of the Philippines," Hearings before the Subcommittee on United States Security Agreements and Commitments Abroad of the Committee on Foreign Relations, United States Senate, 91st Congress, First Session, Part 1, September 30, October 1, 2, and 3, 1969 (Washington: U.S. Government Printing Office, 1969). On Marcos's unprecedented success in winning reelection in 1969 through the mobilization of national state resources, see Shantz, "Political Parties." On U.S. backing of Marcos, see Bonner, *Waltzing with a Dictator*, pp. 85–137.

21. Manapat, *Some Are Smarter Than Others.*

22. On the government's bankruptcy, see De Dios, *An Analysis of the Philippine Economic Crisis*; on the withdrawal of U.S. support, see Bonner, *Waltzing with a Dictator*, pp. 355–440. On the fall of Marcos, see M. Thompson, *The Anti-Marcos Struggle.* For a revisionist account along the more structuralist lines suggested above, see Hedman, "In the Name of Civil Society," esp. chaps. 2 and 5.

23. In 1992 and 1995, the Marcos family's notoriously ill-gotten wealth bankrolled successful congressional campaigns by Ferdinand "Bongbong" Marcos Jr. and his mother, Imelda Marcos (as well as their respective failed senatorial and presidential bids). Yet these financial assets seemed to represent neither an established base in the national economy nor a stable source of productive capital for dynastic self-perpetuation, but rather a cache of reserves for conspicuous consumption and political speculation.

24. Gutang, *Pulisya*; Nolledo, *The Local Government Code of 1991.*

25. J. C. Scott, *Weapons of the Weak*, p. 308. See also Kerkvliet, *Everyday Politics in the Philippines*, pp. 266–73.

26. Migdal, *Strong Societies and Weak States*, p. xiii.

27. Ibid., p. 4.

28. Evans, "Predatory, Developmental, and Other Apparatuses," p. 562.

29. Ibid.

30. For classic historical accounts of the development of caciques, see Brenan, *The Spanish Labyrinth*, pp. 1–16; Carr, *Spain*, 366–79; and Romero-Muara, "Caciquismo as a Political System." On the mafia, see Blok, *The Mafia of a Sicilian Village*; Arlacchi, *Mafia, Peasants.*

31. On India, see, for example, Frankel and Rao, *Dominance and State Power.* On Latin America, see the various fine essays in Kern, *The Caciques.* On caciquism in Mexico, moreover, see Friedrich, "A Mexican Cacicazgo," and "The Legitimacy of a Cacique."

32. See Rouquié, *The Military and the State*, pp. 39–116. On the perhaps paradigmatic case of Venezuela, see Gilmore, *Caudillism and Militarism*, pp. 60–67, 125–57.

33. Rouquié, *The Military and the State*, pp. 153–86.
34. See, for example, Winichakul, *Siam Mapped*.
35. Bunnag, *The Provincial Administration of Siam*.
36. Riggs, *Thailand*.
37. On corruption in Thailand during this period, see J. C. Scott, *Comparative Political Corruption*, pp. 57–75.
38. Riggs, *Thailand*, pp. 242–310. See also Chaloemtiarana, *Thailand*.
39. On these points, see Ockey, "Business Leaders, Gangsters, and the Middle Class," pp. 64–190.
40. B. Anderson, "Murder and Progress in Modern Siam."
41. Anek Laothamatas, "Business and Politics in Thailand: New Patterns of Influence," *Asian Survey* 28, no. 4 (April 1988), pp. 451–70.
42. See Ockey, "Business Leaders, Gangsters, and the Middle Class," pp. 97–190.
43. Ibid., pp. 191–290.
44. Ockey, "Political Parties, Factions, and Corruption in Thailand."
45. See Taylor, *The State in Burma*, pp. 249–70.
46. See Robinson, *The Dark Side of Paradise*, pp. 218–34; Magenda, "The Surviving Aristocracy in Indonesia," esp. chaps. 2–4; and Harvey, "Tradition, Islam and Rebellion.
47. McVey, "The Post-Revolutionary Transformation of the Indonesian Army."
48. For an interesting account of this process in one Outer Island province, see Magenda, *East Kalimantan*, pp. 69–94.
49. See Shamsul, *From British to Bumiputera Rule*.
50. See Ahmad, "The Police and Political Development in Malaysia."
51. See Guyot, "The Politics of Land."
52. Shamsul, *From British to Bumiputera Rule*, pp. 181, 201.
53. On this trend, see Kerkvliet, "Rural Society and State Relations."
54. "Current Data on the Indonesian Military Elite: July 1, 1989–January 1, 1992," *Indonesia* 53 (April 1992), p. 98.
55. See, e.g., Erie, *Rainbow's End*; Key, *Southern Politics in State and Nation*; Mayhew, *Placing Parties in American Politics*; Shefter, "The Emergence of the Political Machine."

# Bibliography

ARCHIVAL PAPERS AND DOCUMENT COLLECTIONS

Commission on Elections, Intramuros, Manila.
Historical Data Papers, National Library, T. M. Kalaw Avenue, Manila.
Ramon Magsaysay Papers, Ramon Magsaysay Award Foundation, Roxas Boulevard, Manila.
Presidential Commission on Good Government, Philcomsat Building, Meralco Avenue, Pasig City, Metro Manila.
Manuel L. Quezon Papers, National Library, T. M. Kalaw Avenue, Manila.
Elpidio Quirino Papers, Ayala Museum, Makati Avenue, Makati.
Securities and Exchange Commission, EDSA corner Ortigas, San Juan, Metro Manila.

OFFICIAL GOVERNMENT DOCUMENTS AND REPORTS

"Administrative Complaint vs. Mayor Daniel Sesaldo for Alleged Involvement in Illegal and Terroristic Activities." Case before the Cebu Provincial Board, 1990–91.
*Aide Memoire on Japanese Kickbacks*. Makati: Office of the Solicitor General, 1991.
*Annual Audit Report of the Province of Cavite for the Calendar Year 1985*. Quezon City: Commission on Audit, 1986.
*The Aquino Administration: Major Development Programs and Projects 1986–1992: Cavite*. Manila: Office of the President, 1992.
*The Aquino Administration: Major Development Programs and Projects 1986–1992: Cebu*. Manila: Office of the President, 1992.

*CAR Case No. 1097*. Avelino Pulido et al., Plaintiffs, versus Cornelio T. Rivera et al., Defendants. Cavite City: Court of Agrarian Relations, 4th Judicial District, Branch 2, 1981.

*Cavite Provincial Profile 1990*. Trece Martires City: Office of the Provincial Planning and Development Coordinator, 1990.

Cebu Portland Cement Company. *Annual Report of the General Manager for the Year Ending June 30, 1950*. Cebu City: Cebu Portland Cement Company, 1950.

*Cebu Provincial Profile*. Cebu City: Provincial Planning and Development Staff, 1987.

*Census of the Philippines 1948*. Manila: Bureau of Printing, 1953.

*Census of the Philippines 1960*. Manila: Bureau of Printing, 1963.

*Civil Case No. 537-91*, Arcadio M. De La Cuesta, Plaintiff, versus Inter-Petal Recreational Corporation, Defendant. Imus: Regional Trial Court of Cavite, 4th Judicial Region, Branch 20.

*Civil Case No. 0012*. Republic of the Philippines, Plaintiff, versus Anos Fonacier, Cesar C. Zalamea et al., Defendants. Manila: Sandiganbayan, 3rd Division, 1987.

*Civil Case No. 0035*. Republic of the Philippines, Plaintiff, versus Benjamin (Kokoy) Romualdez et al., Defendants. Manila: Sandiganbayan, 2nd Division, 1987.

*Civil Case No. 0062*. Republic of the Philippines, Plaintiff, versus Juanito Reyes Remulla, Defendant. Manila: Sandiganbayan, 3rd Division, 1989.

*Civil Case No. 0063*. Go Pok Alias Benito Tan, Petitioner, versus Presidential Commission on Good Government and the People of the Philippines, Respondents. Manila: Sandiganbayan, 2nd Division, 1989.

*Criminal Case No. 13784*. People of the Philippines, Plaintiffs, versus Rebecco Panlilio, Trinidad Diaz-Enriquez, Accused. Manila: Sandiganbayan, 2nd Division, 1989.

*Civil Case No. 144805*. José L. Abueg, Plaintiff, versus Marbella Club Manila, Inc., and Eduardo Dee, Defendants. Manila: Court of First Instance, Branch 26, 1981.

*Civil Case No. CEB-4412*. Hee Acusar, Jesus Y. Acusar, and José Y. Acusar, Plaintiffs, versus Mayor Celestino Martinez Jr., Municipal Mayor of Bogo et al. Cebu City: Regional Trial Court, 7th Judicial District, Branch 8, 1985.

*Civil Case No. CEB-9658*. Malayan Integrated Industries Corporation, Petitioner, versus the City of Mandaue, Mayor Alfredo M. Ouano et al., Respondents. Cebu City: Regional Trial Court, 7th Judicial District, Branch 10, 1990.

*Civil Case No. DC-56*. Ramon Durano Sr., Ramon Durano III, and Elizabeth Hotchkiss Durano, Plaintiffs, versus Spouses Angeles Sepulveda Uy and Emigdio Bing Sing Uy et al., Defendants. Danao City: Court of First Instance, 14th Judicial District, 1974.

*Civil Case No. NC-321*. Trinidad Diaz-Enriquez and Montesol Development Corporation, Plaintiffs, versus Marbella Club (Manila), Inc., Philippine Tourism Authority, et al., Defendants. Naic: Regional Trial Court, 4th Judicial District, Branch 15, 1990.

*Civil Case No. TM-975*. Pura Abueg Nuñez, Plaintiff, versus Marbella Club

(Manila), Inc., Defendant. Trece Martires City: Court of First Instance, 4th Judicial District, Branch 1, 1982.

*Criminal Case No. 143784*, People of the Philippines, Plaintiff, versus Rebecca Panlilio, Trinidad Enriquez, Accused. Manila: Republic of the Philippines, Sandiganbayan, 1987.

*Criminal Case No. BCV-88-49*. Valeriana Cunanan et al., Plaintiffs, versus Municipality of Carmona et al., Defendants. Bacoor: Regional Trial Court, 4th Judicial District, Branch 19, 1988.

*Criminal Case No. CBU-4460*. People of the Philippines, Plaintiff, versus Eleazar Tabar et al., Accused. Cebu City: Regional Trial Court, 7th Judicial District, Branch 21, 1985.

*Criminal Case No. CBU-15864*. People of the Philippines, Plaintiff, versus Rex A. Escario, Accused. Cebu City: Regional Trial Court, 7th Judicial District, Branch 14, 1991.

*Criminal Case No. CBU-20741*. People of the Philippines, Plaintiff, versus Rex A. Escario, Accused. Cebu City: Regional Trial Court, 7th Judicial District, Branch 17, 1991.

*Criminal Case No. CBU-22860*. People of the Philippines, Plaintiff, versus Rogelio Japitana et al. Cebu City: Regional Trial Court, 7th Judicial District, 1991.

*Criminal Case No. CBU-22920*. People of the Philippines, Plaintiff, versus Rufo Fibida, Vicente Mata, et al., Accused. Cebu City: Regional Trial Court, 7th Judicial District, Branch 16, 1991.

*Criminal Case No. CCC-XII-27 Negros Occidental*. People of the Philippines, Complainant, versus Carlos Caramonte, Accused. Bacolod City: Circuit Criminal Court, 12th Judicial District, 1967.

*Criminal Case No. DU-1891*. People of the Philippines, Plaintiff, versus Ruel Ceniza Archua alias Juan Castillo/Taroroy/Roy, Marilyn Balancar y Bomonit et al. Mandaue City: Regional Trial Court, 7th Judicial District, Branch 28, 1991.

*Criminal Case No. NC-579*. People of the Philippines, Plaintiff, versus SPO3 Armando Angue et al., Accused. Naic, Cavite: Regional Trial Court, 4th Judicial District, Branch 15, 1992.

*EAC No. 6-90*. Octavio D. Velasco, Protestant/Appellant, versus Conrado C. Lindo, Protestee/Appellee. Manila: Electoral Contests Adjudication Department, Commission on Elections, 1990.

Economic Intelligence and Investigation Bureau. "Economic Subversion in the Philippines." Manila: EIIB, December 1991.

Economic Intelligence and Investigation Bureau. "Extent Of Smuggling." Manila: EIIB, 1991.

*Election Protest Case No. NC-1*. Octavio D. Velasco, Protestant, versus Conrado C. Lindo, Protestee. Naic: Regional Trial Court, Branch 15, 1988.

*Election Protest Case No. NC-2*. Teodorico C. Ramirez, Protestant, versus Paulito C. Unas, Protestee. Naic: Regional Trial Court, 4th Judicial District, Branch 15, 1992.

*Electoral Case No. 102*, Manuel S. Rojas, Protestant, versus Jose T. Cajulis, Protestee. Manila: Electoral Tribunal of the House of Representatives, 1957.

*Electoral Case No. 137*. Fernando C. Campos, Protestant, versus Justiniano S.

Montano Sr., Protestee. Manila: Electoral Tribunal of the House of Representatives, 1962.

*Executive Order No. 525.* "Designating the Public Estates Authority as the Agency Primarily Responsible for All Reclamation Projects." Manila: Office of the President, Malacañang, February 14, 1979.

*Fact-Finding Survey Report.* Manila: Department of Labor, 1936.

*Fifth Annual Report of the Philippine Commission, 1904.* Washington, D.C.: U.S. Government Printing Office, 1905.

*G.R. No. 57625.* Avelino Pulido et al., Petitioners, versus the Honorable Court of Appeals et al., Respondents. Manila: Supreme Court, 1982.

*Handbook on Philippine Land Resources.* Manila: Bureau of Lands, 1954.

*Land Registration Case No. B-90-6.* Cesar Casal et al., Applicants. Bacoor: Regional Trial Court, 4th Judicial District, Branch 19, 1990.

*Landholdings Covered Under Operation Land Transfer, Municipality of Bantayan.* Bantayan, Cebu: Municipal Agrarian Reform Office, 1992.

*List of Lease Contracts Issued, Province: Cebu.* Cebu City: Bureau of Mines, 1992.

*Masterlist of Landowner 50 Has. and Above.* Trece Martires City: Department of Agrarian Reform, Cavite Provincial Office, 1992.

National Bureau of Investigation. *Annual Report Fiscal Year 1970.* Manila: Department of Justice, 1971.

*1980 Census of Fisheries: Region VII—Central Visayas.* Manila: National Census and Statistics Office, 1980.

*1990 Census of Population and Housing: Cebu.* Cebu City: Provincial Planning and Development Office, 1991.

*1970 Census of Population and Housing.* Manila: Bureau of the Census and Statistics, 1972.

*1971 Census of Agriculture.* Manila: National Census and Statistics Office, 1975.

*PCGG I.S. No. 35.* Presidential Commission on Good Government, Complainant, versus Juanito Reyes Remulla, Respondent.

"Petition," filed February 1, 1980, by Valentino L. Legaspi, in George Baladjay et al., Petitioners, versus Florentino Solon et al., Respondents. Manila: Commission on Elections, 1980.

"Petition of Protest," filed November 3, 1987, by Edgar F. Gica and Elias L. Espinoza, in Emerito S. Calderon, Protestant, versus Crisologo Abines, Protestee. Manila: House of Representatives Electoral Tribunal, 1987.

"Petition of Protest," filed November 13, 1987, by Regalado E. Maambong, in Celestino N. Sybico Jr., Protestant, versus Pablo P. Garcia, Protestee. Manila: House of Representatives Electoral Tribunal, 1987.

Philippine Ports Authority. *Port Directory Cebu District 1985.* Manila: Philippine Ports Authority, 1985.

*Placer Lease Contracts.* Cebu City: Bureau of Mines, 1992.

*Port of Manila and Other Philippine Ports Year Book 1950.* Manila: Bureau of Printing, 1951.

*Province of Cebu: Socio-Economic Profile CY 1990.* Cebu City: Provincial Planning and Development Office, 1991.

*Provincial Bantay Dagat Sugbo Council 1989 Annual Report.* Cebu City: Office of the Vice-Governor, 1990.

*Provincial Bantay Dagat Sugbo Council 1991 Annual Report.* Cebu City: Office of the Vice-Governor, 1992.

*Provincial Profile: Cavite.* Manila: Republic of the Philippines National Statistics Office, 1990.

*Report of the Philippine Commission to the Secretary of War 1908.* Washington, D.C.: U.S. Government Printing Office, 1909.

*Roster of Philippine Legislators: 1907 to 1988.* Quezon City: House of Representatives Congressional Library, 1989.

*RTC-BCV-88049,* Valeriana Cunanan et al., Plaintiffs, versus Municipality of Carmona et al., Defendants. Bacoor, Cavite: Regional Trial Court, 4th Judicial District, Branch 19, 1988.

*Sixth Annual Report of the Philippine Commission, 1905.* Washington, D.C.: U.S. Government Printing Office, 1906.

*Special Civil Action Case No. 73646.* United Nationalist Democratic Organization (UNIDO) and Fernando C. Campos, Petitioners, versus the Provincial Board of Canvassers of the Province of Cavite et al., Respondents. Manila: Supreme Court, 1986.

*S.P. Case No. EC-11.* Clarito J. Dinglasa, Petitioner/Protestant, versus Antonio Singco, Repondent/Protestee. Cebu City: Regional Trial Court, 7th Judicial District, Branch 16, 1992.

*S.P. Proceedings No. 76-SF.* "In the Matter of the Settlement of the Estate of the Deceased Ramon M. Durano, Sr." Danao City: Regional Trial Court, 7th Judicial District, Branch 25, 1988.

*TBP Case Nos. 87-01808 through 87-02029.* Fernando C. Campos et al., Complainants, versus Juanito R. Remulla et al., Respondents. Manila: Republic of the Philippines, Office of the Ombudsman, 1987.

*United States Security Agreements and Commitments Abroad: The Republic of the Philippines.* Hearings Before the Subcommittee on United States Security Agreements and Commitments Abroad of the Committee on Foreign Relations, United States Senate, 91st Congress, 1st Session, Part 1, September 30, October 1, 2, and 3, 1969. Washington, D.C.: U.S. Government Printing Office, 1969.

### NEWSPAPERS AND MAGAZINES

*Ang Pahayagang Malaya* (Manila)
*Asia-Philippines Leader* (Manila)
*Bag-ong Kusog* (Cebu City)
*Bag-ong Suga* (Cebu City)
*Bisaya* (Cebu City)
*Bulletin Today* (Manila)
*Business Day* (Manila)
*Business Star* (Manila)
*Business World* (Manila)

*Cebu Daily News*
*Daily Mirror* (Manila)
*Freeman* (Cebu City)
*Manila Daily Bulletin*
*Manila Chronicle*
*Manila Times*
*Morning Times* (Cebu City)
*New Day* (Cebu City)
*Newsday* (Manila)

*Philippine Daily Globe* (Manila)
*Philippine Daily Inquirer* (Manila)
*Philippines Free Press* (Manila)
*Pioneer Press* (Cebu City)
*Republic Daily* (Cebu City)
*Say* (Manila)

*Star Monthly* (Cebu City)
*Sun-Star Daily* (Cebu City)
*Taliba* (Manila)
*Tulay* (Manila)
*Veritas* (Manila)

## SECONDARY SOURCES

Abueva, José V. *Ramon Magsaysay: A Political Biography*. Manila: Solidaridad Publishing House, 1971.

Agpalo, Remigio. *Pandanggo sa Ilaw: The Politics of Occidental Mindoro*. Quezon City: University of the Philippines, 1965.

Aguilar, Filomeno V., Jr. "Phantoms of Capitalism and Sugar Production Relations in a Colonial Philippine Island." Ph.D. diss., Cornell University, 1992.

Aguinaldo, Emilio. *Mga Gunita Ng Himagsikan*. Manila: Cristina Aguinaldo Suntay, 1964.

Ahmad, Zakaria Hin Haji. "The Police and Political Development in Malaysia: Change, Continuity and Institution-Building of a 'Coercive' Apparatus in a Developing, Ethnically Divided Society." Ph.D. diss., Massachusetts Institute of Technology, 1977.

Alano, Bienvenido, Jr. "Import Smuggling in the Philippines: An Economic Analysis." *Journal of Philippine Development* 11, no. 2 (1984): 157–90.

Alvarez, Santiago V. *The Katipunan and the Revolution: Memoirs of a General with the Original Tagalog Text*. Quezon City: Ateneo de Manila University Press, 1992.

Anderson, Benedict. "Cacique Democracy in the Philippines: Origins and Dreams." *New Left Review*, no. 169 (May/June 1988): 3–31.

———. "Murder and Progress in Modern Siam." *New Left Review*, no. 181 (May/June 1990): 33–48.

———. "Old Corruption." *London Review of Books*, February 5, 1987, pp. 3, 5–6.

———. "Studies of the Thai State: The State of Thai Studies." In Eliezer B. Ayal, ed., *The Study of Thailand: Analyses of Knowledge, Approaches, and Prospects in Anthropology, Art History, Economics, History, and Political Science*. Athens: Ohio University Southeast Asia Series No. 54, 1978.

Anderson, Gerald H., ed. *Studies in Philippine Church History*. Ithaca, N.Y.: Cornell University Press, 1969.

Ansay-Miranda, Evelyn. "Early American Imperialism and the Development of the Philippine Oligarchy: The Case of the Philippine Commission and the Filipino Legislative Elite, 1899–1916." Ph.D. diss., University of the Philippines, 1966.

Arlacchi, Pino. *Mafia, Peasants and Great Estates: Society in Traditional Calabria*. Cambridge: Cambridge University Press, 1983.

Artigas y Cuerva, Manuel. *Los Sucesos de 1872: Reseña Historica Bio-Bibliográphica*. Manila: La Vanguardia, 1911.

Azcarraga y Palmero, Manuel. *La Reforma del Municipio Indigena en Filipinas.* Madrid: Imprenta de J. Noguera, 1871.

Bacani, Cesar S., Jr., and Bernardino L. Cailao. *Raiders of the Philippine Treasury: The Inside Story of the 1978 Cebu Highways Anomaly.* Manila: Bacani and Cailao, 1990.

Baja, Emmanuel A. *Philippine Police System and Its Problems.* Manila: Pobre's Press, 1933.

Baldwin, Robert E. *Foreign Trade Regimes and Economic Development: The Philippines.* New York: Columbia University Press, 1975.

Bankoff, Greg. "Big Fish in Small Ponds: The Exercise of Power in a Nineteenth-Century Philippine Municipality." *Modern Asian Studies* 26, no. 4 (1992): 679–700.

———. "Crime, Society and the State in the Nineteenth Century Philippines." Ph.D. diss., Murdoch University, 1990.

———. "Redefining Criminality: Gambling and Financial Expediency in the Colonial Philippines, 1764–1898." *Journal of Southeast Asian Studies* 22, no. 2 (September 1991): 267–81.

Bardhan, Pranab. *The Political Economy of Development in India.* Oxford: Basil Blackwell, 1984.

Baterina, Virginia F. "A Study of Money in Elections in the Philippines." *Philippine Social Sciences and Humanities Review* 20, no. 2 (June 1985): 39–172.

Berlin, Donald Lane. "Prelude to Martial Law: An Examination of Pre-1972 Philippine Civil-Military Relations." Ph.D. diss., University of South Carolina, 1982.

Bethel, Leslie. *Colonial Spanish America.* Cambridge: Cambridge University Press, 1987.

Billig, Michael S. "'Syrup in the Wheels of Progress': The Inefficient Organization of the Philippine Sugar Industry." *Journal of Southeast Asian Studies* 24, no. 1 (March 1993): 122–47.

Blair, Emma Helen, and James Alexander Robertson, eds. *The Philippine Islands, 1493–1803.* Cleveland, Ohio: Arthur H. Clark Company, 1903–1919.

Blok, Anton. *The Mafia of a Sicilian Village 1860–1960: A Study of Violent Peasant Entrepreneurs.* New York: Harper and Row, 1974.

Bogo-Medellin Sugar Planters Association. *Annual Report: 1958.* Cebu City: Bogo-Medellin Sugar Planters Association, 1958.

Bonner, Raymond. *Waltzing with a Dictator: The Marcoses and the Making of American Policy.* New York: Times Books, 1987.

Borromeo, Soledad. "El Cadiz Filipino: Colonial Cavite, 1571–1896." Ph.D. diss., University of California at Berkeley, 1973.

Boyce, James K. *The Philippines: The Political Economy of Growth and Impoverishment in the Marcos Era.* Honolulu: University of Hawaii Press, 1993.

Brass, Paul R. "National Power and Local Politics in India: A Twenty-Year Perspective." *Modern Asian Studies* 18, no. 1 (1984): 89–118.

Brenan, Gerald. *The Spanish Labyrinth: An Account of the Social and Political Background of the Civil War.* Cambridge: Cambridge University Press, 1990.

Broad, Robin, and John Cavanagh. *Plundering Paradise: The Struggle for the En-

*vironment in the Philippines*. Berkeley: University of California Press, 1993.

Bunnag, Tej. *The Provincial Administration of Siam 1892–1915: The Ministry of the Interior Under Prince Damrong Rajanubhab*. Kuala Lumpur: Oxford University Press, 1977.

Caballero, Isabelo P., and M. DeGracia Concepcion. *Quezon: The Story of a Nation and Its Foremost Statesman*. Manila: United Publishers, 1935.

Campos, Amado C. "Commercial-Scale Poultry Production in Cebu." *Philippine Agriculturist* 37, nos. 1/2 (June/July 1953): 9–15.

Campos, Cicero C. "The Role of the Police in the Philippines: A Case Study from the Third World." Ph.D. diss., Michigan State University, 1983.

Canlas, Corinne. "Industrializing the Countryside or Undermining Agriculture? The Calabarzon Land Conversion Project." *Philippine Development Briefing*, no. 4 (1993): 1–15.

Caoili, Manuel. "Quezon and His Business Friends: Notes on the Origins of Philippine National Capitalism." *Philippine Journal of Public Administration* 31, no. 1 (January 1987): 65–106.

———. "Real Property Tax Administration in the Province of Leyte." *Philippine Journal of Public Administration* 12, no. 3 (July 1968): 310–30.

"Carmona Relocation: The Solution to Urban Problems?" *SGV Group Journal*, no. 1 (1973): 62–67.

Carr, Raymond. *Spain: 1808–1939*. Oxford: Clarendon Press, 1966.

Cartier, Carolyn Lee. "Mercantile Cities on the South China Coast: Ningbo, Fuzhou, and Xiamen." Ph.D. diss., University of California at Berkeley, 1991.

Castillo, J. G. *Property Tax Administration in the Philippines*. Manila: Bureau of Printing, 1957.

Center for Regional Development Operations. *Metro Cebu Business Directory*. Cebu City: U.P. College Cebu, 1982.

Chaloemtiarana, Thak. *Thailand: The Politics of Despotic Paternalism*. Bangkok: Social Science Association of Thailand, 1979.

Chapman, Paul K. *Trouble on Board: The Plight of International Seafarers*. Ithaca, N.Y.: ILR Press, 1992.

Chaudhuri, K. N. *Trade and Civilization in the Indian Ocean: An Economic History from the Rise of Islam to 1750*. Cambridge: Cambridge University Press, 1985.

Chubb, Judith. *Patronage, Power, and Poverty in Southern Italy: A Tale of Two Cities*. Cambridge: Cambridge University Press, 1982.

Clariño, José V. *General Aguinaldo and Philippine Politics*. Manila: Fajardo Press, 1928.

Concepcion, Venancio. *"La Tragedia" del Banco Nacional Filipino*. Manila: 1927.

Connolly, Michael J. *Church Lands and Peasant Unrest in the Philippines: Agrarian Conflict in 20th-Century Luzon*. Quezon City: Ateneo de Manila University Press, 1992.

Corpuz, Onofre D. *The Bureaucracy in the Philippines*. Manila: University of the Philippines Institute of Public Administration, Studies in Public Administration no. 4, 1957.

———. *The Roots of the Filipino Nation.* Quezon City: Aklahi Foundation, 1989.

Crisostomo, Isabelo Tinio. *Governor Eduardo L. Joson: The Gentle Lion of Nueva Ecija.* Quezon City: J. Kriz Publishing Enterprises, 1989.

Crouch, Harold. *Economic Change, Social Structure and the Political System in Southeast Asia: Philippine Development Compared with the Other ASEAN Countries.* Singapore: Institute of Southeast Asian Studies, 1985.

Cullinane, Michael. "The Changing Nature of the Cebu Urban Elite in the 19th Century." In Alfred W. McCoy and Ed. C. de Jesus, eds., *Philippine Social History: Global Trade and Local Transformations.* Quezon City: Ateneo de Manila University Press, 1982.

———. "*Ilustrado* Politics: The Response of the Filipino Educated Elite to American Colonial Rule, 1898–1907." Ph.D. diss., University of Michigan, 1989.

———. "Patron as Client: Warlord Politics and the Duranos of Danao." In Alfred W. McCoy, ed., *An Anarchy of Families: State and Family in the Philippines.* Madison: University of Wisconsin Center for Southeast Asian Studies, 1993.

———. "Playing the Game: The Rise of Sergio Osmeña, 1898–1907." In Ruby Paredes, ed., *Philippine Colonial Democracy.* Quezon City: Ateneo de Manila University Press, 1989.

Curry, James Allan. "The Determinants of Philippine Political Competition in Presidential and Off-Year Elections, 1946–1971." Ph.D. diss., University of Kansas, 1974.

De Dios, Emmanuel. *An Analysis of the Philippine Economic Crisis.* Quezon City: University of the Philippines, 1984.

De Jesus, Ed. C. *The Tobacco Monopoly in the Philippines: Bureaucratic Enterprise and Social Change, 1766–1880.* Quezon City: Ateneo de Manila University Press, 1980.

Dones, Ed. *Visayas Agriculture: Profile of a Crisis.* Quezon City: Philippine Peasant Institute, 1992.

Doronila, Amando. *The State, Economic Transformation, and Political Change in the Philippines, 1946–1972.* Singapore: Oxford University Press, 1992.

———. "The Transformation of Patron-Client Relations and Its Political Consequences in Postwar Philippines." *Journal of Southeast Asian Studies* 16, no. 1 (March 1985): 99–116.

Edgerton, Ronald K. "Americans, Cowboys, and Cattlemen on the Mindanao Frontier." In Peter Stanley, ed., *Reappraising an Empire: New Perspectives on Philippine-American History.* Cambridge, Mass.: Harvard University Press, 1984.

Elliott, John H. *Imperial Spain: 1469–1716.* New York: St. Martin's Press, 1963.

Endriga, José N. "The Friar Lands Settlement: Promise and Performance." *Philippine Journal of Public Administration* 14, no. 4 (October 1970): 397–413.

Erie, Steven P. *Rainbow's End: Irish-Americans and the Dilemmas of Urban Machine Politics, 1840–1985.* Berkeley: University of California Press, 1988.

Evans, Peter B. "Predatory, Developmental, and Other Apparatuses: A Comparative Political Economy Perspective on the Third World State." *Sociological Forum* 4, no. 4 (December 1989).

Fegan, Brian. "Accumulation on the Basis of an Unprofitable Crop." In Gillian

Hart, Andrew Turton, and Benjamin White, eds., *Agrarian Transformations: Local Processes and the State in Southeast Asia*. Berkeley: University of California Press, 1989.

———. "Folk-Capitalism: Economic Strategies of Peasants in a Philippine Wet-Rice Village." Ph.D. diss., Yale University, 1979.

———. *Rent-Capitalism in the Philippines*. Quezon City: University of the Philippines Third World Studies Center, 1981.

Fenner, Bruce Leonard. *Cebu Under the Spanish Flag 1521–1896: An Economic-Social History*. Cebu City: San Carlos Publications, 1985.

———. "Colonial Cebu: An Economic-Social History, 1521–1896." Ph.D. diss., Cornell University, 1976.

Finin, Gerard Anthony. "Regional Consciousness and Administrative Grids: Understanding the Role of Planning in the Philippines' Gran Cordillera Central." Ph.D. diss., Cornell University, 1991.

Forbes, W. Cameron. *The Philippine Islands*. Boston: Houghton Mifflin, 1928.

Foreman, John. *The Philippine Islands*. New York: Charles Scribner's Sons, 1906.

Fox, Jonathan. "The Challenge of Rural Democratisation: Perspectives from Latin America and the Philippines: Editor's Introduction." *Journal of Development Studies* 26, no. 4 (July 1990): 1–18.

———. "The Difficult Transition from Clientelism to Citizenship: Lessons from Mexico." *World Politics* 46, no. 2 (January 1994): 151–84.

———. "Latin America's Emerging Local Politics." *Journal of Democracy* 5, no. 2 (April 1994): 105–16.

Francisco, Gregorio A., Jr., and Raul P. De Guzman. "The '50–50 Agreement': A Political Administrative Case." *Philippine Journal of Public Administration* 4, no. 4 (October 1960): 328–47.

Francisco, Juan. *Indian Culture in the Philippines: Views and Reviews*. Kuala Lumpur: University of Malaya, 1985.

———. *The Philippines and India: Essays in Ancient Cultural Relations*. Manila: National Book Store, 1971.

Frankel, Francine R., and M. S. A. Rao, eds. *Dominance and State Power in Modern India: Decline of a Social Order*. Delhi: Oxford University Press, 1993.

Friedrich, Paul. "The Legitimacy of a Cacique." In Marc J. Swartz, ed., *Local-Level Politics: Social and Cultural Perspectives*. Chicago: Aldine, 1968.

———. "A Mexican Cacicazgo." *Ethnology* 4, no. 3 (July 1965): 190–209.

Friend, Theodore. *Between Two Empires: The Ordeal of the Philippines 1929–1946*. Manila: Solidaridad, 1969.

Gamalinda, Eric. *Saving the Earth: The Philippine Experience*. Makati: Philippine Center for Investigative Journalism, 1991.

Gesick, Lorraine, ed. *Centers, Symbols, and Hierarchies: Essays on the Classical States of Southeast Asia*. New Haven, Conn.: Yale University Southeast Asia Studies Monograph Series no. 26, 1983.

Gilmore, Robert L. *Caudillism and Militarism in Venezuela, 1810–1910*. Athens: Ohio University Press, 1964.

Gleeck, Lewis E. *Nueva Ecija in American Times: Homesteaders, Hacenderos and Politicos.* Manila: R. P. Garcia, 1981.

Gonzales, Dionisio. "A Survey of the Postwar Fishing Industry in the Province of Cebu." M.A. thesis, University of San Carlos, 1954.

Grossholtz, Jean. *Politics in the Philippines.* Boston: Little, Brown, 1964.

Guerrero, Amado. *Philippine Society and Revolution.* Hong Kong: Ta Kung Pao, 1971.

Guerrero, Milagros C. "Luzon at War: Contradictions in Philippine Society, 1898–1902." Ph.D. diss., University of Michigan, 1977.

———. "A Survey of Japanese Trade and Investments in the Philippines, with Special Reference to Philippine-American Reactions, 1900–1941." M.A. thesis, University of the Philippines, 1965.

Gutang, Rod B. *Pulisya: The Inside Story of the Demilitarization of Law Enforcement in the Philippines.* Quezon City: Daraga Press, 1991.

Gutierrez, Eric. *The Ties That Bind: A Guide to Family, Business and Other Interests in the Ninth House of Representatives.* Pasig: Philippine Center for Investigative Journalism, 1994.

Gutierrez, Eric, Ildefonso C. Torrente, and Noli G. Narca. *All in the Family: A Study of Elites and Power Relations in the Philippines.* Quezon City: Institute of Popular Democracy, 1992.

Guyot, Dorothy. "The Politics of Land: Comparative Development in Two States in Malaysia," *Pacific Affairs* 44, no. 3 (Fall 1971): 368–89.

Hagopian, Frances. "Traditional Politics Against State Transformation in Brazil." In Joel Migdal, Atul Kohli, and Vivienne Shue, eds., *State Power and Social Forces: Domination and Transformation in the Third World.* Cambridge: Cambridge University Press, 1994.

———. *Traditional Politics and Regime Change in Brazil.* Cambridge: Cambridge University Press, 1996.

Hall, Kenneth R. *Maritime Trade and State Development in Early Southeast Asia.* Honolulu: University of Hawaii Press, 1985.

Hallare-Lara, Cynthia. "A Profile of the Philippine Corn Industry." *Rural Development Studies* 8, no. 4 (September 1992): 1–51.

Hamilton, Nora. *The Limits of State Autonomy: Post-Revolutionary Mexico.* Princeton, N.J.: Princeton University Press, 1982.

Harvey, Barbara. "Tradition, Islam and Rebellion: South Sulawesi, 1950–1965." Ph.D. diss., Cornell University, 1974.

Hawes, Gary. *The Philippine State and the Marcos Regime: The Politics of Export.* Ithaca, N.Y.: Cornell University Press, 1987.

Hayden, Ralston. "The Philippines: An Experiment in Democracy." *Atlantic Monthly* (March 1926): 403–17.

———. *The Philippines: A Study in National Development.* New York: Macmillan, 1947.

Hedman, Eva-Lotta E. "In the Name of Civil Society: Contesting Free Elections in the Post-Colonial Philippines." Ph.D. diss., Cornell University, 1998.

Hernandez, Carolina G. "The Extent of Civilian Control of the Military in the

Philippines: 1946–1976." Ph.D. diss., State University of New York at Buffalo, 1979.

Hingco, Therese Gladys, and Rebecca Rivera. *The History of Trawling Operations in Manila Bay*. Quezon City: Tambuyog Development Center, 1990.

Hinkle, Harry B., and Justo C. Aquino. *A Report on Factors Affecting the Cost of Ice in the Philippines*. Manila: Philippine Fishery Program, U.S. Fish and Wildlife Service, 1949.

Hollnsteiner, Mary R. *The Dynamics of Power in a Philippine Municipality*. Quezon City: University of the Philippines, Community Development Research Council, 1963.

Hutchcroft, Paul D. "Oligarchs and Cronies in the Philippine State: The Politics of Patrimonial Plunder." *World Politics* 43, no. 3 (April 1991): 413–50.

———. "Predatory Oligarchy, Patrimonial State: The Politics of Private Domestic Banking in the Philippines." Ph.D. diss., Yale University, 1993.

Hutterer, Karl L., ed. *Economic Exchange and Social Interaction in Southeast Asia: Perspectives from Prehistory, History, and Ethnography*. Ann Arbor: Michigan Papers on South and Southeast Asia no. 13, 1977.

Japan International Cooperation Agency. *The Master Plan Study of the Project Calabarzon*. Manila: Department of Trade and Industry, 1991.

Jocano, F. Landa. *The Philippines at the Spanish Contact: Some Major Accounts of Early Filipino Society and Culture*. Manila: MCS Enterprises, 1975.

Juario, Jesus V., Enrique M. Avila, and Hilda D. Lastimosa. "Vanishing Swamps and Ruined Reefs: Trouble in Visayan Waters." *Data Links* 1, no. 4 (June 1992): 1–6.

Kaplan, David E., and Alec Dubro. *Yakuza*. New York: Macmillan, 1986.

Kathirithimby-Wells, J., and John Villiers, eds. *The Southeast Asian Port and Polity: Rise and Demise*. Singapore: Singapore University Press, 1990.

Kelly, Amzi B. *His Majesty King Torrens: An Impartial Constructive Criticism of Our Land Registration Under the Torrens Title System*. Manila, 1920.

Kerkvliet, Benedict J. Tria. *Everyday Politics in the Philippines: Class and Status Relations in a Central Luzon Village*. Berkeley: University of California Press, 1990.

———. *The Huk Rebellion: A Study of Peasant Revolt in the Philippines*. Berkeley: University of California Press, 1977.

———, ed. *Political Change in the Philippines: Studies of Local Politics Preceding Martial Law*. Honolulu: University Press of Hawaii, 1974.

———. "Rural Society and State Relations." In Benedict J. Tria Kerkvliet and Doug J. Porter, eds., *Vietnam's Rural Transformation*. Boulder, Colo.: Westview Press, 1995.

Kerkvliet, Benedict J., and Resil B. Mojares, eds. *From Marcos to Aquino: Local Perspectives on Political Transition in the Philippines*. Quezon City: Ateneo de Manila University Press, 1991.

Kern, Robert, ed. *The Caciques: Oligarchical Politics and the System of Caciquismo in the Luso-Hispanic World*. Albuquerque: University of New Mexico Press, 1973.

Key, V. O., Jr. *Southern Politics in State and Nation*. Knoxville: University of Tennessee Press, 1984.

Kirsch, A. Thomas. *Feasting and Social Oscillation: Religion and Society in Upland Southeast Asia*. Ithaca, N.Y.: Cornell University Southeast Asia Program, 1973.

Kohli, Atul. *Democracy and Discontent: India's Growing Crisis of Governability*. Cambridge: Cambridge University Press, 1990.

Kummer, David M. *Deforestation in the Postwar Philippines*. Quezon City: Ateneo de Manila University Press, 1992.

Landé, Carl H. *Leaders, Factions, and Parties: The Structure of Philippine Politics*. New Haven, Conn.: Yale University Southeast Asia Studies, 1964.

———. *Southern Tagalog Voting, 1946–1963: Political Behavior in a Philippine Region*. De Kalb: Northern Illinois University Center for Southeast Asia Studies, 1973.

Larkin, John A. *The Pampangans: Colonial Society in a Philippine Province*. Berkeley: University of California Press, 1972.

Legarda, Benito Fernandez, Jr. "Foreign Trade, Economic Change and Entrepreneurship in the Nineteenth-Century Philippines." Ph.D. diss., Harvard University, 1955.

Leichter, Howard M. *Political Regime and Public Policy in the Philippines: A Comparison of Bacolod and Iloilo Cities*. De Kalb: Northern Illinois University Center for Southeast Asia Studies Special Report no. 11, 1975.

Lewis, Henry T. *Ilocano Rice Farmers: A Comparative Study of Two Philippine Barrios*. Honolulu: University of Hawaii Press, 1971.

Lieberman, Victor. "Local Integration and Eurasian Analogies: Structuring Southeast Asian History, c. 1350–1830." *Modern Asian Studies* 27, no. 3 (1993): 475–572.

Lopez, Salvador P. *Isles of Gold: A History of Mining in the Philippines*. Singapore: Oxford University Press, 1992.

Lorenzo-Abrera, Ma. Bernadette G. *Ang Numismatika ng Anting-Anting: Panimulang Paghawan ng isang Landas Tungo sa Pag-Unawa ng Kasaysayan at Kalinangan Pilipino*. Quezon City: Unibersidad Ng Pilipinas, Programang Kaalamang Bayan, Tanggapan Ng Dekano, Dalubhasaan Ng Agham Panlipunan At Pilosopiya, 1992.

Love, Robert S. "The Samahan of Papa God: Tradition and Conversion in a Tagalog Religious Movement." Ph.D. diss., Cornell University, 1977.

Luna, Eufrosino U. *Ang Bogohanong Kasaysayan*. Cebu City: Cebu Star Press, 1980.

Lynch, Frank, and Alfonso de Guzman II, eds. *Four Readings on Filipino Values*. Quezon City: Ateneo de Manila University, Institute of Philippine Culture, 1973.

Lynch, John. *Bourbon Spain: 1700–1808*. Oxford: Basil Blackwell, 1989.

———. *The Spanish American Revolutions: 1808–1826*. New York: W. W. Norton, 1973.

Lynch, Owen J., Jr. "Invisible Peoples and a Hidden Agenda: The Origins of Contemporary Philippine Land Laws (1900–1913)." *Philippine Law Journal* 63, Third Quarter (September 1988): 249–320.

————. "Land Rights, Land Laws and Land Usurpation: The Spanish Era (1565–1898)." *Philippine Law Journal* 63, First Quarter (March 1988): 82–111.

————. "The Legal Bases of Philippine Colonial Sovereignty." *Philippine Law Journal* 62, Third Quarter (September 1987): 279–316.

————. "The Philippine Colonial Government: Attraction and Disenfranchisement." *Philippine Law Journal* 63, Second Quarter (June 1988): 112–60.

Machado, Kit G. "From Traditional Faction to Machine: Changing Patterns of Political Leadership in the Rural Philippines." *Journal of Asian Studies* 33, no. 4 (August 1974): 523–47.

————. "Leadership and Organization in Philippine Local Politics." Ph.D. diss., University of Washington, 1972.

Magenda, Burhan Djabier. *East Kalimantan: The Decline of a Commercial Aristocracy*. Ithaca, N.Y.: Cornell Modern Indonesia Project Monograph Series no. 70, 1991.

————. "The Surviving Aristocracy in Indonesia: Politics in Three Provinces of the Outer Islands." Ph.D. diss., Cornell University 1989.

Magno, Francisco A. "Politics, Elites and Transformation in Malabon," *Philippine Studies* 41, Second Quarter, (1993): 204–16.

Mamoru, Tsuda, and Yokoyama Masaki, eds. *Japan, Inc. in Asia: A Documentation on Its Operations Through the Philippine Polity*. Tokyo: Akashi Shoten, 1992.

Manalili, Jesus M. "Historical Suffrage in the Philippines and Its Present Problems." Ph.D. diss., University of Santo Tomas, 1966.

Manapat, Ricardo. *Some Are Smarter Than Others: The History of Marcos' Crony Capitalism*. New York: Aletheia Publications, 1991.

*Manila Bay Research*. Quezon City: Tambuyog Development Center, 1990.

Manuel, E. Arsenio. "Biography of Tomas Tirona." *Diliman Review* 14, no. 4 (1966): 287–380.

*The Master Plan Study on the Project Calabarzon*. Manila: Republic of the Philippines Department of Trade and Industry and Japan International Cooperation Agency, 1991.

May, Glenn, A. *Battle for Batangas: A Philippine Province at War*. New Haven, Conn.: Yale University Press, 1991.

————. "Civic Ritual and Political Reality: Municipal Elections in the Late Nineteenth Century." In Ruby Paredes, ed., *Philippine Colonial Democracy*. Quezon City: Ateneo de Manila University Press, 1989.

————. "Filipino Revolutionaries in the Making: The Old School Tie in Late Nineteenth-Century Batangas." *Bulletin of the American Historical Collection* 9 (July–September 1981): 53–64.

Mayhew, David. *Placing Parties in American Politics: Organization, Electoral Settings, and Government Activity in the Twentieth Century*. Princeton, N.J.: Princeton University Press, 1986.

Mayo, Katherine. *The Isles of Fear: The Truth About the Philippines*. New York: Harcourt, Brace, 1925.

McAndrew, John P. *The Impact of Corporate Mining on Local Philippine Communities.* Davao City: ARC, 1983.

———. "Urbanization and Social Differentiation in a Philippine Village." *Philippine Sociological Review* 37, nos. 1–2 (January–June 1989): 26–37.

———. *Urban Usurpation: From Friar Estates to Industrial Estates in a Philippine Hinterland.* Quezon City: Ateneo de Manila University Press, 1994.

McBeth, John. "A Life for a Life." *Far Eastern Economic Review* (July 29, 1993): 16–17.

McCoy, Alfred W. "Baylan: Animist Religion and Philippine Peasant Ideology." In David K. Wyatt and Alexander Woodside, eds., *Moral Order and the Question of Change: Essays in Southeast Asian Thought.* New Haven, Conn.: Yale University Southeast Asia Studies Monograph Series No. 24, 1982.

———. "Quezon's Commonwealth: The Emergence of Philippine Authoritarianism." In Ruby R. Paredes, ed., *Philippine Colonial Democracy.* Quezon City: Ateneo de Manila University Press, 1989.

———. "The Restoration of Planter Power in La Carlota City." In Benedict J. Kerkvliet and Resil B. Mojares, *From Marcos to Aquino: Local Perspectives on Political Transition in the Philippines.* Quezon City: Ateneo de Manila University Press, 1991.

———. "Sugar Barons: Formation of a Native Planter Class in the Colonial Philippines," *Journal of Peasant Studies* 19, nos. 3/4 (April/July 1992): 106–41.

———, ed. *An Anarchy of Families: State and Family in the Philippines.* Madison: University of Wisconsin Center for Southeast Asian Studies, 1993.

McCoy, Alfred W., and Ed. C. de Jesus, eds. *Philippine Social History: Global Trade and Local Transformations.* Quezon City: Ateneo de Manila University Press, 1982.

McVey, Ruth. "The Post-Revolutionary Transformation of the Indonesian Army." *Indonesia* 11 and 13 (April 1971 and April 1972): 131–76 and 147–81.

Medina, Isagani R. "Cavite Before the Revolution, 1571–1896." Ph.D. diss., University of the Philippines, 1985.

Mejia, Patricia Torres. *Philippine Virginia Tobacco: 30 Years of Increasing Dependency.* Quezon City: University of the Philippines Third World Studies Center, 1982.

Migdal, Joel S. *Strong Societies and Weak States: State-Society Relations and State Capabilities in the Third World.* Princeton, N.J.: Princeton University Press, 1988.

Miyagi, Dale S. "Neo-Caciquismo: Origins of Philippine Boss Politics 1875–1896," *Pacific Asian Studies* 1, no. 2 (April 1976): 20–34.

Mojares, Resil B. *Escaño: A Family Portrait.* Cebu City: Hijos de F. Escaño, 1989.

———. *The Man Who Would Be President: Serging Osmeña and Philippine Politics.* Cebu City: Maria Cacao, 1986.

———. *Theater in Society, Society in Theater: Social History of a Cebuano Village, 1840–1940.* Quezon City: Ateneo de Manila University Press, 1985.

————. *Vicente Sotto: The Maverick Senator*. Cebu City: Cebuano Studies Center, 1992.

*The NAMFREL Report on the February 7, 1986 Philippine Presidential Elections*. Manila: National Citizens Movement for Free Elections, 1986.

Nolledo, José N. *The Local Government Code of 1991*. Manila: National Book Store, 1992.

Norman, Jerry. *Chinese*. Cambridge: Cambridge University Press, 1988.

Nowak, Thomas C., and Kay A. Snyder. "Clientelist Politics in the Philippines: Integration or Instability?" *American Political Science Review* 68, no. 3 (September 1974): 1147–70.

Ocampo, Romeo B., and Elena M. Panganiban. *The Philippine Local Government System: History, Politics, and Finance*. Manila: Local Government Center, 1985.

Ockey, James Soren. "Business Leaders, Gangsters, and the Middle Class: Societal Groups and Civilian Rule in Thailand." Ph.D. diss., Cornell University, 1992.

————. "Chaopho: Capital Accumulation and Social Welfare in Thailand," *Crossroads* 8, no. 1 (1993): 48–77.

————. "Political Parties, Factions, and Corruption in Thailand." *Modern Asian Studies* 28, no. 2 (1994): 251–77.

Omohundro, John T. *Chinese Merchant Families in Iloilo: Commerce and Kin in a Central Philippine City*. Athens: Ohio University Press, 1981.

Parayno, Guillermo. "The Extent of Smuggling." Unpublished MS., 1991.

Paredes, Ruby, ed. *Philippine Colonial Democracy*. Quezon City: Ateneo de Manila University Press, 1989.

Phelan, John Leddy. *The Hispanization of the Philippines: Spanish Aims and Filipino Responses 1565–1700*. Madison: University of Wisconsin Press, 1959.

Poethig, Richard. "An Assessment of the Carmona Resettlement Project." *Impact* 5, no. 7 (July 1970): 11–18.

Political Science 130 Class and Carolinian Political Science Society, 1975–76. *An Inquiry into the Visayan Electric Company, Inc. Power Failures*. Cebu City: University of San Carlos, 1976.

Porter, Gareth, with Delfin Ganapin, Jr. *Resources, Population, and the Philippines' Future: A Case Study*. Washington, D.C.: World Resources Institute, 1988.

Putzel, James. *A Captive Land: The Politics of Agrarian Reform in the Philippines*. Quezon City: Ateneo de Manila University Press, 1992.

Quirino, Carlos. *Amang: The Life and Times of Eulogio Rodriguez, Sr.* Quezon City: New Day, 1983.

————. *History of the Philippine Sugar Industry*. Manila: Kalayaan Publishing Company, 1974.

————. *Philippine Tycoon: The Biography of an Industrialist, Vicente Madrigal*. Manila: Madrigal Foundation, 1987.

————. *Quezon: Paladin of Philippine Freedom*. Manila: Filipiniana Book Guild, 1971.

Ragas, E. L. *Handumanan mga Punoan Lungsodnon (Ubos sa Balaod Jones) sa 1916–1937 sa Kabisayan ug Mindanaw*. Cebu City: Ragas Brothers, 1938.

Ramsey, S. Robert. *The Languages of China*. Princeton, N.J.: Princeton University Press, 1987.

Reid, Anthony. *Southeast Asia in the Age of Commerce: 1450–1680*. Vol. 2: *Expansion and Crisis*. New Haven, Conn.: Yale University Press, 1993.

———, ed. *Southeast Asia in the Early Modern Era: Trade, Power, and Belief*. Ithaca, N.Y.: Cornell University Press, 1993.

Reid, Anthony, and Lance Castles, eds. *Pre-Colonial State Systems in Southeast Asia*. Kuala Lumpur: Malaysian Branch of the Royal Asiatic Society, 1975.

Riggs, Fred W. *Thailand: The Modernization of a Bureaucratic Polity*. Honolulu: East-West Center Press, 1966.

Rivera, Temario Campos. "Class, the State and Foreign Capital: The Politics of Philippine Industrialization 1950–1986." Ph.D. diss., University of Wisconsin at Madison, 1991.

Rivera, Temario C., and Kenji Koike. *Chinese-Filipino Business Families Under the Ramos Government*. Tokyo: Institute of Developing Economies Joint Research Program Series no. 114, 1995.

Robles, Eliodoro G. *The Philippines in the Nineteenth Century*. Quezon City: Malaya Books, 1969.

Robinson, Geoffrey Basil. *The Dark Side of Paradise: Political Violence in Bali*. Ithaca, N.Y.: Cornell University Press, 1995.

Romani, John H., and M. Ladd Thomas. *A Survey of Local Government in the Philippines*. Manila: Institute of Public Administration, 1954.

Romero-Muara, J. "Caciquismo as a Political System." In Ernest Gellner and John Waterbury, eds., *Patrons and Clients in Mediterranean Societies*. London: Duckworth, 1977.

Rosenberg, David A., ed. *Marcos and Martial Law in the Philippines*. Ithaca, N.Y.: Cornell University Press, 1979.

Rouquié, Alain. *The Military and the State in Latin America*. Berkeley: University of California Press, 1987.

Roxas, Gerardo M. "The Pork Barrel System." *Philippine Journal of Public Administration* 7, no. 4 (October 1963): 254–57.

Sagalongos-San Luis, Felicidad. *Gobernador Felicisimo T. San Luis: Buhay na Alamat ng Laguna*. Antipolo: Detail Printing, 1991.

Sahlins, Marshall D. "Poor Man, Rich Man, Big-Man, Chief: Political Types in Melanesia and Polynesia." *Comparative Studies in Society and History* 5, no. 3 (April 1963): 285–303.

Saulo, Alfredo B., and Esteban A. de Ocampo. *History of Cavite*. Trece Martires City: Provincial Government of Cavite, 1985.

Schmidt, Steffen W., Laura Guasti, Carl H. Landé, and James C. Scott, eds. *Friends, Followers, and Factions: A Reader in Political Clientelism*. Berkeley: University of California Press, 1977.

Scott, James C. *Comparative Political Corruption*. Englewood Cliffs, N.J.: Prentice-Hall, 1972.

———. "The Erosion of Patron-Client Bonds and Social Change in Rural Southeast Asia." *Journal of Asian Studies* 32, no. 1 (November 1972): 5–37.

———. "Patron-Client Politics and Political Change in Southeast Asia," *American Political Science Review* 66, no. 1 (March 1972): 91–113.

———. *Weapons of the Weak: Everyday Forms of Peasant Resistance.* New Haven, Conn.: Yale University Press, 1985.

Scott, James C., and Benedict J. Kerkvliet. "A Theory with Special Reference to Southeast Asia." *Cultures et Développement* 5, no. 3 (1973): 482–512.

Scott, William Henry. *Barangay.* Quezon City: Ateneo de Manila University Press, 1997.

———. *Slavery in the Spanish Philippines.* Manila: De La Salle University Press, 1991.

Shalom, Stephen R. *The United States and the Philippines: A Study of Neocolonialism.* Philadelphia: Institute for the Study of Human Issues, 1981.

Shamsul, A. B. *From British to Bumiputera Rule: Local Politics and Rural Development in Peninsular Malaysia.* Singapore: Institute of Southeast Asian Studies, 1986.

Shantz, Arthur Alan. "Political Parties: The Changing Foundations of Philippine Democracy." Ph.D. diss., University of Michigan, 1972.

Shefter, Martin. "The Emergence of the Political Machine: An Alternative View." In Willis D. Hawley, ed. *Theoretical Perspectives on Urban Politics.* Englewood Cliffs, N.J.: Prentice-Hall, 1976.

———. *Political Parties and the State: The American Historical Experience.* Princeton, N.J.: Princeton University Press, 1994.

Simbulan, Dante C. "A Study of the Socio-Economic Elite in Philippine Politics and Government, 1946–1963." Ph.D. diss., Australian National University, 1965.

Skowronek, Stephen. *Building a New American State: The Expansion of National Administrative Capacities 1877–1920.* Cambridge: Cambridge University Press, 1982.

Sobritchea, Carolyn I. "Banditry in Cavite During the Post World War II Period." *Asian Studies* 22–24 (1984–1986): 10–27.

Soriano, J. Clark S. *Political Clans and Electoral Politics: A Preliminary Research.* Quezon City: Institute For Popular Democracy, 1987.

———. "The Return of the Oligarchs." *Conjuncture* 1, no. 2 (October 1987): 4–8.

Sorongon, Arturo. *A Special Study of Landed Estates in the Philippines.* Manila: U.S. International Cooperation Administration, 1955.

Stanley, Peter W. *A Nation in the Making: The Philippines and the United States, 1899–1921.* Cambridge, Mass.: Harvard University Press, 1974.

———, ed. *Reappraising an Empire: New Perspectives on Philippine-American History.* Cambridge, Mass.: Harvard University Press, 1984.

Starner, Frances Lucille. *Magsaysay and the Peasantry: The Impact of Philippine Politics, 1953–1956.* Berkeley: University of California Press, 1961.

*The Story of Aboitiz & Company, Inc. and the Men Behind It.* Cebu City: Aboitiz, 1973.

Szanton, David L. *Estancia in Transition: Economic Growth in the Rural Philip-*

*pine Community*. Quezon City: Ateneo de Manila University Press, Institute of Philippine Culture Papers no. 9, 1972.

Szanton, Maria Cristina Blanc. *A Right to Survive: Subsistence Marketing in a Lowland Philippine Town*. University Park: Pennsylvania State University Press, 1972.

Tancangco, Luzviminda. *The Anatomy of Electoral Fraud: Concrete Bases for Electoral Reforms*. Manila: MJAGM, 1992.

Tarling, Nicholas. "Some Aspects of British Trade in the Philippines in the Nineteenth Century." *Journal of History* 11, nos. 3 and 4 (September–December 1963): 287–327.

Taussig, Michael. *Shamanism, Colonialism, and the Wild Man: A Study in Terror and Healing*. Chicago: University of Chicago Press, 1987.

Taylor, Robert H. *The State in Burma*. Honolulu: University of Hawaii Press, 1987.

Thompson, Edward P. *Customs in Common*. New York: Basic Press, 1991.

———. *The Poverty of Theory and Other Essays*. London: Merlin Press, 1978.

———. *Whigs and Hunters: The Origins of the Black Act*. New York: Pantheon Books, 1975.

Thompson, Mark R. *The Anti-Marcos Struggle: Personalistic Rule and Democratic Transition in the Philippines*. New Haven, Conn.: Yale University Press, 1995.

———. "Searching for a Strategy: The Traditional Opposition to Marcos and the Transition to Democracy in the Philippines." Ph.D. diss., Yale University, 1991.

Tiglao, Rigoberto. *The CDCP Sting: Or How the Marcos-Cuenca Construct Built a Highway to Haven*. Quezon City: Freedom from Debt Coalition, 1992.

———. *Looking into Coconuts: The Philippine Coconut Industry*. Manila: ARC Publications, 1981.

———. "Stacked Decks: Philippine Shipowners Fear Keppel Repair Monopoly." *Far Eastern Economic Review* 25 (November 1993): 60.

Tria, Melinda C. "The Resistance Movement in Cavite, 1942–1945." M.A. thesis, University of the Philippines, 1966.

Umehara, Hiromitsu. "Green Revolution for Whom? An Inquiry into Its Beneficiaries in a Central Luzon Village, Philippines." In Antonio J. Ledesma, S.J., Perla Q. Makil, and Virginia A. Miralao, eds., *Second View from the Paddy*. Quezon City: Ateneo de Manila University Press, 1983.

Van Velzen, H. U. E. Thoden. "Robinson Crusoe and Friday: Strength and Weakness of the Big Man Paradigm." *Man* 8, no. 4 (December 1973): 592–613.

Vandermeer, Canute. "Corn on the Island of Cebu, the Philippines." Ph.D. diss., University of Michigan, 1962.

Vergara, Ernesto M. "The Fiscal Position of Philippine Local Governments, 1962–1966." Ph.D. diss., University of Kansas, 1971.

Vidallon-Cariño, Ledivina. *The Politics and Administration of the Pork Barrel*. Manila: Local Government Center, College of Public Administration, University of the Philippines, 1966.

Villamor, Ignacio. *Criminality in the Philippine Islands: 1903–1908*. Manila: Bureau of Printing, 1909.

Villanueva, Buenaventura M., Patrocinio S. Villanueva, Elsa V. Perez, Juanita F. Pua, and Caridad G. Cuento. *Government and Administration of a Municipality*. Quezon City: Community Development Research Council, 1966.

Villegas, Bernardo M. "The Story (So Far) of the Philippine Economic Crisis." *Economics and Society* (April 1985): 1–11.

Vitug, Marites Dañguilan. *Power from the Forest: The Politics of Logging*. Pasig: Philippine Center for Investigative Journalism, 1993.

Walsh, Thomas. "Perceptions of Gubernatorial Authority: Aspects of the 'Reality World' of the Philippine Provincial Governor." *Philippine Journal of Public Administration* 20, no. 1 (January 1976): 68–102.

Wernstedt, Frederick L. *The Role and Importance of Philippine Interisland Shipping and Trade*. Ithaca, N.Y.: Cornell University Southeast Asia Program Data Paper no. 26, 1957.

Wickberg, Edgar. *The Chinese in Philippine Life: 1850–1898*. New Haven, Conn.: Yale University Press, 1965.

———. "The Chinese Mestizo in Philippine History," *Journal of Southeast Asian History* 5, no. 1 (March 1964): 62–100.

Winichakul, Thongchai. *Siam Mapped: A History of the Geo-Body of a Nation*. Honolulu: University of Hawaii Press, 1994.

Williams, Arthur R. "Center, Bureaucracy, and Locality: Central-Local Relations in the Philippines." Ph.D. diss., Cornell University, 1981.

Wolters, Oliver W. *History, Culture, and Region in Southeast Asian Perspectives*. Singapore: Institute of Southeast Asia Studies, 1982.

———. "Khmer 'Hinduism' in the Seventh Century." in R. B. Smith and W. Watson, eds., *Early South East Asia: Essays in Archaeology, History and Historical Geography*. New York: Oxford University Press, 1979.

Wolters, Willem. "Rise and Fall of Provincial Elites in the Philippines: Nueva Ecija from the 1880s to the Present Day." *Sojourn* 4, no. 1 (February 1989): 54–74.

Wurfel, David. "The Bell Report and After: A Study of the Political Problems of Social Reform." Ph.D. diss., Cornell University, 1960.

———. *Filipino Politics: Development and Decay*. Ithaca N.Y.: Cornell University Press, 1988.

———. "The Philippines." *Journal of Politics* 25, no. 4 (November 1963): 757–73.

Yoshihara, Kunio. *Philippine Industrialization: Foreign and Domestic Capital*. Singapore: Oxford University Press, 1985.

# Index

Abello, Remedios. *See* Escario, Remedios (née Abello)
Abello, Salvador, 97
Abines, Apolonio, Jr., 117, 122
Abines, Apolonio, Sr., 116–17
Abines Bus Company, 121
Abines, Crisologo ("Sol"): *muro-ami* fishing protected by, 122; offices held by, 117; photograph of, 118; protégés of, 90
Abines family, 116–22; cockfighting operations, 120; described, 174; election tactics of, 121–22, 184; family store of, 118; illegal immigration operations, 119–20; land transportation enterprises, 120–21; longevity of reign, 99–100; mistreatment of workers by, 119–20; monolithic economic control by, 121; *muro-ami* fishing industry controlled by, 117, 119–20, 182–83; Sumilon operations of, 121, 183; supramunicipal empire of, 117
Aboitiz family, 132, 133–34, 188
Aboitiz, Paulino, 133
Agravante, Januario B., Jr., 86
Agriculture: Casal's control of economy in Carmona, 43–44; commercialization in Cebu, 86
Aguinaldo, Emilio, 55–61; Bonifacio executions approved by, 53, 165; Bureau of Lands confiscation of his estate, 60–61; complaints about election of (1935), 57; consolidation of power under Americans, 56–57; defeat by Quezon, 61; emergence of, 55–56; friar

landholdings of, 55, 58–59, 61; Philippine Revolution activities, 55–56, 166; surrender to Americans (1901), 56; ties with Quezon, 58–59, 60; ties with Tirona, 57–58, 60
*Alcades mayores* (provincial governors), 14, 15
Aller, Benito, 85
Almendras, Jovenal, 107
Almendras, Paulo, 106
Alvarez, Mariano, 56
Ambagan, Santos, 35
American colonial rule, 16–18; Aguinaldo's surrender, 56; "bossism" and "bosses" emphasizing institutional structures of, 6; Cavite criminal activities during, 30; elections during, 16, 17; electoral system and political machines, 60; entrenchment of bossism during, 18–19; governorship elections of 1907, 57; hierarchy of authority in, 17; importance of scholarship regarding, 4, 6, 12; subordination of state apparatus during, 13, 16, 17, 158
Amoy dialect, 174
Aquino, Corazon C., 113, 126, 138
Assassinations and murders: before and after the Montano era, 37; of Borromeo, 110–11; of Cavite municipal leaders, 29, 51–53; by Cavite municipal leaders, 29; in Cebu, 83, 172; by Durano Sr., 105, 107, 110–11; during Remulla's reign as governor, 39; by Escario family, 97; of Maquinay, 47; Maragondon

Massacre of 1952, 53; Montano-Camerino rivalry and, 53; of Tecala, 110; of Velasco, 51–53, 165
Aznar family, 132

Baguio, Sergio, 85
*Bale* (credit receipt), 120
Bantayan: before Escario family's rise to power, 90–91; mayors (1901–37), 92; oligarchy in, 91; Rubio's landholdings in, 91. *See also* Escario family
Barbas family, 85
Bayots of Amadeo, 35
Beduya, Gaudencio, 180–81
Bendebel family, 86
Bifactionalism: Cavite nonconformance, 48; mayoral monopolies vs., 24; patron-client relations and, 8; post-Marcos period and, 9; in pre-martial-law years, 8; "premodern" view of, 23–24
Binamura, Ramon, 120
Bocalan, Lino: defeat of Delfin Montano, 71, 170; defection to Marcos camp, 71; Malacañang courting of, 69; photograph of, 67
Bonifacio, Andres, execution of, 53, 165
Bonifacio, Procopio, execution of, 53, 165
Borromeo, Raul, assassination of, 110–11
Bosses: Abines family, 116–22; Aguinaldo, 53, 55–61; Casal, 41–48; Cuenco family, 102, 105–6, 108–9, 124; defined, 19; Durano family, 102–15; Escario family, 90–98; *hacendados* and fishing magnates, 115–22; large landowners of Cebu, 85; local bosses outside Cavite and Cebu, 141–42; local élite families of Cebu, 85–86; longevity of small-town bosses, 49–50; Marcos, 6, 11, 69–73, 75, 110, 112, 113, 137–38, 142–45; Montano, 35, 36, 41, 43, 53, 61–71; municipal executives' discretionary powers, 26–27, 33, 83–84, 128–29; Osmeña family, 124–39; as power brokers, 141; Remulla, 37, 39, 45, 46, 52, 53, 71–78; subcategories of, 142; use in this book, 6, 19. *See also* District-level dynasties of Cebu; Provincial warlords of Cavite; Small-town bosses of Cavite; Small-town dynasties of Cebu; Strongman rule
Bossism: in Burma, 151; comparative analysis needed for, 19–20; comparative perspective for Philippine bossism, 145–47; currency of term, 6; defined, 19; entrenchment during American colonial era, 18–19; factors affecting, 19–20; global perspective, 147; in Indonesia, 151; institutional structures supporting, 50; mafia-style bosses in Cavite, 35, 37, 39, 49; in Malaysia, 151–52; state agencies and, 145–47; in Thailand, 11, 147–51; trends in the Philippines, 153–54; use in this book, 4, 6, 19; in Vietnam, 152. *See also* District-level dynasties of Cebu; Provincial warlords of Cavite; Small-town bosses of Cavite; Small-town dynasties of Cebu; Strongman rule
Brazil, authoritarian control in, 2
Briones, José, 134
Briones, Maria Luisa Cabrera, 134
Buddhism, Southeast Asian politics and, 13
Bureau of Customs, "monkey business" in, 34, 163
Bureau of Lands: Aguinaldo estate confiscated by, 60–61; corruption in, 32, 59
Burma, bossism in, 151

Cabaron, Pedro, 85
*Cabezas de barangay* (village headmen), 14, 15, 30, 55
Cacique democracy, 6
Caciquism, 6, 155. *See also* Spanish colonial rule
Calderon, Beatriz, 86
Calderon, Emerito S., 184
Camerino, Dominador: Casal's ties with, 46; fall from favor, 35; photographs of, 38, 39; replaced by Montano protégé, 41; rivalry with Montano, 41, 53, 64; rivalry with Remulla, 73; suspension by Malacañang, 64
Campos, José Yao, 45, 137
Camposes of Dasmariñas, 35
Canlubang Estate, 44
Capitalism: bossism as outgrowth of, 145–47; introduction during Spanish colonial rule, 15; "Old Corruption" in England, 140–41, 147; "primitive accumulation," 18, 146–47
Carmona: before Casal's ascendance to mayorship, 41; highways linking Manila to, 45, 46, 71–72; landownership issues in, 42–44; rice and sugar processing in, 44; suburbanization of, 44–46. *See also* Casal, Cesar E.
Carmona Resettlement Project, 45
Carnapping in Cavite in the 1950s, 31
Casal, Alfred, 42
Casal, Cesar E., 41–48; agricultural economy controlled by, 43–44; Carmona before his ascendance to mayorship,

41; communal landownership manipulated by, 43–44; economic opportunism by, 40, 42–44, 164; election as mayor, 42; Land Reform Act of 1955 and, 42–43; Manila's impact on his fiefdom, 44–46; photograph of, 40; political involvement used to protect his properties, 47–48; political success of, 47–48; on provincial board, 46–47; reelection and entrenchment of, 44, 164; semiretirement of, 46; ties to Montanos, 35, 41–42, 44; ties with Camerino, 46; ties with Remulla, 46

Causing, Benigno, 91

Cavite: abuse of franchises and concessions in, 33–34, 162; Casal's mayorship in Carmona, 41–48; as case study, 20–21; Cavite politics and presidential elections (1946–69), 64; Cebu contrasted with, 81–82, 89, 90, 99–100, 101, 142; construction boom scams in, 34; criminal activities in, 30–31; demographics, 21, 62, 71, 167; friar estates in, 31–32, 55, 58–59, 61; gangster-style competition in, 28–29; high turnover among mayors, 27; highways linking Manila to, 45, 46, 71–72; landed "commercial élite" in, 34–35; landownership issues in, 30, 31–33, 34–35; mafia-style mayors in, 31, 35, 37, 39, 49; Manila's impact on, 33, 34, 44–46, 49, 62, 78–79, 162; Marcos's impact on, 71–72; Montano era, 35–37, 61–71; municipal politics in, 28–41; political economy of, 29–30, 31–34, 54–55; socio-economic transformation during postwar era, 62; suburbanization of, 33, 34, 44–46, 49, 62, 162. *See also* Casal, Cesar E.; Provincial warlords of Cavite; Small-town bosses of Cavite

Cavite-Carmona Development Project, 45

Cavite Electricity Development Authority (CEDA), 65, 75

Cavite Export Processing Zone, 71

Caviteño bandits (*tulisanes*), 30, 55–56

"Ceboom," 138

Cebu: abuse of franchises and concessions, 84–85; as case study, 20–21; Cavite contrasted with, 81–82, 89, 90, 99–100, 101, 142; Chinese mestizo élite in, 86–89; commercialization of agriculture in, 86; correlation between Manila administration and Cebu mayors, 89; demographics, 21–22; diverse economy of, 123; election "anomalies" in, 82–83; friar estates in, 86, 128; high

turnover among mayors, 27; Hokkien-speaking immigrants in, 88; mayoral powers in Cebu City, 128–29; merchant dynasties, 132–33; Osmeña family, 124–39; state patronage and municipal elections, 89. *See also* District-level dynasties of Cebu; Osmeña family; Small-town dynasties of Cebu

Cebu Autobus Company, 131

Cebu Ice and Cold Storage Plant, 134

Cebu Portland Cement Company (CEPOC), 106–7

Cebu Shipyard and Engineering Works, 133

CEDA (Cavite Electricity Development Authority), 65, 75

CEPOC (Cebu Portland Cement Company), 106–7

Cerna family, 85

*Chao pho* ("godfathers") in Thailand, 150–51

Chinese mestizo élite in Cebu, 86–89; crystallization into oligarchy, 87–88; diversification by, 88; municipal politics of, 88–89; prominent families, 90–91; rise of, 86–87; sugar crisis and, 87

Chiongbian family, 132, 134–35

Chiongbian, James, 188

Chiongbian, Victor S., 134

Chiongbian, William, 134

Chiong Veloso, Estefania, 127

Chiong Veloso, Nicasio, 127, 185

Christian Democrat Party (Italy), 5

Chubb, Judith, 5

Chulalongkorn (Rama V), 148

Clientelism. *See* Patron-client relations

Climaco, Juan, 127

Cockfighting: Abines family operations, 120; Cebu political battles over, 84–85, 173

Coconut Producers' Federation (COCOFED), 85, 115, 173

Cojuangco, Eduardo ("Danding"), Jr., 77–78, 137

Cojuangco, Jose ("Peping"), Jr., 77

Comelec. *See* Commission on Elections

Commission on Appointments, 158, 192

Commission on Elections: Cavite monitored by, 28; Cavite towns place under control of PC by, 42; documentation of local ills, 24; election fraud by, 170; "sensitive hot spots" noted in Cebu, 110; Velasco assassination and, 51

Commonwealth Act 725 of 1946, 176

Commonwealth period (1935–41): conditions shaping Cavite politics during,

61–62; election-related skullduggery in Cavite during, 28; land sales in Cavite during, 33. *See also* Montano, Justiniano S., Sr.

Comparative analysis: need for, 19–20; of Philippine bossism, 145–47

Competition, bifactional. *See* Bifactionalism

Comprehensive Agrarian Reform of 1988, 47

*Conquistadores,* grants awarded to, 14

*Coronelismo,* 3

"Credit bondage" tactics of Abines family, 120

Criminal activities: in Cavite, 30–31; in Cebu, 83–84; Escario family profits from, 92–93; *jueteng* (illegal lottery) syndicates, 30, 31, 37, 59, 60, 63; smuggling under Montano's "protection," 67–68, 169. *See also* Assassinations and murders; Election fraud; Violence and intimidation regarding elections; Vote-buying

Crisologo, Floro, 142

*Cuadrilleros* (town policemen), 30

Cuenco family: conflict with Rodriguez family, 105–6; election tactics of, 108, 109; Liberal Party power of, 108–9; longevity of reign, 102; provincial hegemony of, 124; Special Police Forces of, 109; ties with Quezon and Roxas, 137

Cuenco, Manuel, 89, 108

Cuenco, Mariano J., 92, 105–9

Cuenco, Miguel, 105, 108

Cuenco-Rodriguez conflict, 105–6

Cushing, James, 107

Dalusag, Rafael, 35

Danao Coal Mines, 107

*Datus,* 13

*Datu*-ships, 13–14

DC (*Democrazia Cristiana*) Party (Italy), 5

De Dios, Elpidio, 85

De La Rama, Esteban, 131

De La Rama Steamship Company, 131–32, 134

Dela Serna, Vicente ("Tingting"), 124

De Leons of Ternate, 35

Delgado, Francisco, 136

Democracy in the Philippines: after Marcos's downfall, 6, 9; American colonial research and, 9; bossism as outgrowth of, 145–47

Democratization, 148

*Democrazia Cristiana* Party (Italy), 5

Demographics: of Cavite, 21, 62, 71, 167; of Cebu, 21–22

Department of Agrarian Reform, 48

Department of Finance, local agents of, 26–27

Despotism: superior attitudes toward, 1–2; by traditional élites, 2, 3–4

Discretionary powers of municipal executives, 26–27, 83–84, 128–29

District-level dynasties of Cebu, 101–23; Abines family, 116–22; Durano family, 102–15; *hacendados* and fishing magnates, 115–22; Martinez clan, 115–16; Osmeña family contrasted with, 125; Osmeña family (provincial dynasty), 124–39. *See also* Abines family; Durano family; Osmeña family

District-level dynasties of Negros Occidental, 142

Donaire, Tiburcio, 89

Dosdos, Tereso, 106, 178

Dragon, Renato, 73, 170

Durano, Beatriz, 86, 114, 180

Durano, Elicia, 106

Durano family, 102–15

Durano, Jesus ("Don"), 113, 114, 181

Durano, Paulo M., 180

Durano, Ramon M., Sr.: burial site of, 102–5; death of, 113; defeat by Cuenco, 107; dynastic success of, 102, 122–23; economic opportunism by, 108, 111–13, 180; election tactics of, 109–10; election to Danao municipal council, 106; enduring empire of, 102–3; murders by, 105, 107, 110–11; NACOCO profits embezzled by, 108; photograph of, 103; private army of, 110, 111; protégés of, 89; provincial power approached by, 124; religious roots of power of, 104; ties with Cuenco, 108; ties with Garcia, 112, 137, 180; ties with Magsaysay, 112; ties with Marcos, 110, 112, 113; violent methods of, 109–11

Durano, Ramon ("Nito"), III: congressional candidacy of, 114; inheritance of dynastic form by, 102; as new family patriarch, 114–15; photograph of, 104

Durano Sugar Mills, 113, 114

Durano, Thaddeus ("Deo"), 113, 114, 181

Economics. *See* Finances and economics; Landownership

Economistic approach to Philippine politics, 9

Election fraud: in 1960s and 1970s, 24; by Abines family, 121–22; by Casal, 44, 164; in Cavite, 28–29, 48, 57, 160; in Cebu, 82–83; by Commission on Elections, 170; by Cuenco family, 109; by Durano Sr., 105; by Escario family, 97; by Liberal provincial governors, 108, 178; media reports, 156; by Montano, 63–64; in post-Marcos period, 9; in pre-martial law period, 9; by Remulla, 72; in senatorial elections, 192; in Thailand, 150

Elections: Abines family tactics, 121–22, 184; Cavite politics and presidential elections (1946–69), 64; correlation between Manila administration and Cebu mayors, 89; Cuenco family tactics, 108, 109; Durano's tactics, 109–10; during American colonial rule, 16, 17; Escario family tactics, 91–93, 97–98; Montano's tactics, 63–64; national realignments and provincial politics (1947–71), 65; Osmeña family tactics, 127–28; Remulla's tactics, 72–73; schoolteachers' counting of ballots, 97, 176; state patronage and municipal elections in Cebu, 89; view during 1960s and 1970s, 23. *See also* Election fraud; Violence and intimidation regarding elections; Vote-buying

Élites: Chinese mestizo élite in Cebu, 86–89; landed "commercial élite" in Cavite, 34–35; local élite families of Cebu, 85–86; machine politics and, 4, 5; traditional, 2, 3–4

*El Nuevo Dia*, 127

*Encomiendas* (grants) to Spanish *conquistadores*, 14, 157

Enrile, Juan Ponce, 137

Erie, Steven, 4, 5

Escamilla, A. G., 58

Escaño, Asuncion, 135

Escaño family, 132, 135

Escaño, Teresita, 135

Escario family, 90–98; alliance with immigrant Chinese families, 95; commercial ports controlled by, 94–95, 176; economic control by, 92–96; election tactics of, 91–93, 97–98, 176; future endurance of, 98; monopoly privileges seized by, 93–94; as patrons and providers to the poor, 96–97; profits from illegal activities, 92–93; share of control by, 95; ties to congressmen, 96

Escario, Felixberto, 91

Escario, Isidro: election as mayor, 91–92, 97, 176; as patron of the poor, 96; as sole labor broker for sugar plantations, 93–94

Escario, Jesus, 92, 95

Escario, Nicolas G., 96

Escario, Rafael, 175

Escario, Remedios (née Abello): as beneficiary to the poor, 96–97; marriage to Isidro Escario, 91; mayorship of, 86, 92, 98; ties with Martinez, 116

Escario, Rex, 92, 93, 175

Espinelis of Magallanes, 35

Espiritu, Pedro, 58, 63

Estimo, Geronimo, 85

FCECI (First Cavite Electric Cooperative, Inc.), 75–76

Fees and licenses, discretionary powers over, 26–27, 33, 83–84, 128, 162

Feinstein, Aaron, 107

Fenton, Harry, 107

Ferrers of General Trias, 35

Feudalism, 6, 10

Fil-Estate Realty Corporation, 45

Finances and economics: Abines family's monolithic control, 121; abuse of franchises and concessions, 33–34, 84–85, 162; Casal's control in Carmona, 43–44; Casal's economic opportunism, 40, 42–44, 164; Cavite political economy, 29–30, 31–34, 54–55; discretionary powers over, 26–27, 83–84, 128; diverse economy of Cebu, 123; Durano's economic opportunism, 108, 111–13, 180; "ecological" features of local economies, 28; economistic approach to Philippine politics, 9; Escario family's economic control, 92–96; Montano's economic opportunism, 66–68, 168; Osmeña family's economic opportunism, 131–32; political economy of Cavite, 29–30, 31–34, 54–55; Remulla's economic opportunism, 77; Thailand's incorporation into world economy, 148–49. *See also* Landownership

First Cavite Electric Cooperative, Inc. (FCECI), 75–76

Fishing magnates. *See Hacendados* and fishing magnates

Fox, Jonathan, 2, 3

Frabal Fishing and Ice Plant Corporation, 119, 182–83

Fragmentation of social control, 2–3

Friar estates: Aguinaldo's holdings in Cavite, 55, 58–59, 61; in Cebu, 86, 128; extent of, 156; *inquilino* dynasties in Cavite, 31–32

GAB (Game and Amusements Board), 65–66
Gaisano family, 132, 133
Gaisano, Modesta Singson, 133, 187
Game and Amusements Board (GAB), 65–66
Gangster-style competition in Cavite, 28–29
Gantuangco family, 85
Gapud, Rolando, 137
Garcia, Carlos P., 112, 137, 180, 190
Garcia, Jesus, Jr., 136
Garcia, Pablo, Sr., 125
General Mariano Alvarez housing project, 45
Genuiono, Ernesto Trias, 35
*Gobernadorcillos* (town executives), 14, 15, 30, 55
"Godfathers" (*chao pho*) in Thailand, 150–51
Gokongwei, John, Jr., 133
Gotianun, Andrew, 133
Gotianuy, Manuel, 133, 187
Gotiaoco family, 132, 133
Gotiaoco Hermanos, Inc., 133
Gotiaoco, Pedro, 133
Grants, Spanish, 14, 15
"Great Tradition" religions, 13–14
Guinto, Benigno, 33

*Hacendados* and fishing magnates, 115–22; Abines family, 116–22; Martinez clan, 115–16. *See also* Abines family
Hagopian, Frances, 2, 3
*Hakot* (ferrying voters), 82
Harrison, Francis Burton, 128
Hebron, Bernardo, 41
Hereditary succession in Spanish colonial era, 14
Hinduism, Southeast Asian politics and, 13
Historical materialism, 7
Hokkien-speaking immigrants in Cebu, 88, 132, 174, 187

Iglesia Ni Cristo (INC), 73, 170
Illegal activities. *See* Criminal activities
Ilocos Sur, bossism in, 142
Import-substitution industrialization, 62
INC (Iglesia Ni Cristo), 73, 170
Indic religions, 13–14

Indonesia, bossism in, 151
Industrialization: export-led, 71; import-substitution, 62; Remulla as "godfather" of, 76–77
Industrial Security Action Group, 77
INP (Integrated National Police), 26
*Inquilinos,* 32, 34, 55–56
Insular Navigation Company, 133
Integrated National Police (INP), 26
Intergovernmental alliances in U.S. machine politics, 4–5
Interviews conducted by the author, 158–59
Intimidation in elections. *See* Violence and intimidation regarding elections
Islam, Southeast Asian politics and, 13
Italy, machine politics in, 5

*Jao poh* ("godfathers") in Thailand, 150–51
*Jueteng* (illegal lottery) syndicates: in Cebu, 84; Espiritu's manipulation of, 63; "protection" of, 30, 31, 59, 60; Remulla's financing from, 37

Kao Sing, 91
Keppel Philippines Shipyard, 133
Kiamzons of Silang, 35
Killings. *See* Assassinations and murders
Kintinar clan, 102
"Kokoy" (Benjamin Romualdez), 75
Kuok, Robert, 136

Lacson, Arsenio, 53
La Naviera Filipina, 134
Landownership: Aguinaldo as land broker, 59; Carmona development projects, 44–46; Casal's landgrabbing, 42–44; in Cavite during postwar era, 62; in Cavite's political economy, 30, 31–33, 34–35; friar estates in Cavite, 31–32, 55, 58–59, 61; friar estates in Cebu, 86, 128; landed "commercial élite" in Cavite, 34–35; landgrabbing by Cavite small-town bosses, 32; Land Reform Act of 1955, 42–43; lot-grabbing in Carmona Resettlement Project, 45; of Osmeña family, 128, 130–31, 186; political longevity and, 35; "strong oligarchy, weak state" thesis and, 11, 157
Land Reform Act of 1955, 42–43
Land Tenure Administration (LTA), 43
Latin American authoritarian control, 2
Laurel, José P., 108
Law enforcement, discretionary powers over, 26, 29, 155, 158

Laysan, Ho, 95
Lhuiller family, 132
Lhuiller, Michel, 135–36
Librando family, 85–86, 121
Licenses. *See* Fees and licenses
Lineages of the Philippine state, 12–19;
American colonial rule, 13, 16–18;
*datu*-ships in pre-Hispanic era, 13–14;
Spanish colonial rule, 14–16; strong-
man power aided by, 12–13, 14
"Little Chicago," Cavite City as, 31
Local Government Code of 1991, 129, 173
Lotteries, illegal. *See Jueteng* (illegal lot-
tery) syndicates
Lozada, Pedro, 91, 92
LTA (Land Tenure Administration), 43
Lu Do & Lu Ym Corporation, 135, 137
Lu Do, Cayetano, 135
Lu family, 132, 135
Luico, Mauricio, 25
Lu Ym, Douglas, 135, 137

Macapagal, Diosdado, 65–66, 69
Machine politics: American-installed electoral system and, 60; as élite-created,
not mass-created, 4, 5; institutional
structures and alliances supporting,
4–5, 60; of Montano, 66; of Osmeña
family, 128–30; of Remulla, 73; in
southern Italy, 5; as tool for understanding Third World politics, 4; in the
U.S., 4–5
"Mafia democracy," 6
Mafia-style bosses in Southeast Asia,
150–53
Mafia-style bosses in the Philippines. *See*
Provincial warlords of Cavite; Small-
town bosses of Cavite
Magdalo Council (Sangguniang Magdalo), 56
Magdiwang Council (Sangguniang Magdiwang), 56
Magsaysay, Ramon: ties with Durano, 112;
ties with Montano, 41, 64–65
Malacañang: Bocalan courted by, 69;
Camerino suspended by, 64; crackdown
on private armies by, 51; Durano's rela-
tions with, 112; firearms ban by, 70
Malaysia, bossism in, 151–52
"Ma Mediong." *See* Escario, Remedios
(née Abello)
Manecio, Leonardo (Nardong Putik), 53
Manila: correlation between Manila administration and Cebu mayors, 89; impact on Cavite, 33, 34, 44–46, 49, 62,
78–79, 162; legislators' influence dur-

ing American colonial rule, 16–17;
opened to foreign trade by Spanish, 15;
town mayors implicated in newspapers
of, 25, 159. *See also* Cavite
Manila Banking Corporation (MBC),
74–75
Manila Electric Company (Meralco), 75,
79
Manila Southwoods Residential Estates
and Golf and Country Club, 45
Maningo, Margarito, 89
Maquinay, Felino, assassination of, 47
Maragondon Massacre of 1952, 53
Marcos, Ferdinand, 142–45; conflicts with
Osmeña family, 137–38; downfall of, 6,
145–46; impact on Cavite, 71–72;
landownership and power of, 11; Mon-
tano's antagonism with, 69–71; obsta-
cles to power overcome by, 142–44;
reign of, 144, 193; ties with Durano,
110, 112, 113; ties with Remulla,
72–73, 75
Marcos, Imelda R., 75
Martinez, Celestino ("Junie") E., Jr., 90,
115–16, 176–77
Martinez clan, 115–16
Martinez, Mariano, 116
Martinez, Nilda E., 116
Mayors. *See* Bosses; Small-town bosses of
Cavite; Small-town dynasties of Cebu
MBC (Manila Banking Corporation),
74–75
Melencio, José P., 58
Meralco (Manila Electric Company), 75,
79
Merchant dynasties of Cebu, 132–33
Migdal, Joe, 1–2, 5
Miranda, Victor, 162
Mitra, Ramon ("Monching"), Jr., 77, 114
Modernization: in municipal political lead-
ership, 24; theory of Philippine politics,
8–9
Monsanto, Pedro, 89
Montano, Delfin: defeat by Bocalan, 71,
170; election to governorship, 41, 66;
photograph of, 39; smuggling "protection" and, 68, 169
Montano, Justiniano N., Jr., 40, 65–66
Montano, Justiniano S., Sr., 61–71; administration during the Montano era,
37; as assistant provincial fiscal,
62–63, 168; Cavite Electricity Development Authority (CEDA) manipulated by, 65; discretion over national
government agency officials, 66; downfall of, 69–71; economic opportunism

by, 66–68, 168; election tactics of, 63–64; exile during Marcos's reign, 71; external conditions shaping politics, 61–62; influence of, 35, 36; Land Reform Act of 1955 and, 43; Maragondon Massacre of 1952 and, 53; Marcos's antagonism with, 69–71; mayors "created " by, 35; photographs of, 36, 38, 69; political ascendancy of, 62–63; political machine of, 66; pork barrel policies of, 66, 68, 169; presidential elections manipulated by, 64; private army of, 66; private law practice of, 63; rivalry with Camerino, 41, 53, 64; smuggling operations "protected" by, 67–68, 169; ties with Macapagal, 65–66, 69; ties with Magsaysay, 64–65; ties with Quezon's machine, 62; ties with Remulla, 73–74; Tirona defeated by, 61

Montemayor, Isabelo ("Beloy"), 93

"Mother of thieves," Cavite as, 30

Municipal Board of Canvassers (Cavite), intimidation regarding (1988), 29

Municipal leaders. *See* Small-town bosses of Cavite; Small-town dynasties of Cebu

Murders. *See* Assassinations and murders

*Muro-ami* fishing, 117, 119–20

NACOCO (National Coconut Corporation), 108

NAMFREL (National Citizens Movement for Free Elections), 72

National Citizens Movement for Free Elections (NAMFREL), 72

National Coconut Corporation (NACOCO), 108

National Development Company (NDC), 106, 131

National Housing Authority, 45

Nazareños of Naic, 35

NDC (National Development Company), 106, 131

Negros Occidental: bossism in, 142; landgrabbing during American colonial rule, 17

Neo-Marxist views of Philippine politics, 9–10

"New men," 9, 35

Nicklaus, Jack, 45

Norte, Ilocos, 137–38

"No-strike zone," Remulla's enforcement of, 76–77

Nueva Ecija landgrabbing, 17

Nuñez, Jorge, 51, 53, 165

"Old Corruption" in England, 140–41, 147

Oligarchies: in Bantayan, 91; Cebu merchant dynasties, 132–33; Chinese mestizo élite in Cebu, 87–88; factors undermining in Cavite, 49; neo-Marxist view of, 10; Osmeñas as brokers for Cebu oligarchy, 132–38; scholarly view of, 2, 3–4; "strong oligarchy, weak state" thesis, 10–12, 157

Osmeña, Emilio ("Lito"), Jr.: "Ceboom" and, 138; photograph of, 126; as provincial governor, 126; real-estate deals of, 131; ties with Manila-based magnates, 136; ties with merchant dynasties, 135–36

Osmeña family, 124–39; as brokers for local oligarchy, 132–38; conflicts with hostile presidents, 137–38; contrasted with mafia-style bosses and other dynasties, 125, 138, 139; economic opportunism by, 131–32; founding of the dynasty, 125–28; ingredients of success for, 127–28; landholdings and real-estate deals of, 128, 130–31, 186; offices held by, 125–26; powers in Cebu City, 128–29; provincial-level power of, 124–25; ties with Aboitiz family, 133–34; ties with Aquino, 138; ties with Chiongbian family, 134–35; ties with Gotiaoco family, 133; two-tiered pattern of entrenchment, 138–39; urban political machine of, 128–30

Osmeña, John ("Sonny"), 126

Osmeña, Lourdes, 135

Osmeña, Sergio ("Serging"), Jr.: conflicts with Garcia, 137; conflicts with Marcos, 137–38; offices held by, 125–26, 185; as presidential candidate, 70; real-estate deals of, 131; ties with Quirino, 89, 137

Osmeña, Sergio, Sr.: charged with real-estate speculation, 130–31; conflicts with Quezon and Roxas, 137; discretion over friar estates, 128; early life of, 127; emergence of, 127; offices held by, 125; "real" father of, 133, 187; rivalry with Cuenco, 92; ties with Manila-based magnates, 136

Osmeña, Severino, 127

Osmeña, Tomas ("Tommy"): "Ceboom" and, 138; landslide reelection of, 130;

offices held by, 126; ties with merchant dynasties, 135; ties with Ramos, 130

Pace, Librada, 85, 86
Palanca, Carlos, Jr., 136
*Panghulga* (intimidation), 82
Patron-client relations: bifactionalism and, 8; breakdown after martial law declared, 8–9; Cavite disparities regarding, 48; historical materialism and, 7; limitations of view, 9, 11–12; scholarly view of, 3, 5, 7–10; as social adhesive, 7–8, 9
PCGG (Presidential Commission on Good Government), 45, 78, 113, 114
PC (Philippine Constabulary), 26, 42
Peña, Macario, 33, 35
People's Homesite and Housing Corporation, 44–45
Pepitos family, 85
Peralta, Macario, Jr., 68
Personalism. *See* Patron-client relations
Philippine Assembly during American colonial era, 16–17
Philippine Constabulary (PC), 26, 42
Philippine Corn Products, 135
Philippine Revolution, 55–56
Philippines: Liberation and independence of, 18; lineages of the state, 12–19; as test case of views toward strongmen, 4, 5–6; trends in, 153–54
Police, discretionary powers over, 26, 29, 155, 158
Political economy of Cavite, 29–30, 31–34, 54–55
Political machines. *See* Machine politics
Post-Marcos period: bifactionalism in, 9; election fraud and vote-buying in, 9; limitations of patron-client relations view in, 9; neo-Marxist view of, 9–10
Postwar era (1946): Cavite criminal activities during, 31; socio-economic transformation of Cavite during, 62
Poultry farmers, 98, 177
"Premodern" political view, 23–24
Presidential Commission on Good Government (PCGG), 14, 45, 78, 113
Presidential Committee on Illegal Fishing and Marine Conservation, 120
"Primitive accumulation," 18, 146–47
Private armies: crackdown on, 51; Cuenco family Special Police Forces, 109; of Durano, 110, 111; of Montano, 66; of provincial warlords of Cavite, 53, 54
Provincial bosses in Ilocos Sur, 142

Provincial governors: during Spanish era (*alcades mayores*), 14, 15; first elections of, 16; warlords elsewhere in the Philippines, 142. *See also* Provincial warlords of Cavite
Provincial warlords of Cavite, 51–80; Aguinaldo, 53, 55–61; assassinations and killings by, 51–53; factor influencing longevity of, 53–54; Montano, 35, 36, 41, 43, 53, 61–71; Osmeña family contrasted with, 125; parallels elsewhere in the Philippines, 80; private armies of, 53, 54; Remulla, 37, 39, 45, 46, 52, 53, 71–78. *See also* Aguinaldo, Emilio; Montano, Justiniano S., Sr.; Remulla, Juanito ("Johnny")
Proxy rule by wealthy individuals, 15
Pugeda, Fabian, 62, 63
Putik, Nardong (Leonardo Manecio), 53
*Puwesto* (position), 14
Puyat clan, 74–75
Puyat, Gil, 74
Puyat, Gonzalo, 74

Quezon, Manuel: Aguinaldo defeated by, 61; conflicts with Osmeña family, 137; Cuenco appointed by, 92; discretionary powers granted to Cebu City mayors by, 128–29; government control in the 1930s by, 17–18; Rabellana's letter of grievance to, 24–25; Soriano supported by, 59; ties with Aguinaldo, 58–59, 60; ties with De La Rama, 131
Quirino, Elpidio, 89, 108, 137

Rabellana, Juan, 24–25
Ramos, Alfredo, 136
Ramos, Fidel, 77, 78, 126
Reciprocity in patron-client relations, 7–8
Remulla, Juanito ("Johnny"), 71–78; assassinated Cavite mayors and, 39, 52, 53; Casal's ties with, 46; Cavite-Carmona Development Project and, 45, 46; downfall of, 77–78; economic opportunism by, 77; election tactics of, 72–73; electricity franchise manipulated by, 75–76; as "godfather" of industrial revolution, 76–77; influence of, 37, 39; "no-strike zone" enforced by, 76–77; photograph of, 70; political machine of, 73; Ramos's antagonism toward, 77, 78; rise to power of, 73–74; rivalry with Camerino, 73; Sarino's antagonism toward, 78; ties with Dragon, 73; ties with Marcos, 72–73, 75; ties

with Montano, 73–74; ties with Puyat clan, 74–75; Velasco assassination and, 52, 53

Republic Act 1400, 42–43

Revilla, "Bong," 78

Revilla, Ramon, 78

Reyes, Augusto, 60

Riego de Dioses of Maragondon, 35

Rodriguez, Buenaventura, 105, 106

Rodriguez, Celestino, 105, 106

Rodriguez-Cuenco conflict, 105–6

Rodriguez, José V., 105

Rodriguez, Pedro, 105

Rojas, Honorio ("jueteng king"), 63

Rojases of Cavite City, 35

Romualdez, Benjamin ("Kokoy"), 75

Roxas, Manuel, 89, 107, 137

Rubio, Manuel, 91

Rural political clans of Cebu, 82–90; Chinese mestizo élite, 86–89; correlation between Manila administration and Cebu mayors, 89; entrenchment of, 89–90; Escario family, 90–98; large landowners, 85; local élite families, 85–86; long-time mayors, 85–86; state patronage and municipal elections, 89. *See also* Escario family; Small-town dynasties of Cebu

*Sacadas* (migrant workers), exploitation of, 94

Samonte, Ramon, 60, 63

Sanchez, Antonio, 25, 26

Sangguniang Magdalo (Magdalo Council), 56

Sangguniang Magdiwang (Magdiwang Council), 56

Sangley Point naval station (U.S.), 29–30, 31

San Miguel beer, 94, 175

Sarino, Cesar, 78, 172

Senate resistance to bossism, 143, 192

Sepulveda, Pedro, 110

Sernat (Chief of Police), 29

Sernat (Councilor), 29

Shefter, Martin, 4, 5

Singson, Luis, 142

Small-town bosses of Cavite: assassinations, 29, 37, 39, 47, 51–53; Casal, 41–48; Cebu dynasties contrasted with, 81–82, 89, 90, 99–100; discretionary powers of, 26–27; during the Montano Era, 37; "ecological" factors affecting, 27–28, 160; factors leading to entrenchment of, 27; high turnover

among, 27; landgrabbing in by, 32; mafia-style mayors, 35, 37, 39; Montano's "creations," 35, 37; Osmeña family contrasted with, 125; power abuses by, 24–26. *See also* Bosses; Casal, Cesar E.

Small-town dynasties of Cebu, 81–100; Cavite bosses contrasted with, 81–82, 89, 90, 99–100; Chinese mestizo élite, 86–89; correlation between Manila administration and Cebu mayors, 89; discretionary powers of mayors, 83–84; entrenchment of, 89–90; Escario family, 90–98; large landowners, 85; local élite families, 85–86; long-time mayors, 85–86; Osmeña family contrasted with, 125; rural political clans, 82–90; state patronage and municipal elections, 89. *See also* Escario family

Smuggling operations: Abines family illegal immigration operations, 119–20; in Bureau of Customs, 34, 163; in Cebu, 84; Montano's "protection" of, 67–68, 169

Soriano, Antero, 59–60

*Sorteo* in Carmona, 43–44

Southeast Asian bossism, 150–53

Spanish colonial rule, 14–16; Cavite criminal activities during, 30; friar estates in Cavite during, 31–32, 55, 58–59; hereditary succession during, 14; institutional features, 15–16; minimal presence of Spanish, 14; Philippine Revolution, 55–56; private capital introduced by, 15; proxy rule by wealthy individuals, 15; strongman power preserved by, 14–15

Strategies of survival in Third World states, 3

Strongman rule: in American colonial era, 17–19; conventional views of, 2–4; *datu*-ships, 13–14; Philippines' importance as case study, 4, 5–6; in Spanish colonial era, 14–16. *See also* Bossism; District-level dynasties of Cebu; Osmeña family; Provincial warlords of Cavite; Small-town bosses of Cavite; Small-town dynasties of Cebu

"Strong oligarchy, weak state" thesis, 10–12, 157

*Strong Societies and Weak States,* 2

Suburbanization: of Carmona, 44–46; of Cavite, 33, 34, 44–46, 49, 62, 162

Sumilon operations of Abines family, 121, 183

Survival strategies in Third World states, 3
Sybico, Celestino, Jr., 184

Taiwanese immigrants, illegal, 119–20
Taxes: discretionary powers over, 26–27, 83–84, 129, 186; punishment of Cavite political rivals through, 33–34, 162
Tecala, Pedra, assassination of, 110
Technology Resource Center (TRC), 45–46
Tenant petitioners' cause, 42–43
Thailand, 147–51; armed revolutionary movements in, 149; *chao pho* ("godfathers") in, 150–51; constraints on bossism in, 148–49; democratization in, 148; economic boom in, 149; incorporation into world economy, 148–49; mafia-style bossism in, 150–53; Philippine bossism vs., 150–51; "strong oligarchy, weak state" thesis and, 11; Vietnam War's effect on, 149–50
Third World states, 2–3
Thompson, E. P., 140
Tinio, Manuel, 17, 158
Tirona, Candido, 57
Tirona, Daniel, 57–58, 60, 61
To-ong family, 85
Town executives (*gobernadorcillos*), 14, 15, 30, 55
Town policemen (*cuadrilleros*), 30
Traditional élites, 2, 3–4
"Traditional Filipino values," 24, 26
TRC (Technology Resource Center), 45–46
Trias, Mariano, 57
*Tulisanes* (bandits), 30, 55–56
Tumulak family, 85
Tumulak, José, 85, 117
Two-party system. *See* Bifactionalism

Unas, Telesforo, 35, 49, 99
United Coconut Mills, 137
United States, machine politics in, 4–5. *See also* American colonial rule
Universal Cement Company, 113
Urot, Florencio S., 109–10, 179
Ursal family, 85
Uytengsu, Tirso, 190

*Vale* (credit receipt), 120
Velasco, Epimaco, 78
Velasco, Octavio, assassination of, 51–53, 165
Vice-mayors. *See* Bosses; Small-town bosses of Cavite; Small-town dynasties of Cebu
Vietnam, bossism in, 152

Vietnam War's effect in Thailand, 149–50
Villacarlos family, 85
Village headmen (*cabezas de barangay*), 14, 15, 30, 55
Violence and intimidation regarding elections: in 1960s and 1970s, 24; by Abines family, 121–22, 184; by Casal, 44, 164; in Cavite, 28–29, 48, 57; in Cebu, 82–83; by Cuenco family, 109; by Durano Sr., 105, 110; by Escario family, 92, 97, 176; by Liberal provincial governors, 108; media reports, 156; by Montano, 63–64; in post-Marcos period, 9; in pre-martial law period, 9; by Remulla, 72. *See also* Assassinations and murders
Visayan Electric Company, 134, 135
Visayan Surety and Insurance Corporation, 133
Vote-buying: in 1960s and 1970s, 24; by Abines family, 122; by Casal, 44, 164; in Cavite, 28–29, 48, 57; in Cebu, 82; by Liberal provincial governors, 108; in post-Marcos period, 9; in pre-martial law period, 9; by Remulla, 72; study of, 156; in Thailand, 150

Warlordism, 6. *See also* Provincial warlords of Cavite
"Weak state, strong oligarchy" thesis, 10–12, 157
Weblike societies, 2–3
William Lines, 134, 188–89
Wood, Leonard, 58, 60

Yan, Manuel, 39
Yaptinchay estate, Casal's expropriation of, 43, 48, 164
Yray, Manuel, 110
Yuchengo, Alfonso, 137
Yulo, José, 44

Zosa, Manuel, 89–90, 102, 180, 184

# CONTEMPORARY ISSUES IN ASIA AND THE PACIFIC

A Series from Stanford University Press and the East-West Center

*Political Legitimacy in Southeast Asia: The Quest for Moral Authority*
Edited by Muthiah Alagappa

*Chiefs Today: Traditional Pacific Leadership and the Postcolonial State*
Edited by Geoffrey M. White and Lamont Lindstrom

*Making Majorities: Constituting the Nation in Japan, Korea, China,
Malaysia, Fiji, Turkey, and the United States*
Edited by Dru C. Gladney

*Capital, Coercion, and Crime: Bossism in the Philippines*
John T. Sidel

Library of Congress Cataloging-in-Publication Data

Sidel, John Thayer
  Capital, coercion, and crime : bossism in the Philippines / John
T. Sidel
     p.    cm. — (East-West Center series on contemporary issues in
Asia and the Pacific)
  Includes bibliographical references and index.
     ISBN 0-8047-3745-2 (cloth : alk. paper). — ISBN 0-8047-3746-0
(paper : alk. paper)
     1. Local government—Philippines. 2. Local officials and
employees—Philippines.   I. Title.   II. Series: contemporary issues
in Asia and the Pacific.
JS7303.A2.S55  1999
352.14'09599—dc21                                            99-37230

Original printing 1999
Last figure below indicates year of this printing:
08   07   06   05   04   03   02   01   00   99

Typeset by Robert C. Ehle in 10/12 Sabon and Friz Quadrata display.